"Wade has the soul of a dolphin and [illegible] oceans on a quest for deep knowledge. The *Swiss Family Robinson*-style adventures among the atoll-dwellers and dolphins of the South Seas exemplifies Wade's fearless journey to seek for greater understanding of the non-Western mind. This is an important book which will change our views of the ocean and our human purpose."



— Ric O'Barry, author of *Behind the Dolphin Smile* and star of *The Cove*, which won the 2010 Academy Award for Best Documentary

"This celebration of the interconnectedness of all life is a gift from the soul of a man at the apex of his life. His insights into the ocean worlds and their inhabitants are deeper than most because he has lived it. A consummate storyteller he communicates exceptionally well."

— Hardy Jones, founder of BlueVoice.org, oceans activist, producer of over 70 films on marine mammals, and author of *The Voice of the Dolphins*

"This is a rare and intriguing record of exploring both the oceanic hemisphere of our globe and the right hemisphere of our own minds. Wade Doak is a mariner/philosopher who knows that hidden within us, long forgotten — and hidden within in all life on earth — are dimensions and interconnections of which we can barely dream. Sailing his own boat through the South Pacific he encounters eerily communicative wild dolphins, psychic shark callers, luminous corals in dark caves, and kite fishermen using sticky balls of spider silk, while all the time brushing shoulders with other poet-scientists of the Mind in the waters and forests of Gaia."

— Lawrence Blair, writer/producer of the *Ring of Fire* book and television series

WADE DOAK

# GAIA CALLS

*South Sea Voices, Dolphins, Sharks & Rainforests*

DIVINE
ARTS

Published by DIVINE ARTS
DivineArtsMedia.com

An imprint of Michael Wiese Productions
12400 Ventura Blvd. #1111
Studio City, CA 91604
(818) 379-8799, (818) 986-3408 (FAX)

Cover design by Johnny Ink. www.johnnyink.com
Cover Art: Steve Moase (www.moaseart.com)
Editor: Geraldine Overton
Copy Editor: Matt Barber
Printed by McNaughton & Gunn, Inc., Saline, Michigan

Manufactured in the United States of America


Library of Congress Cataloging-in-Publication Data
Doak, Wade.
Gaia calls : south sea voices, dolphins, sharks & rainforests / Wade Doak.
p. cm.
ISBN 978-1-61125-005-3
1. Doak, Wade. 2. Gaia hypothesis. 3. Dolphins--Behavior. 4. Human-animal communication. 5. Seafaring life. 6. Philosophy of nature. 7. Biology--Philosophy. 8. Life. I. Title.
QL31.D59A3 2012
599.53--dc23

2011039289

Printed on Recycled Stock

MIX
Paper from responsible sources
FSC® C011935
FSC
www.fsc.org

# CONTENTS

# A WORD FROM THE PUBLISHER

I had just finished *Dolphin*, an hour-long TV documentary on interspecies communication, and was researching a sequel when someone told me that I should contact Wade Doak, as he was "Mr. Dolphin" and knew more about human-dolphin encounters than anyone on the planet. So I wrote to him asking if he'd be interested in seeing my film. Typically, Wade responded that he would love to hear all about it. In addition, he told me that he'd just received a set of roundtrip tickets to the U.S. which was the First Prize in a short story contest he had won with a piece on dolphins. Since Wade and his wife Jan were not keen to travel just then, he offered the tickets to me and my wife and suggested we meet them in New Zealand.

We jumped at the chance! New Zealand was extraordinarily beautiful and the Doaks had laid claim to one of its most exquisite spots. This was in 1979 and already they were living "off the grid" with sustainable eco-friendly systems to supply their own electricity, water, and food. Wade introduced us to Jan, their kids, and their pet pig, Lucky. (The pig was a test, he told us later. If we liked the pig, and the pig liked us, he'd like us.)

Wade was indeed Mr. Dolphin. His pride and joy was a Polynesian-style catamaran designed especially for dolphin interaction. He had kitted out a specially designed monopod wetsuit that had built-in appendage dorsal fins, pectorals, a dolphin tail fluke, and space for a radio sound transmitter installed in the diving suit's hood to imitate a dolphin's frontal lobe. I asked him if he really thought this fooled the dolphins into thinking he and Jan were dolphins too and he said, "Certainly not, but it enhances our ability to communicate with them through mimicry."

Wade showed us all the local beauty spots, including his beloved Poor Knight's Islands. His passion for Mother Nature was deeply moving. He was pioneering deep ecology. More than just lip service, he and his family walked the talk, and swam it too!

And what a consummate storyteller! We spent many nights listening to Wade tell remarkable stories that fired our imagination about finding not only sunken treasure, but the riches and ecologies of atoll island life that are quickly disappearing. Wade and Jan have spent half their lives immersed, or as he would say, "flying underwater" in a new world which most of us only know from the surface.

His "water-biography" reads like an ancient myth. Shortly after birth Wade was dipped in the sea by his young mother who believed that salt water was good for babies. She lost her grip on him when a wave snatched the infant away only to toss him back to her on the next roller! Could this explain Wade's childhood obsession to venture beneath the sea at a time when diving equipment was in its infancy?

At fifteen, the water boy invented his own diving system by putting an ice cream can on his head which was linked to the surface by a garden hose and ventilated by a car pump. Then he walked on the seabed picking up his first treasure: an old pewter and marble chalice. The sea gods were calling.

That same year during a high school history class he was caught building his own scuba regulator under his desk and the teacher, thinking he was "up to no good," caned him severely.

It was apparent that the sea gods favored their aquatic son when they led Wade to uncover a massive undersea treasure trove of thousands of gold and silver coins. This boon allowed him to spend his life exploring the ocean intensively with Jan, and sharing his discoveries through 19 books and many television programs.

The high tides of Wade's life roll on like a fairy tale. From the Atlantic to the Pacific, he's been places and done things that most of us only dream about. His gratitude for the sea, the rainforests, wetlands and mangroves, shows in his celebration of the interconnectedness of all life.

Jan and Wade have heard the ocean sirens' call, which has led them through a life well lived. It is my great pleasure to know Wade and be the publisher of this fine collection of his work. It is my hope that through the stories of this incredible couple that you too will rejoice in the abundant gifts the natural world has given us and listen quietly as *Gaia Calls*.

Michael Wiese
November 2011
Cornwall, England

# PART ONE

## A MIND JOURNEY

Now it can be told. Finding the *Elingamite* treasure in 1966 was a *déjà vu* experience. Down deep and chilled to the bone, I was cruising along the rocky ocean floor. Suddenly, before I looked, I knew it was there — like reaching for slippers under the bed and finding them exactly where I knew they would be.

Without a culture or literature of other levels of awareness and other human capacities, we cannot talk about them. We censor ourselves to maintain our precious credibility. We maintain the status quo. Although I described every other aspect about the *Elingamite* find in my very first book, I never dared to tell my diving mates how I came to locate that bullion hoard.

That ocean treasure, some 10,000 silver and gold coins, changed our lives: I left teaching high school to write a book about the adventure, and — with my wife and diving partner Jan's help — seventeen more about marine life. And thus, when the invitation came, we were free to travel on R.V. *El Torito* to remote parts of the Pacific with Dr. Walter Starck — a marine biologist/philosopher equally interested in consciousness and non-western cultures — to investigate the shark-calling Melanesian people of Laulasi and the remote Polynesian atoll dwellers of Luaniua.

Things we learned about other levels of consciousness among those South Sea islanders became hugely important when we returned to New Zealand, talked with our Maori neighbours, and set out on what would become a fifteen-year research project studying "ocean mind" (the capacities of wild dolphins and whales) and "mind at large" (the interconnectedness of life in the sea and in the rainforests).

The following is the story of our initial coin discovery.

## FINDING THE TREASURE OF THE *ELINGAMITE*

At 150 feet the sea can be a pretty hostile place to men. You don't see much there that's not eating or being eaten. There isn't much colour, and it's always as cold as fish blood. You don't even feel like a human down there. No weight, nothing to plant your feet square on so you can size things up. Like a patient under an anaesthetic you have a mouthpiece between your teeth and the queer, thick stuff you breathe sets your lips tingling with nitrogen narcosis. *You feel as if you're not inside yourself*. Rather like after the first few drinks at a wedding party, where you don't really feel wanted and you start analysing how alcohol is affecting your version of reality.

That's how it was when I came across the *Elingamite* treasure: finning quietly from rock to rock, feeling very wet and groggy, some part of the half-boozed brain still ticking over, sensible to the 150 feet of liquid cutting it off from the sky.

"Soon have to make it back up there again, but below it's so quiet and peaceful." I could easily have fallen asleep: no struggling in the fierce current up there and all the cold work of taking off my gear.

Life topside in the cramped quarters of the *Ahiki*, sleeping on the diesel fuel tank, was hell anyway. No really deep sleep such as seemed possible down below. Still, that smart part of the brain kept the fins flicking and head swivelling among the wreckage.

"Feel like a blasted ballet dancer down here." Weightless and clad in tights, it was a lot easier to move with grace and poise in liquid space than to barge around like a he-man. I kept thinking I was a fish as schools of butterfly perch swam close in front of my mask, pirouetted around me or darted under a rock.

"Suppose it saves energy if you copy them." Besides, any sudden effort sent an icy squirt of water through the neck of my wet suit and sluicing around my armpits. Then I would get a bit dizzy and have to screw my mind into focusing on what I was doing.

"Looking for the bullion. But there wouldn't be a chance of finding it amongst all this junk. The rest of the boys must be close by hunting for souvenirs. They don't reckon there's a tinker's chance in hell of finding the treasure here." I'd passed Jag and John Pettit struggling in the current to attach a shotline to a couple of port-holes. And Kelly was waltzing around with his huge camera rig and flash gun trying to get some smart pics of the wreck.

Trouble was, this area of seabed didn't look much like a ship. Earlier in the dive I'd posed for Kelly with a few seagrowth-covered wine bottles gathered from under a rock. Nearby was a white, twisted length of lead plumbing. This would show we were actually over a wreck. Then we'd come across a huge, mossy mangle of wreckage, which turned out to be the propeller, sitting boss uppermost, blades awry and jagged. While Kelly juggled with his light meter and aperture controls, I'd balanced over the prop, holding on to the tip of one six-foot blade, like a gymnast doing a single-handed handstand. Then he had signalled me to snuggle up close to some more debris — some sort of winch bristling with sea urchins and finger sponges. Now as I swam by myself my fingers still burnt with those damned spines you pick up from touching sponges. "Like bits of fibre glass-spicules! Fancy my depth-fuddled brain throwing up that scientific word for sponge skeleton! Not as water-logged as I thought."

Anxiety struggled to resist nitrogen narcosis: "Wonder how my air supply is lasting. Be good when it's cut and I can get out of here. I'm getting too cold to feel sleepy now." Trouble is, the insulating bubbles in these wet suits get so squeezed up under pressure there's no warmth left in them.

I was starting to get clumsy. If I curved gracefully and swooped down under the rock ledges cold water would swill up and down my spine, so I moved as little as possible, just my big flippers. They kept going without even thinking about it. Like the heart, a reflex action and a big drain on energy and body heat. The thick compressed air, which I gulped from my regulator was cold too, my lungs acting as a heat radiator with each breath.

I felt flayed and water-sodden. I tried to imagine sitting down to a good meal, all dry and warm in the cosy cabin. A bit of salty water in my mask made my eyes smart like onions.

"Body just keeps on working for me while the mind hikes off on little trips of its own. Like shelling peas. Why does a man like diving? What a hellish torment it can become near the end of a deep dive. Fortunately we forget this and remember only the pleasure.

In these stressful physical conditions I must have slipped into an altered state for the first time in my life. I knew I would see a pile of coins under that rock *before I looked!*

"Hey! Can I really be here?" Coins: a mound of scattered discs in the white sand. This was like watching a film and telling yourself it was not real. But they were! A handful in my plastic bag. Gold? I plunged my hand back in feverishly. "Too light — just pennies. May as well keep digging. Could be something better below."

Varying sized coins began to tumble into view. These could not all be pennies but they were not heavy enough for gold. Everywhere in the rocky recess coins were scattered, coral encrusted or sulphated black.

"How the hell will I find this spot again when I go up?" I should have brought down a marker buoy to fix to the kelp growing on top of the rock.

"Hey — where are the other divers? Who can give me a hand before my air runs out? Need someone else to help me get a good fix on this spot."

This was the last dive of the expedition and I hardly dared leave off to call someone else in. Doubling sideways I saw John Pettit finning past. I gave him the "OK" sign, which means on a treasure wreck: COINS. Like a fish taking bait he streaked beside me and we scrounged furiously in the sand together for more and more coin. We could not see much in the sandstorm of particles being stirred up, so we worked by touch, groping blindly until our fingers met. It did not feel deep any more. I was no longer cold. My brain was working perfectly and methodically hyper-aware.

I knew my air was getting very low and I shepherded every breath. The decompression meter on my wrist indicated that ascent should be soon if I was to avoid a fatal "bend."

John tapped my shoulder and signalled "up." His air was finished already as he had been toiling hard raising portholes. Off up into the blue tide race he went, to tell the boys we were on to it. Frantically I scooped up as much as possible, thinking: "This is our last dive here." That day the weather had begun to deteriorate and our supply of air tanks was finished. A tap on my leg. I did not even react. Then it sunk in: I turned and there was Kelly wanting to know what I was doing. I flashed some coins at him. Gasping the remaining air from his tank he snapped some photos of me with his electronic flash, and ascended.

My own tank was giving me the last air we would be able to breathe on the *Elingamite* site. "Pit-a-pit-a-pit," my sonic air pressure gauge triggered off its staccato warning, forcing me to accept that it was all over. Hiccupping bubbles it drew a cloud of fish around me as I made a last rummage through the sand, squeezed the water out of my coin bag and backed out from the underhang.

It was getting twilight and no one else remained below. A blue wall of current was sweeping down over the wreck. I kicked off into it but I could not rise far from the bottom with the weight of coins. Removing my mouthpiece, my chilled lips fluttered uselessly around the tube of my buoyancy compensator as I puffed in some air; like a yellow halter around my neck it swayed and tilted, inflated by my exhaust. I lightened and lifted off. The current started to bear me away. Slanting up from the wreck I tried wildly to fix some landmarks in my mind. From forty feet above, the wreck looked so different: just jumbled rocks festooned with kelp plants streaming out in the current.

"The prop — can't miss that. One-two-three-four... Four rocks down the slope from the prop. A valley of girders, a square hatch cover to one side and..." but by then the wreck site was fading from view as I started to soar. My eyes lifted upward towards the surface glitter: far above a buckling sheet of tinfoil, so good to see after a long dive. As the pressure of the water diminished, my compensator bulged tight around my neck. Reaching forty feet I purged the air from it so it would not rupture. Had I ascended too fast my own lungs would also have swollen and burst. I kept breathing steadily and the sonic air gauge kept up its staccato cluck-cluck warning. Attracted by this sound, trevally and kingfish swarmed around me in the warmer surface waters. I clutched the precious bag firmly in my hand.

"Hell, when will I ever get back to what I'm leaving below me? Wait till the boys see this bullion!" My mask burst through the surface into another world and a fresh set of problems. It was a mad, white confusion in the tide race. A wind could just be heard howling amidst the roar of the waves slamming into the face of the island. The *Ahiki* was soaring or plummeting with the deep swells as she cruised as close in as she dared. "Weather is brewing something up."

Despite the evening sunlight my yellow buoyancy compensator was quickly noticed. Sea birds swooped low over me. Bucking violently, the *Ahiki* swung her bow around and came surfing down. One moment her red bottom was indecorously exposed, the next I was looking down on her foredeck winches and gear. It always seemed an impossibility to transfer from this mad welter of water on to that runaway stallion of a ship, wearing such a burden of lead and scuba tank. But this time I had only one hand free to snatch the ladder with.

"Time it right." I finned hard to close the gap between the ship and myself. Strangely, it was not a matter of moving horizontally but getting on the same level as the ship even long enough to grab the diving ladder before she crashed below me. Alternately I soared high on a crest or dropped under her hull. She could not use her propeller in case it hacked into me, and I had to back off smartly to avoid her crashing bilge. "How could Kelly make it with his great, unwieldy camera rig?" flashed through my mind.

The current did not matter much now: both the ship and myself were being swept north, away from the sea-lashed island. With a series of strong fin thrusts I snatched the ladder and friendly arms reached down to help me aboard.

"Hey! Wait a minute," I yelled, letting drop my mouthpiece. My bullion hand was empty. They had grabbed the bag from me to safety. Well I now had two hands to hoist myself aboard with, so why worry! By the time I had flung my gear off the boys were crouched in a circle on the counter of the ship: John Gallagher (Jag), John Pettit, John Young, Kelly Tarlton, Jeff Pearch and Mr. Tarlton, Kelly's father. On a sack in their midst was a small heap of gritty, rust-covered coin. Jag wielded a hefty diving knife and started to hack, scratch and gouge at a coin, hopeful of a golden gleam. The stainless blade flashed on the dirty coin. "Might just be a penny from a passenger's cabin," said John Pettit, voicing a thought in all our minds: "Could this really be the bullion?"

"It's silver," was Jag's verdict.

"More likely this is just the purser's change from the ship's bar," ventured Kelly, who remembered all the wine bottles I'd been posing with. My heart was sinking as the flush of discovery started to fade away. I began to shiver in my wet suit. The sun was setting. We were a lot of pessimists. First we had thought we would never locate the wreck, back in 1965 when we had made our first expedition and chanced upon the wreck's perimeter on our very last dive.

Now we thought we were never to find the bullion. Down below, they all admitted, no one else had given the least consideration to looking for coins. Artifacts: bath tiles, wine bottles, portholes, or photos, that was all the *Elingamite* wreck seemed likely to yield. The search area was just too vast and too deep. At least the proverbial needle in the haystack was on dry land with no limit on time or air. Despite these doubts we were bursting to go below again, but this was impossible.

Our skipper Peter Sheehan was tapping the glass. Our air supply was exhausted and the fine spell was over. Just as the year before, we were heading for home on the verge of a fresh discovery, scurrying into the shelter of North Cape before the storm broke.

The setting sun glowed red in our faces and our knives scraped and clinked. "Say — this one is a half-crown," said Jag.

"Nineteen-hundred." Queen Victoria's stately plump head was just visible through a mud pack of corroded iron rust and adhering coraline growth. Kelly's father, our boatman, was methodically scraping at a smaller coin. "This is a shilling," he announced. "Eighteen seventy-nine."

As others scraped clean more shillings, all with varying dates — 1880, 1875, 1899 — things really began to look grim.

"This can't be the bullion. They wouldn't send a lot of old, used coins across from one bank to another," said Kelly. At that time we did not know much about the *Elingamite* or her cargo, except that her £17,300 consignment was a mixture of silver coin and gold half-sovereigns, dispatched from a Sydney bank to its New Zealand branch in 1902.

"Must be some passenger's savings. Still it is silver coin — let's count it," I urged, excitement still on the simmer. So over the small heap our hands plied until it was all sorted into coin piles. There were a few threepences and sixpences, a dozen pennies and the balance was shillings, florins and half-crowns, totalling in all £15-11 shillings and 8d. Some coins soon cleaned up handsomely, especially those stuck in clumps. Six shillings, cemented together by iron rust, readily fell apart with the tap of a knife to reveal blue-faced Queen Victorias oxided from the small amount of copper in each coin. Three differently designed heads marked successive mintings of the old monarch's likeness, each increasing in severity. My hopes sagged. Clearly this was not bullion: each shilling a different date, even when stuck together in lumps.

As more and more florins and half-crowns were cleaned it was noticed that these were all dated 1900 — two years old when the ship sank. A new theory arose: "Surely no passenger or bar-till would hold so much silver of the same year?" Jag said.

"Might have been a collector with a craze for that date," John Young put in. John was the spearfisherman on our expedition, and a quiet humorist. We could not find a single florin, half-crown, three-pence, sixpence or penny, which was not dated 1900.

The Bullion Theory began to gain deck space. After all, the shillings could just have been dispatched from circulated coin stocks held in the bank vaults. New Zealand and Australia were both using English coinage in 1900, and it was highly unlikely that all the other denominations were not part of a consignment of specie, being without exception of the same minting.

Anyway, while our expedition members argued and scraped and theorised, with a following sea the *Ahiki* surged southward from the Three Kings Islands to New Zealand. Once it grew too dark I went below to my bed on the diesel fuel tank and wrote up my diary for this final day of the trip.

There has always been a rather humorous pattern to our Three Kings diving trips. We have invariably started off pessimistically. Each time, on our last dive, we have been both staggered by a sudden success and frustrated by the relentless verdict of reality. In this remote and exposed area it says: "Get back to the shelter of New Zealand; you have no more air supplies and you can't dive anyway."

So it was in 1966 with this initial coin discovery. And in 1965, without a thought of treasure, we had gone up to the Three Kings on a spear fishing safari, only to make a fluke discovery of the *Elingamite* on our very last dive.

In my 26th year when I found undersea treasure, at this stage in my life I had never experienced any other form of consciousness, not even an anaesthetic. But deep diving produces its own weird chemistries. Later I realized I had undergone an episode of *déjà vu*. Having no cultural context or vocabulary for such a thing, I just dismissed it. I did not dare mention such a "fruit loop" thing to my diving mates. We were all as straight as flagpoles. But a few years later, on an expedition to Stone Age Melanesian societies, I found people living in altered states as part of normal existence.

A Solomon islander with a Ph.D. in anthropology once stayed with us on our Ngunguru rainforest land. As I reviewed my more unusual island experiences [next chapter] with Laurence, he explained that his people don't realise that what westerners refer to as coming from a "sixth sense" are experiences which to them are part of their normal reality. I jumped at that. He went on to explain many episodes I related from our travels that locals had explained as arising from "custom radio." *Custom* is pidgin English for traditional. Custom dress, custom songs, custom carvings, and custom dance.

I realized that during our *El Torito* voyage through Laurence's archipelago we had not grasped the significance of all those explanations given to us that involved a transmitted knowledge of events, as coming from "custom radio"! We had been travelling in a world where 'E.S.P.' was a normal part of living. So many mysteries we had encountered were then comprehensible. I now know that these realities extend from Tibet to Mexico; from the Amazon jungles to ancient cultures of the east. When you encounter them on far flung Pacific Islands it makes you think about how persistent they are; how universal are some aspects of human culture; and often so remote from western minds.

# PART TWO

## NON-WESTERN MIND: THE SHARK CALLERS OF LAULASI

In 1938 Sir Harry Luke, Governor and Commissioner in Chief of Fiji, was making a tour of the Solomon Islands. Late in June he visited Auki Island, in Langalanga Lagoon, Malaita. His journal entry for June 22:

> "It is really beautiful, and in the pearly flush of dawn reminiscent of the lagoon of Venice ... the shark is a sacred and totem animal of the place, and on occasions the particular tutelary fish of the neighbourhood, the 'steady' so to speak, who is marked with a smudge of tar* on his back to be easily recognised, comes along, perhaps accompanied, as today, by a mate, to be fed by three dreadful-looking old priests of the cult. The sharks come swimming slowly from the open sea into a little cove or canoe camber, where the old men feed them with the entrails of dead pig — the pig on this occasion provided by me. The water in the camber is quite shallow — barely a foot or so and the old men tickle the

> sharks and scratch their backs. The sharks seem quite tame, at all events with the old men and the natives of the village who not only have no fear of them and swim in the shark-infested waters unconcernedly, but actually regard them as their protectors . . . ."
>
> — *A South Seas Diary 1938-1942*

[*This "smudge" reference enhances the authenticity of Sir Harry's words: the sharks involved have a black smudge on their dorsals: black-tipped reef sharks.]

January 1973: There it was, the diving ship I had heard so much about. R.V. *El Torito* — a short, squat, steel hull that lay restively against the Sydney wharf; beamy as a tennis court, with the simple, functional lines of an ocean-going barge; her foredeck a sophistry of sea-exploring machines, including a yellow submarine.

I'd heard a lot about Dr. Walter Starck, owner of *El Torito*, and it had all served to make my curiosity keener. Which one was he? Then I saw a lean, lightly-built man standing about five foot eleven in baggy, knee-length pants, nondescript shirt, on bare prehensile feet. He was checking up on the oil flow, topping off one of the stern tanks and filling the other. Surrounded by expedition people loading gear on the after-deck he stood out by his sheer unobtrusiveness. A quiet man, withdrawn in a crowd but radiating capability; effacing himself, it seemed, by being totally there.

In a world in which the pursuit of knowledge is often a staid and serious business, Walt Starck, an American marine biologist, brings a lively and questing spirit as I discover when I join Walt's underwater research vessel, *El Torito*, in Sydney. Our expedition to Melanesia should prove to be a stimulating experience on many levels. A major objective will be to study the habits of sharks, in particular their seemingly unpredictable aggression. Would the wearing of a zebra-striped wet suit, modeled on the sea snake, counter their attacks on divers? As *El Torito* moves northward from Lord Howe Island to New Caledonia, the New Hebrides (now Vanuatu) and the Solomon Islands, Walt and our party will test this theory, learning at the same time much more about these "piranhas of the sea." Eventually our research will takes us to Laulasi off the Malaita coast, where the shark is being worshipped in the old way by a people who have rejected many aspects of Western culture. Walt wants to study these people and document how they reputedly "call sharks" on ceremonial occasions.

## *EL TORITO* SAILS INTO AUKI HARBOUR

After an overhaul, clean-bottomed and full-powered, *El Torito* sets out for Auki, the only town on Malaita. Most populous and least civilised island in the Solomons, Malaita we had heard, still harbours old customs in defiance of missionary zeal.

Through a gap in the coral barrier *El Torito* sails into Auki Harbour: a green bay fringed with grass huts standing on stilts in the shallows and a river running swiftly from the steep jungle clad mountains behind the settlement.

On the morning of our arrival, Terry Hannigan and I take a stroll through the one-street town past the Chinese shops and the Golden Dragon bar. Along the Sunday road we dawdle to the sliding blue river past best-shirted greeters, the kapok trees with their pendulous fruits, the bamboo groves and the *rao* palms. On our singing way back a parrot leaps from a hand. It is beside me on the table as I write. A yellow-bibbed lorrikeet: red body, green wings, royal blue thighs, lemon yellow throat. Its owner, sitting on a tree-shaded canoe hull, tells us it is called Nixon. Walt very much wants a ship's parrot and here it is. We buy Nixon for $3.50.

On the ship Nixon takes over the table, stealing the butter with his furry tongue. That evening we go up to the Auki Club for drinks, hopeful of some leads on the shark cultists. In a valley of palm trees, above the river arced with a rainbow, the eaves of the Auki Club drip from a sudden rain squall. Crickets shriek in dense waves. Glistening frogs hop on the tonsured lawn slopes; passersby on the river road, umbrella-ed, burden-bearing, wharf-bound. We can hear the churchgoers singing while we drink our whisky and below in the town the *Golden Dragon* bar is roaring.

Next day we visit Ambu, the Seventh Day Adventist village adjacent to the town. A packet of *Omo* soap powder on the window ledge of a grass hut speaks eloquently. Such products cost more in Auki than in the United States, yet for people of the Solomons the average wage is a dollar a day. A policeman in Honiara told me proudly he was getting $42 a month.

Encountering the consumer goods, medicine and living standards of the Western world, the Solomons people are easily persuaded to toss aside their traditional beliefs in exchange for Western culture, its religions and money system — a new twist to the cargo cult. Who could resist the teachings of men from big steel ships, with transistor radios, firearms and bulldozers? On the shirt tails of Western technology, the evangelists ride.

At present in Malaita, nine Christian sects are competing vigorously for members. Some people whose parents or grandparents were shark cultists have already belonged to two or three Western faiths. Young men are tossing up apprenticeships in agriculture or as mechanics to become church teachers and convert relatives. Village gardens are neglected for intensive religious services and observances. The tragedy of it all is that these island peoples, on the brink of self-government, are greatly in need of unifying influences. Tribes a few miles apart have quite different languages and customs. Now they also belong to several different religions, most of them of the more fundamentalist, self-righteous brands.

Unable to find adherents in educated areas, proselytisers gain easy pickings among the naive and friendly peoples of the Pacific and whip up cohesion among churchgoers at home with Sunday collections: "Penny in the plate for the savages in the Solomons."

We notice that with many fundamentalist religions outward observances such as dietary restrictions, which have been eased in Western countries, are strongly enforced in the islands. For example, on the outlying Polynesian island of Rennell, the S.D.A. church has convinced the people they should not eat eels, crabs, lobsters, or pork, as being "unclean." With one blow this religion wiped a major part of the islanders' source of protein. Much of what they eat now comes from cans imported from the West. Their rich traditions of music, song and dance have likewise been repressed.

"Hullo friends. My name is Gabriel. I got Jesus. We are all happy in this village, we all got Jesus. Why are you happy?" the native preacher addresses Terry. "Because you have Jesus. We all got Jesus, brothers."

Soap powder too! Ambu children visit the ship. They sing for us. They know no traditional songs, just a saccharine monotony of Bible Belt tunes.

In Ambu village we meet Sadeus who goes fishing with a kite and a ball of spider web.

Sadeus offers to show us how it is done. Behind the village he gathers the webs of the *Nephiles* spider. One of the strongest known, it can even ensnare small birds. A bunch of this web is the bait. Skimming along the surface beneath the kite, the sticky web will entangle the teeth of needlefishes which grab at it.

Sadeus climbs a *rao* palm and tosses down some leaves. These he pins together with slivers of bamboo to form a broad sheet, which he fashions into a bird-shaped kite and attaches to a light bamboo frame.

Out on the lagoon Sadeus lofts his kite, holding the string in his teeth as he paddles. The hank of web dances behind his canoe and the bird-kite flutters thirty feet above; it takes only the slightest breeze to raise it. On a good day Sadeus can catch up to twenty silvery needlefish in this way.

At Auki we hear stories about the Laulasi people. "Never let them on your ship. They are criminals. They are pagans and worship sharks. Soon they are going to have a huge feast and make sacrifices to the sharks."

That was enough for Walt. Hell bent, we headed along the Malaitan coast for the man-made island of Laulasi!

## THROUGH THE TABOO PASS

The old headmasters and priests by the taboo huts cannot believe their eyes: a small white ship is approaching their island. It is heading for the sacred pass in the reef on which their ancestors built the island seventeen generations ago. "Missionaries!" Tofi spits his red betel juice on the coral cobbles. But there is a white girl in a bikini up on the bow. Tourists?

Through the pass, *taboo to all women*, by the taboo huts where the ancestors' skulls are stored, past the canoe landing to which the spirit sharks come for sacrifices, a ship has pushed its way into their lagoon, a ship with *women* aboard. The anchor chain rattles and clangs in their ears. Old Georgi, head priest for the weather, puts on his WWII lemon-squeezer army hat. He calls to Brown Noni, son of Bosikoru the shark priest. Brown paddles him out to the ship.

"Here comes a canoe. Dig that island, man," says Terry. It is like a dream: tall palm trees, grass huts, wisps of woodsmoke. Four solid stone walls, each about 100 metres long, form a square which contains the island. On the seaward side it opens out on to the reef flat of the coral barrier that encloses Langalanga lagoon. On two sides the island is bordered by passes such as the one we just came through. On the landward side the stone wall drops into the deep waters of the lagoon. One hundred metres out we are anchored in ninety feet.

For a dozen miles running down from Auki this lagoon is dotted with artificial islands, some built on the reef itself; others on sand-banks and mangrove clumps. We've passed several stilt villages standing on coral rubble islands out in the lagoon, a series of huts linked by causeways and plank paths. But this one, Laulasi, is a more coherent structure.

Up over our stern a New Zealand army lemon-squeezer hat appears. Proudly the old Laulasi man steps on deck, sucking at a dry pipe. We invite him into the wheel house and give him some stick tobacco. As he stokes up his furnace Georgi begins to tell us about Laulasi. How his people keep the old customs. No missionaries can come on the island. We assured him we aren't missionaries. We explain that we are interested in sharks, that we are making a film about them and that we would like to make one about his village. We would like to stay here until the big feast and film all the customs, and the dances and the sacrifices to the sharks.

Georgi tells us about the war. He shows us a deep, jagged scar on his shoulder. Although there had been no fighting on Malaita, an American plane for some odd reason, maybe just to jettison its load, had dropped three bombs over their tiny island. The explosion killed and injured many villagers. Others, terrified, fled into their huts and were burnt in the conflagration. Georgi tells us the island was bombed because one of the bushmen, their inveterate enemies on the mainland, had tipped off the Americans that the island was giving refuge to some Japanese.

Another canoe arrives. It is Jack Kamada, a powerfully built, middle-aged man, Georgi's stepson, with his little boy called Tommy. Then Georgi tells us what he's come for. All the rest was just small talk. Maybe he doesn't like to come down on us but Jack's arrival brings him to the point.

"Why you come through taboo pass? You got missee on ship?"

Aside, Jack tells Terry and me that if somebody makes his father very angry, he will get some of that man's food and feed it to a spirit shark. Then the shark will attack that man.

We will never know what did it. Maybe it is the sight of all the strange apparatus on the ship when we show them around, or the fact that we are genuinely very sorry at breaking their taboo, of which we are ignorant. Perhaps it is because we are saltwater people like them and so interested in sharks. He sees many pictures of them around. Or is it the tobacco?

Anyway, Georgi forgives us. He invites us to bring the ship over alongside the village for our own safety. All the other villages dotted along the reef and around the lagoon are Christians, he explains. A whole string of different religions are ensconced on the artificial islands of Langalanga lagoon. "They will steal from you if you stay here," he warns us. "Bring your ship close to Laulasi and we will watch it at night."

Our initial uptightness drops away — we will be okay with these people, pagans like ourselves!

Walt makes it clear that we will give them no money. We will help them any way we can, but we will not pay them. That is okay too and it is not long before our chance comes.

The village goes wild with joy when we up-anchor and shift *El Torito* over, accompanied by a huge convoy of canoes and kids. Laulasi is like a dock. A gang plank links our manmade island of technology to their stone-age fortress. And the kids invade the ship. Scores of canoes surround us from dawn to dusk. Naked, laughing boys use the stern platform as a meeting ground. *El Torito*'s sloping steel decks, they discover, make a tremendous slide. Sluicing the decks with the hose renders them slippery to bare skin. Pretty soon there is a living cascade of bare bodies slithering from bow to stern.

"Grab the camera, Walt, the movie has started."

But not once in all our months with them do the kids get out of hand. They never tamper with anything, steal anything or annoy us in the least. On *El Torito* we are late risers. The parents must have noted this and their kids are never allowed on board until one of us appears on deck. We have the same access to their village as they do to *El Torito*.

The next visitor to the ship is Bosikoru Noni, a shark priest. In his forties, a handsome intelligent man, Bosikoru is renowned as a diver. He can reach depths of one hundred feet. He can see a turtle on the bottom, dive down in his blind spot and grab him for *kai-kai*. He tells us that most of the people in the village are divers. The women and the girls dive in the shallows for clam shells to make white shell money. The men dive in the lagoon to depths of sixty feet or more for the red-shelled oyster, from which the precious red-shell money is made. Laulasi and other villages of the lagoon are the *mint* where shell money is manufactured for use throughout the Solomons and even up into the highlands of New Guinea.

We take Bosikoru out in the skiff to show us around the area so we will not break any more taboos. Returning to the island he takes the controls and speeds towards the canoe landing at thirty miles an hour. The kids whoop for joy. Bosikoru, the leading shark priest, is a very important person in the village. He often travels to Honiara, and even to a South Seas Art Festival in Fiji as leader of a Solomon's dancing troupe. He understands our purpose fully and undertakes to help us in every possible way to make a good film of life in Laulasi including the manufacture of shell money, skull houses, the sacrifices and other special ceremonies leading up to their big feast in about six weeks' time.

## LOST CANOE: A PSYCHIC EPISODE

When something goes wrong on Laulasi, everybody is aware in next to no time. Old Georgi comes downstairs beside himself with worry. A canoe has sunk. It is Jack's canoe with a precious outboard on it. Jack is away at the gardens on the mainland. Georgi borrowed the canoe and sent his youngest son over to the mainland to get a load of stones. Maintaining an artificial island is a never-ending job: walls must be repaired with blocks of coral rock and the interior resurfaced with canoe-loads of porous white coral gravel. The boy overloaded the canoe. Crossing the lagoon, the afternoon breeze lashed the water surface into a short chop. Jack's canoe disappeared into the green murk of the lagoon. We decide we just had to find that canoe. If it is not located, with all the diving gear we have, its loss might be interpreted as a bad omen, casting a pall on the big feast.

Our first day's search only serves to show us how difficult the task will be. The boy has very little idea as to where it went down. Next day we do an intensive hunt for the lost canoe. Six canoes tow six divers in a patterned search. Visibility is fifteen feet and the bottom, at around 100 feet, is a series of ridges and valleys, huge basket sponges, staghorn coral, soft corals and lots of small fish. *But no canoe.*

That night a medium in the village, Angiso, dreams how we can find the canoe. We must take nothing red with us, nor any women from the island. All her guidelines are followed. The canoe is swiftly found and towed back to Laulasi. At the sacred canoe landing, by the taboo huts, Bosikoru purges it of evil spirits with special prayers. Then Walt takes the outboard back to *El Torito,* strips it down, cleans and reassembles it.

Jack, who returned to the sadness of a lost canoe and a distraught Georgi, are all smiles. Everyone is happy. From our desperation to please the island elders, and our initial failure, we divers are re-instated in the village because we listened to that medium and followed her instructions to the letter.

That night we run a power cable ashore and set up a slide projector in the village. About 120 people gather to see our pictures of sharks, the submarine and reef fishes, which they recognise with delight. Then Terry plays the guitar and sings their favourite songs: hillbilly, country and western, the music their transistors bring them from Honiara radio. The boys dance and sing. The girls sing in unison but never dance with the boys. That is not the custom. One boy, Stanley, is a star performer. Like a limbo dancer, undulating and grimacing hideously, he folds himself slowly to the ground backwards, his elbows and shoulders writhing sideways rhythmically, his whole body contorting, convulsing in spasms, with hoots of laughter, bloodcurdling screams and whoops of joy. I match his antics. The kids squeal with pleasure.

"They encourage their eccentrics," says Terry, "not ostracising them or forcing them to conform."

Damn Nixon. He won't let me reload my Rollei camera! In the wheel house he pulls at the stitching on my wet suit seams, and when I mend it, he eats the neoprene glue, old sticky beak. "Nixon's shit on my shirt," growls Terry.

Georgi, Bosikoru and Jack come down, when the drowned outboard is running sweetly, and invite us to the taboo ground. We are welcome to bring our cameras and they will explain everything to us: a rare opportunity. When we reach a point two-thirds along the island, Georgi shows us an invisible demarcation line beyond which it was taboo for women. Leaving the fair sex to see the taboo-to-men maternity hut, and the moonblood hut (menstruation quarters), the male chauvinists go on towards the three ancient grass huts with their high-pitched, shaggy-thatched roofs and low walls. Above each hut is a signboard with a totem carved on it.

We approach the main hut. The board reads "Headmaster Macmadama (name of guardian priest) *Aniboni* 1947." Beside this the frigate bird totem perches on a pointed canoe paddle. *Aniboni*, I learn, means "counting the days."

Nodding respectfully to Moses, the chief priest and ancient guardian of this hut, we step over a sill into an antechamber where two shark altars stand, mounds of flat coral stones and ashes where sacrifices are prepared. The headmasters also cook their own food here once they become priests. They cannot eat anything touched by a woman. We step over another sill into the hut proper. There are no windows, just the dim light filtering between woven walls. Beneath our bare feet the earth is dank and greasy. I shudder. It feels as if the sweat of sacrificial victims has soaked into the floor. Nowadays pigs are used for sacrifices, but this same ground was used for human sacrifices only a few generations ago when captured bushmen died here.

At the far end, a pile of skulls show green or gleaming pale in the half-light. Cigar-shaped fish traps made from split bamboo hang on the rear wall. These hold the most distinguished skulls. A shelf stores several more that belonged to priests and headmasters of the past; some might be centuries old. Six days after death, Jack explains to me, the head of the deceased is removed according to a special ritual and placed in a fish trap in the ocean until it is clean.

When the custom feasts or *maoma* are held, at irregular intervals of twenty to thirty years, all the skulls are removed so that they can participate in the feasts. The spirits thus placated, any skulls no longer of importance can then be disposed of. At this time special, large-scale sacrifices to the ancestral spirits must be made. This we will see within a few weeks as they are preparing for a huge *maoma,* the first since just after the war.

Among the skulls are several coconuts. Bosikoru explains that during the disastrous cyclone that hit the island last year, the worst in its history, the hut was damaged, sweeping some of the skulls into the lagoon. "Some turned into coconuts," Georgi says.

At the very end of the island, next to the taboo pass we've infringed, the third skull house holds the sacred basket of *Chama* shells, a rock oyster from which shell money is made. Now heavily calcined with age, these shells were placed there by the first comers to the island. They commemorate Avelaua, the shell money lady, who had led the Laulasi people to the island and taught them how to make shell money. From this the shark cult arose, as the spirits of ancestors, whom they worship, take the form of guardian sharks. Whenever they dive for shell money the spirit sharks protect them, enabling them to dive deeper — provided they do everything right by them, observing the rituals and taboos of the shark cult. Otherwise the sharks will kill them. This basket is the most taboo and sacred object on the island. Not even the chief priest, Moses, nor Ansiagallo the headmaster of this hut, can touch the shell basket.

The main support of the hut is a stout post which bears the design of a fish, its tail skywards, its head plunging towards the earth; at the foot of this post is a mound of coral stones. Beneath the mound, Bosikoru tells us, there is the spirit of the man who holds the hut up. When it was built long ago, a deep pit was dug for the post. A captive bushman was told that if he got into the pit he would be released. The post was thrust down on his body and now his spirit forever strengthens the hut against cyclones and disasters.

Just outside this hut, on the northwest corner of the island, we are shown a rectangular stone enclosure, part of the seaward wall, elevated three feet and boxed off. In one corner is a neat, tent-shaped pile of small coral stones thatched with palm leaves. In this place, Bosikoru says, the chief priest gives departing warriors talismans, which will ward off danger. We are told that no men who had these stones were killed in the last war.

On the very corner of the island is a three-forked stick. Georgi, the weather priest, explains that this stick, plus another across the taboo channel on the mangrove bank adjacent, is to ward off cyclones or huge waves and protect the island. At special ceremonies such as we will see, their power is renewed.

Gradually I begin to see a meaning in it all. These people, living in a stone-age society that is stable and unchanging, find it natural to worship their ancestors, who have all the knowledge necessary for survival. In our society every time we visit a library we're doing the same.

Since men have to undertake many dangerous tasks, such as deep diving, for which they need spiritual reinforcing, it is natural that there should be an area taboo to women. The reinforcement "magic" is strongest on all-male ground: since they alone must face such dangers, they prepare for them alone.

This community has no dominant chief but works by a consensus process, with greatest influence vested in the elders who traditionally have had the most knowledge. Women can act as spiritual mediums, magical healers and midwives. Since men lead the community in most other respects the old priests are revered. They live apart, and care for themselves, close to the skulls of their predecessors. In this way a continuity of spiritual contact is maintained. Consulted by the villagers for guidance and advice in their everyday lives, minor crises and problems, the old men are able to exert authority and leadership over the village without there being any one chief, any dictator. In this society consensus emerges by finding out what the ancestors would have done in a given situation. The priests on the taboo ground are there to provide the answers and to teach the villagers all the complex rituals and taboos they must follow to preserve the village from disasters, both physical and spiritual.

The women of Laulasi make rope from plant fibres, tend mainland gardens, gather and prepare food, and manufacture shell money. Men catch fish, tend gardens, make long canoe journeys to trade, build huts and dive deep for the most precious red shells.

We pass the island's stonewalled pig pens or *banisi*. Each pig is owned by a leading male. The pens are scrupulously clean — living on coral rubble must be ideal for pig raising — and flies are seldom seen at Laulasi. Adjacent to the pig pens is the moonblood hut.

During menstruation Laulasi women have a complete break from routine household duties. They must not prepare food but live apart, in the *moonblood* hut. They swim daily in the sea alongside — gossip, sing and relax.

In the village's big communal hut women are making shell money. Malaitan shell money is a manufactured item involving a complicated process and not just the stringing together of natural shells. The women sit around in groups, each engaged in some stage of manufacture. A couple are chipping pieces of broken shell into roughly rounded discs about 3cm across. These discs are placed in circular depressions on the face of a block of white stone: ten small, saucer-shaped craters. A grinding paste of wet sand is smeared over them and the stone is rubbed on a large rock slab until the discs are ground smooth and of uniform thickness.

At this stage a hole must be drilled in each disc, using an agate-tipped pump drill. I try one and it takes only a few attempts to get the pendulum rhythm, which makes the drill spin on the down-stroke of the crossbow and wind up again in a spiral. Momentum comes from a wooden or turtle shell flywheel just above the fibre binding which secures the agate tip. This igneous stone bit, orange-yellow and slightly translucent, is sharper and harder than steel. To get a sharp edge on the agate, it is chipped with a large cockle shell. (Georgi uses a pair of shells like this to pluck his beard out, bristle by bristle.) It is hard to make the initial indentation in the shell, but as soon as the indentation is made, working from each side to avoid splitting, the hole is quickly made. The pierced discs are threaded on palm fibre string.

The outside edges are made perfectly round and reduced to the correct diameter by a laborious grinding process, the only part of the operation which men undertake. A strand is stretched along a plank. At each end a man sits astride the strand. They have a brick-shaped grinding stone grooved along its underside. Smearing this with a grinding paste they fit the stone groove over the shell strand and shunt the stone back and forth. The strand is rotated and the finished article is a long cylinder of thin shell discs. The smaller the diameter to which they are ground, the more valuable they are. In our currency, a red shell-money bride belt with turtle shell spacers can be worth three hundred dollars. Shell-money discs of various colours, red, white, orange and black, are threaded together on fresh strings to make elaborate patterns.

The strands are interwoven and laid up into necklace bands of five or ten, or fashioned into armbands and bracelets.

Besides its use in transactions involving food for feasts and canoes, the most important function of shell money is for the bride price. The parents of a boy must present gifts of shell money in the form of bride belts to the bride's parents in payment for their daughter and in recognition of their efforts to rear her as a good and capable wife.

We have heard of this bride price system from the European viewpoint, which makes it sound as though the islanders are buying and selling their women like a commodity. The churches, especially the fundamentalist ones, detest this bride price system and object to the wearing of any decorative artwork. In destroying the bride price system they are tearing apart the fabric of a complex and intricate culture. The result is often the break-up of village life and the inevitable drift to the town, where island people work for a dollar a day, their rich village culture replaced by cheap movie houses and bars.

The girls of Laulasi, we learn, are virgins until they are married. By Malaitan custom a man caught in an affair with a young woman must either pay the bride price, through his own family, or her family will kill him. The girl at the marriage ceremony holds a sprouting coconut. Symbolic of fertility it is also (like a white wedding dress) a token of her virginity, for by custom she knows that only a virgin can hold such a symbol at her wedding. If she breaks this custom she believes she will die. Autosuggestion would probably ensure this. So, as we will find later, when we join in *moongames* with the young people, Laulasi teenagers have a relationship strangely free of sexual tensions. Since parents choose and arrange marriages, doing the very best they can for their sons; and since daughters are groomed to the highest possible degree for marriage, the young people don't worry about courtship, jealousies, self-doubt, and all the tortures of adolescence.

Ironically, in discouraging the bride price system among their converts, Christian missionaries are destroying one of the few non-promiscuous cultures in the modern world. As in our own culture, Christian girls are fair game. For some of the young Laulasi bucks the sight of a pretty Christian girl with a cross around her neck, from one of the adjacent villages, is enough to start the pulse racing.

## FUNERAL DANCE TO A MEDIUM'S SONG

The day after our village tour we plan to go out with Jack and Peter Kia, two of the best shell money divers in the village, to film them diving for red-shell oysters deep in the lagoon. But the news comes that Jack's mother Naoli has died during the night. The old lady has been critically ill for some time. She has been in hospital in Honiara but returns to Laulasi to die. On her deathbed her daughters, living in an adjacent Christian village, convert her to their faith and take her away. So she does not die in Laulasi, but has spent her entire life here.

Jack has to buy cabin biscuits, sugar, tea and cocoa for the funeral celebration. We give him a ride down to Auki in the skiff. According to tradition the village will dance all through the night until first light, sustained by Jack's supplies. In the morning the burial will take place.

Towards dusk the villagers begin to gather in the communal hut and in the adjacent square. Georgi invites us to join in the funeral celebrations and we are provided with traditional clothes; men wear tapa cloths (tree bark) and women, grass skirts. We decide it is good form to see it right through to dawn. This is to be no mournful occasion, but a real festivity. Walt runs a power cable ashore from the ship and rigs up lights over the village square. Laulasi people arrive from the mainland, wherever they have intermarried or shifted (last year's cyclone displaced a large number) and are shining with excitement at coming home. Rufalua, a medium, begins to wail. I think, here it comes, a keening concert. I have a loathing of that ever since the time I'd acted the part of a dead body in an Irish play. Under a bit of hessian cloth, with Irish women wailing over me, my nose started to itch. It was hell, and I couldn't move. The curtain came down. End of the tragedy. Thunderous applause. I sat up and scratched my nose. The clapping continued and the curtain rose. There was the corpse... the clapping went wild.

But no, this wailing gives way to a tune. The tune develops and strengthens. She is composing it on the spot for her friend. The village women rehearse the tune, crooning it together. Then Rufalua starts to develop a ballad story of Naoli's life, her husband, her children, finding food, all the daily tasks the dead woman knew and performed so well. The women rehearse, rephrasing each idea with different words and sing them in harmony. Jack is telling us what the words are about when Rufalua starts to include *El Torito* in her spontaneous song:

*A ship comes to Laulasi*
*We live with the people in that ship*
*They are very honest, good people*
*Now they are staying with us like brothers and sisters*
*We do not know where they come from*
*But while they are here they are very friendly*
*We want them to come back and see us*
*Happy that they are being here with us today*
*At the funeral dance of Naoli.*

The singers then begin to develop a dance routine. Each grasping a long pole, they move in a huge circle to a series of fast steps and pauses, syncopated with blows of their sticks on the coral gravel. The song and the dance go on all through the night, a marathon performance. Old Georgi, in full regalia, walks around with tape recorder and microphone, his betelnut bag around his neck — a fantastic anachronism. Bosikoru urges the dancers on, whipping things along until they are in a trance state — an effortless, timeless patterned performance. Georgi offers Terry and me some betel, really bitter betel. We find it a mind-changing euphoriant, although few Westerners would persist in chewing it, being so astringent. But within the ambience of village life, you must persist or appear rude. And so, in the cultural context it gets through to us and makes us high.

"What did you say Georgi?"

"Not any something," he replies with a broad, stoned grin, not wanting to be recorded on my tape just then.

At midnight we share their favourite drink, a pleasant concoction of tea, cocoa and sugar with thick slabs of cabin biscuits, and we appreciate what a treat it really is.

A strange figure joins the dancers. Contortions, grimacing and outrageous posturing; Stanley in a grass skirt, coconut shells for breasts, the village clown livening up the funeral dance.

Next morning, in a downpour of rain, we cross to the adjacent island. In a simple coffin of wooden planks, Naoli is buried in a sand pit. His prayer book protected by a banana leaf, a preacher reads a Christian burial service. Jack is not there, nor is his father, just Naoli's daughters, their girlfriends from Laulasi, and people from the Christian village where she died.

The pagans have the last word. As the Laulasi girls set about to paddle their canoe back to their island it is seized by violent rocking, which eventually capsizes all the girls, screaming with laughter, into the sea. We are told this is Naoli's spirit, communicating that it is free and has escaped the Christians.

From our anchored skiff we can clearly see the women sitting in their canoe totally relaxed and smiling. They are not clutching the sides or making any physical effort. Their hands are clasped in their laps. Yet that canoe rocks so vigorously it turns right over!

With Jack and Peter Kia we set off two miles down the lagoon towards Auki. Peter has made red ochre patterns on his cheekbones with chewed betelnut. This is the tradition for the shell diver to show that he has made peace with the shark spirits.

At forty feet in the gloom of the lagoon Walt and I film Peter moving around looking for the red-shelled rock oyster. The only gear he has is a thirty-cent pair of plastic goggles. His endurance is excellent. The shells, encrusted with sponge growths, are very hard to find even when you know what to look for. On each dive Peter gets four or five. With scuba on it took me ages to locate one to photograph. Peter and Jack firmly believe that keeping the shark custom enables them to stay down longer. They say there has never been a shark attack on a Laulasi diver in the lagoon or on the outer reef.

Maybe there is something in this. I recall the experimental work done by Ted Hobson at Eniwetok Atoll. This outstanding fish scientist has made a study of the feeding behaviour of greys, blacktips and whitetip reef sharks. He found the grey "is often highly excited by and attracted to a source of rapid and/or erratic movement." (*Pacific Science Vol. 17*, April 1963).

Such would be the case with a diver who, feeling no bond with the sharks, reacted in panic when they approached.

It was also found that all three species can detect by smell the presence of an uninjured but distressed fish. A captive grouper with no external injury whatsoever was held in a plastic container. At intervals the fish was agitated with a pole. When water from the container was discharged downcurrent, sharks were attracted.

According to the degree of distress, the fish released some stimulating olfactory substance. This metaboloid or *schreckstoff*, which sharks can detect, might also be released by frightened humans. Perhaps the Laulasi divers, unafraid of sharks because of their religion, are avoiding giving certain biological cues, which stimulate shark attack.

As Walt says of the shark cult: "In our culture sharks are viewed as dangerous, unpredictable animals, at best something to be avoided, but in these Pacific islands man has lived for thousands of years in close relationship with sharks. And so in some areas people have come to look upon sharks not as dangerous enemies but as guardians and benevolent spirits, as animals which can actually help them. Naturally enough these beliefs were embodied in their traditional religions, which unfortunately have now been largely supplanted and destroyed with the influence of Christian missionaries. In a few isolated areas such as Laulasi the traditional religious beliefs involving sharks are still maintained. I'm curious to know if perhaps, in their special relationship with sharks, island people know anything about them that we don't."

On our return to Laulasi, we begin to understand what the divers meant. "Quick, come to the taboo ground. Kulani is speaking with the voice of the ancestors." Ramo, the coolest guy in the village, is shaking with excitement. We grab cameras and tape recorders.

In front of the three taboo huts we find everyone seated in clusters under trees, on canoes and around hut entrances. One man is speaking, or rather shouting in a breathless, wild manner. Sentences explode in staccato bursts, hoarse guttural words are repeated at machinegun speed, his voice rising to breakpoint and sobbing. All the while this powerfully built man, Kulani, about fifty years old but in perfect shape, is pacing to and fro wearing only a bark cloth. He is dancing on his toes, waving his arms, leaping and pirouetting like a ballet star. I know Kulani is a very quiet and gentle man, a priest for fertility and famine. The transition is incredible. I realise now that *Kulani is a shaman*, and that he is in a state of ecstatic trance.

Among primitive peoples all over the world the possessed shaman incarnates ancestor spirits and at ritual seances exhorts his people to shun social evils, emphasising the value of harmony in social relations. The shaman gives expression to the sentiments of his people. He is called on to settle disputes and is asked to decide issues concerning succession to priesthoods and chieftainships. Kulani follows the standard pattern described in anthropological literature.

This day Bosikoru has chosen to go to Buma village on an errand. Is it by chance that Kulani's trance occurs during this absence? A year before, Bosikoru left the island to visit Fiji with a dancing troupe on a government sponsored tour. On his return, he dallied one day in the town of Honiara. Had he returned home as scheduled things may have been different, but the day he was supposed to return Cyclone Ida, the worst in the island's history, hit Laulasi. Cyclones originate in this area but seldom cause damage. The portion of the island where Bosikoru has three huts was completely destroyed by the sea. It vanished into the lagoon. All the rest of the island survived, beaten but intact. Bosikoru returned to chaos.

Now the spirit of the ancestors, through Kulani, is warning the villagers that Bosikoru, who was appointed to be the chief shark priest when the old one had died, must sacrifice a pig and prepare to take up his duties. My young friend Wale takes the tape recorder and translates Kulani's words for me with surprising fluency.

Kulani: "There is one trouble that should be fixed before the feast. We must offer sacrifice to the sharks. Unless we do this, the whole village will be wiped out. A serious problem exists to do with the sea. All the shark spirits must be placated, the spirits of our ancestors." Eyes closed, he wails: "Aieeee, aieee." His voice pleads, rising to a crescendo. Then he howls and grunts and he leaps about. "Aagh, aagh." He looks exhausted, like a man exercising heavily, his energy failing. A brief rest and he resumes.

Now Moses, chief priest for wind and the weather, and other priests put questions to the spirits speaking through Kulani.

"Everybody must do this to save the village. This island originated from the sea. Sharks and sea spirits largely control the island. Those who know the sharks best must intercede with the shark spirits, or with tidal waves, fierce storms, earthquakes and bloodshed they will wipe out the whole island.

"It is your duty to think about this and work it out in your minds — a very important thing in the lives of the people of Baekwa, the shark worshippers. Bosikoru must fix the problem. When this island was founded originally, it was linked with the sharks. The shark cult must be followed, or trouble will arise.

"Six months ago this problem should have been fixed. If the feast is to go well it must be done."

After two hours, Kulani sags and falls silent. Throughout his tirade the villagers have shown neither tension nor anguish. They just sit around at ease, looking quite casual. Now every man and boy wipes his hands with leaves of the sacred tree growing between the taboo huts and troops down to the taboo canoe landing where they stoop to rinse their hands. Ramo says this signifies that they have been in a sacred place and are ready to go home again. We join in, all the *El Torito* men, ready to resume our ordinary lives.

Bosikoru tells us he is going to sacrifice a pig to the sharks tomorrow and that we should get ready to film it. We can watch the ritual in the taboo hut, and then film the sharks when they come in.

We discuss with him the preparations for the feast. The Laulasi people want to go over to Honiara to sell shell money and wood carvings in order to buy supplies for the feast. Walt offers to take a party over. Poor Bosikoru — he has the task of selecting the thirty voyagers.

Talking over the funeral I ask him how they can maintain the custom ways with the Christian influence on young people at school. He says that many will return to custom ways. He himself has been a Christian once and so have many men at Laulasi. He says the church people think Naoli's spirit has gone to heaven but they know it is in a shark, a good shark that will help her husband and children.

When *El Torito* returns to Laulasi in the afternoon, Bosikoru leads Terry and me down to the taboo huts to observe preparations for his sacrifice. He takes some earth from beneath the sacred tree. He places it on the shark altar fire on which a pig has been sacrificed earlier by another priest. He heats the earth and speaks to the spirits. Then he takes the earth to the canoe landing, immerses it and mixes it to paste. Each shark priest rubs some on his palms and purges his hands clean in the sacred cove. Bosikoru then takes some pig remnants, scraps from various parts of the body — feet, belly, head, etc. — from a rattan bag, and heats them over a low fire at the rear of the taboo hut. Murmuring to the shark spirits he eats them.

## SHARK SACRIFICE AND CUSTOM SONGS

Within the antechamber of *Aniboni*, Bosikoru is preparing a fire on his shark altar, aided by the other shark priests. Split logs are arranged in a square stack with a layer of black cooking stones on top, and then set alight.

In front of Walt, Terry and myself lies a forty-pound pig, its legs trussed securely. Bosikoru enters the main chamber of the hut and returns with a knife and a woven rope. He places a hitch around the pig's head, near the ears, and begins to bind the muzzle tightly, working towards the snout. The pig's horrified squeals subside as it struggles and snuffles for breath. It is a favourable omen: the pig dies at the last turn of the rope and no blood comes from the nostrils. Bosikoru chants words to the shark spirits about the offering he is making. The other priests hold the legs steady and with bundles of burning palm fronds they singe off the hair while Bosikoru scrapes the skin with clam shells. The hut is full of smoke but the priests must not smoke their pipes.

From *El Torito* a cable is running through the village to this hut, for our movie floods. Funny to think of the generator spinning in the engine room, lighting for televiewers this weird scene in the smoky taboo hut as the pig is eviscerated, its legs cut off the body and the rib cage removed so that the torso is transformed into a big sheet of flesh. The entrails are placed on a long wooden tray shaped like a fish.

By now the fire has burned down, leaving a heap of very hot stones in the ashes. The legs are seared over an open flame and then wrapped in banana leaves with the hot stones. The meat sheet is placed on these covered with banana leaves and edible green leaves from the sacred *rara'ava* tree growing beside the hut. Alternate layers of hot stones and leaves are placed over the meat in a mound, with flat slabs of coral on top to keep the heat in. Now everybody must leave the hut while the pig cooks. It will then be eaten as a sacrament by Bosikoru and his fellow priests.

Shark priest Tofi Atakwa walks down from the taboo hut to the canoe landing. On the large, fish-shaped tray the nude man carries the entrails of the freshly sacrificed pig. He is threading the entrails on a palm fibre string secured to a lump of coral stone.

Waist-deep in the water he is sorting out the cord with the entrails on the end.

The men of the *El Torito* team stand on the corner of Laulasi. Janice is watching the ceremony from a distance; no women can come on this taboo ground.

Tofi swims out over the clear blue waters of the reef passage, and anchors the offering in fifteen feet of water. The spirit of an ancestor in the form of a shark may take the offering. If a shark appears it is a good omen, showing acceptance by the spirits. The entrails are bobbing in a pink cloud as Tofi swims back inshore underwater.

At this time we have been on the island two weeks and have not seen a single shark. The children swim here every day and we have often dived in the area. There is no current just now to carry the scent. We wonder how long it will take for the sharks to appear, or if one will appear at all. Above us, beside the old taboo hut, the other shark priests are intoning prayers to the shark spirits as the ritually killed pig cooks on the altar stones. With tape recorder, movie and still cameras, we await the sacred sharks. Less than a hundred feet away a group of children are laughing and splashing. Nobody seems in the least concerned.

"There's a shark!" shouts Walt. "A blacktip!"

Only five minutes have elapsed before the first one appears. Two more join it, circling the food offering, mouthing it but not swallowing until they've made a number of turns and manoeuvres. Our cameras hum and click. They are small blacktips, up to five feet long, but quite capable of inflicting serious injury. Then they strike. A snout comes out of the water, a tail lashes around, and there is nothing left. Still the children, playing in the same warm sea and the village life continuing unperturbed: the swish, swish of people grinding shell money strings on wooden planks, roosters crowing, girls singing.

Waiting to film the next sequence, when the priests will eat their sacrament, Walt and I sit on the wall stones looking out over the calm lagoon as canoes come and go.

Almost every activity now is in preparation for the *maoma*, the biggest feast in the lives of most of the Laulasi people. Only the old priests know the pattern of rituals and ceremonies that will follow these initial shark sacrifices, culminating with the sharks' enormous banquet when scores of pigs will be slaughtered here in the same way.

From the mainland come canoe loads of firewood to fuel the altar fires; from sand cays on the main reef, loads of coral rubble to resurface the floors of every hut on the island and all the open spaces; clean and white, musically tinkling under bare feet.

As we swelter there on the taboo ground the village is a hive of industry. New huts are springing up in every available space: men are lashing framework and thatching roofs, women weaving walls. There will be many visitors coming to the *maoma*, families of Laulasi men and women who have married outside the village but who still feel the tug of the shark cult.

"Sharks apparently live a very long time," Walt says, as we chew over the things we've seen. "From the very slow growth of those Jack Randall and I have tagged and some other growth studies, a large shark may be fifty to eighty years old, maybe more; we can't be sure, but certainly much older than the average bony fish. If this is the case then there's a good chance that individual sharks can become conditioned over a period of years, living around a village.

"Wow, look at that!" A shark swims right in beneath us. Five feet away and two feet beneath the surface it swoops in and snaps up a stray piece of pig gut that some little barred *pomacentrids* are feeding on.

Just a few hundred yards away in the taboo pass, four Laulasi men with two canoes are herding fish towards a long net floating just beneath the surface. One man in a canoe is beating the water with a stick. Three swimmers are driving the school towards the net, leaping out like polo players and flailing their arms on the surface to confuse the fish. With so many sharks about their sangfroid is too much to believe!

Bosikoru comes down from the taboo hut, chewing a piece of pork. "Lucky for you. Lucky you come and join us at this time. Wherever you go in the world now luck must follow you. This will make you lucky with the sharks. When you show your films you must be lucky." Over near the hut, Ansiagallo and the other priests are all chewing.

"*Funabu*," Bosikoru explains. The pig's belly is the part that is forbidden for other people. Only the priests and their helpers can share this bit. They chew it, speak quietly to their ancestors, and then come down to the water's edge and wash the tray. Fishes snap up bits of tree cabbage and morsels of pork.

Bosikoru tells us a strange story which I have heard from several others, including a man at Auki, and the Malaitan church minister who officiated at the burial of Jack's mother. Each account is identical in most respects.

Four men are travelling in a cutter from Malaita to Florida to get pigs for a feast. The cutter sinks. There are two men from Laulasi and two from the coast. They start to swim. At six in the morning, on their third day in the water, a shark comes along and takes one of the Laulasi men on its back. He holds its fin and is taken to a small island on the south end of Florida. People are amazed to see him arrive. He says: "You wait. My brother will soon be here." Next day his brother is deposited on the beach. The two non-Laulasi men are lost.*

*CHILD RESCUED BY A SHARK — *Solomon Islands Radio* 16/12/74:

"A Tulagi correspondent claims a boy who fell off a boat earlier this month was rescued by a shark. The boy, Philip Naotaraha, was eating a meal perched on the rail of the catcher-boat, *Chohachi Maru*, sailing between Savo and Gela on December the fifth. The sea was very rough and the boy fell overboard. No one else aboard the boat noticed him fall. Our correspondent, Xachary Taihu, says Philip spent the night in the sea. In the morning he says the boy saw a shark coming towards him, and for his life. But the boy spoke a custom spell of his people, and the fish pushed him ashore at Sandfly on Gela. Exhausted, Philip spent a day and a night there, before local people returned him to Tulagi. There have been many reports from different parts of the world of people being pushed ashore by dolphins, but none of any being saved by a shark."

Then Jack Kamada comes over to me and explains the events of the past few days. Somehow he knows I am puzzled and he certainly finds a good opportunity to explain.

One night there was a big stir in the village. John Makoro, Jack's brother-in-law from a neighbouring Christian village, arrived at Laulasi with two other men, known as troublemakers. All three men were drunk, waving a bottle of methylated spirits and orange juice around. Meths drinking is a serious problem in the islands. When a man earns a dollar a day, whisky costs a week's work; but he can buy a bottle of this more effective nerve poison for twenty cents.

The drunks were sent away. Next morning Bosikoru and Georgi came down to the ship and asked us to radio the police at

Honiara. John was missing. Jack's wife was weeping inconsolably for her brother. Poor Jack — the lost canoe, his mother's death, and now this.

An expert fisherman, John often makes eighty-mile trips across to Honiara to sell his catch. He is a polio victim, a huge man down to the waist, his legs are shrivelled to the size of a child's. Later that night, it appears, John had headed his outboard powered canoe straight out to sea, alone in the middle of the night.

Just as Kulani said, there would be trouble in the village. John Makoro wasn't keeping the customs. He had been earning good money from his fishing but he did not make any sacrifices to the spirit of his grandfather. Because of this, an evil spirit had seized him and his canoe when he was drinking meths. He didn't know where he was going yet he arrived at Ngella (in the Florida Group) and returned to the lagoon some days later. Then he had brought a pig down to the taboo ground for Ansiagallo to sacrifice — that was the offering that had preceded Bosikoru's.

Jack looks sleepy. I ask him why. He says he is scared that people from the Christian villages may sabotage *El Torito* to bring shame on his people. So every night he and other Laulasi men stay up in the custom hut to keep an eye on the ship. Tonight, Jack says, old Amoko wants me to come to his hut again. He will sing me some more custom songs and old stories about Laulasi.

After sundown Jack comes for me. Taking my hand, as is the custom with friends and brothers, I set out with him through the village with the Akai tape deck to the hut of old Amoko. I run a power cable through Laulasi village to Amoko's hut. People working by firelight smile and call "Wadey" softly as I pass by, groups weaving walls for new huts, stacking firewood from canoes, knotting palm fibre dancing skirts, labouring far into the night in readiness for the *maoma.*

I met Amoko weeks ago as he sat outside his hut making intricate shell money armlets. He asked me for some tobacco. I brought him three sticks from Auki. Like an ascetic, biblical figure Amoko hobbles around the village with a long pole, instead of using a crutch. One knee joint is in a permanent bandage, stuffed with special leaves. A gap-toothed, betel-stained grin.

One day he seizes my hand firmly, leans forward on his stick and tells me to bring tobacco to his hut. He will sing me some custom songs. That is the first of four visits to Amoko's hut. Thereafter the old man sends word that he has some more songs for me to hear. I think he understands the value of the tape recorder. He knows that his songs should be passed on to the young people. They like listening to Dusty Springfield broadcasts from Honiara on their transistors. They like tape recorders too. Whenever Amoko and his friends sing for me, young people gather around and listen. Each recording has to be played back for them.

My friend Ramo translates each song for me. This is a complex process as the songs are in an archaic language understood only by the old men. After each song they explain its content to Ramo in the Laulasi language. Ramo then relays it to me on the tape in pidgin English. This was really an interview; if I can't follow something I ask Ramo. Sometimes he rephrases his meaning for me. Quite often it is necessary for him to question Amoko further. This clearly pleases the singers. They can see it is coming across and they willingly explain.

Tonight Walt asks me to make some really high quality recordings for his film sound track. I set the tape up on a sleeping bench and operate it by remote control. I sit with the old Laulasi men in the thatched hut: just the glow of the embers of a wood fire on the coral floor and their pipes winking in the warm darkness.

"Ungh, Ungh. Yi Yi Yiii." Then Amoko in a high, quavering voice leads off, the other three harmonising, establishing a clean rhythm with their wooden instruments. Amoko holds a pair of batons, which give a high-pitched, staccato beat. Two others strike sticks on a section of bamboo or a spearshaft: bop Bop, bop Bop, bop Bop: a rhythm exactly twice as fast as my heart beat at rest, or the same as when I'm dancing. A deep bass voice trails behind, giving the sound a broad spectrum in time and space: "Kiorakia, kiorakia, o sali, sali."

Each song, expressed in the first person, conveys a facet or cameo of the Laulasi culture. Often tragic, they seem to represent the people's longing to conform to the village code by putting both listener and singer in the place of somebody who, having broken the custom, has been exiled from the village. Others tell of courage in repelling giant invaders; of transporting the spirit of a dead relative across the sea; of journeys and famines; shell diving and spirit sharks; sexual peccadilloes and black-birders (European kidnappers of endentured labour).

During one session a blood-curdling wailing joins their voices. "Aieee!" It is Jack. I am told that sometimes when such songs are being sung, the spirit of an ancestor may speak through a man in this way. Jack had reason enough for the blues.

1. Ari sings this song. He is on a canoe journey to Marau Sound (South Guadalcanal). They are preparing a feast at Laulasi and he is going to find some pigs. On his way to Marau at night he sings about what he is doing as he paddles his canoe.

2. Walmae has fled for his life to Marau. In olden days people in the lagoon fought one another. Living at Marau he sings this song about fleeing from his enemies.

3. This song is about a shark. Laulasi people are travelling by canoe to the Florida islands. On the way over the sea the canoe sinks.

The people do not know which way to swim. They cry out for the shark. The shark helps them and when they are safely ashore, one man sings this song about it.

4. This song is about a dead body. A man dies at Florida Island while on a journey from Laulasi. His name is Mahilo. They put his body in the canoe for the return to Laulasi. Over his body they put a cover and they say: "He is not dead, he is just sleeping." This is the custom because if you take a dead body across the sea from Florida this would bring trouble to the relatives. When they arrive at Laulasi they say: "You are awake now," and they carry the body of Mahilo ashore and place him in his house as they sing this song.

5. A giant called Ria comes with a tribe from the north. He stays at Alite, a village near Laulasi. He wants to make trouble with a girl. The father tells all his people to chase the giant away. All the canoes surround him and they chase him towards the pass near Buma. As they are going through the pass a man called Kilalia goes out on the reef and throws his spear at the giant. The giant falls dead in his canoe. Everybody fights and all the tribe of the giant are killed.

6. Tolman is singing about when he is diving. On every reef in the lagoon he dives; he knows each rock on the reef. When looking for shells to make shell money, the custom shark helps him to find them.

7. Tolman sings this song for his people. He wants to make for himself an altar, round like a pen. When he dies he wants his people to gather around the altar and his spirit will come through to each one of them. They will always remember him because of this altar.

8. Mokobo is out fishing. Mr. Lawman comes in a sailing ship and captures him. He is taken away to work in Queensland on a sugar plantation for three years. He knows his relatives are very worried

about him because their spirits come to his mouth, as he sings about his journey.

9. Aria has fled to Marau with two women. Over there his ancestor's spirit comes to him and he sings about how he wants to come home to Laulasi.

10. Walmai is singing because his engagement to a girl has been broken off. There has been some trouble between her parents and his.

11. Nutoli is in love with the wife of another man. In the night he breaks through the wall of her hut and touches her breast. Then he gets frightened and runs away. But she doesn't wake up and her husband never finds out.

12. Walmai is a Laulasi man who has been fighting with the bush people. To save his life he flees to Marau. Over there he has more fights and kills some people. The people there are angry and want him to go home so he thinks about this and sings about how he wants to come back to Laulasi.

13. The Laulasi people go to the Siwan River in Ari Ari Lagoon. There, they are ambushed by the Koio people. A man called Fiaka from Kwaloefala Island has paid the Koio people to do this. In the fighting, one man, Sieta, is killed. When the Koio eat his flesh, they die.

14. Fiaka, when he goes to Marau, is killed by the people there because the Laulasi people pay them to. Tolman, a Laulasi man, escapes and he sings this song.

15. Watara sings about three brothers — Fideli, Ragia, and Ogali — who fight over their parents' shell money. When Ragia takes the money the other two angrily go to Fiji to work. While there, a cat eats some of their food scraps. This is taboo for shark worshippers

and they die in Fiji. Their spirits come back to Laulasi to Watara and he sings this song.

16. This song is about famine all over the land. The people go to the priest (a man in Kulani's lineage) and they say to him: "You are priest. You are making famine in our land." When the priest hears this he tells the people they must bring him shell money. Then he talks to his spirit and offers sacrifice. Then each one must tie a piece of tree bark around his neck. After that they receive plenty of food from the bush people on the mainland. So before a feast the Laulasi people must still put palm fibre around their necks to remind them of famine.

17. A giant comes from the north and nobody will give him food. On the eastern side of Laulasi a man called Taria kills the giant and sings this song.

At times I find that these hypnotic tunes and the steady, metronomic beat carry my mind off in a reverie: a powerful contact high or altered state. Ramo is affected too as are all the other villagers who crowd into the hut or stand around the doorway.

Beside the spirit box, where his father's spirit dwells, a belt of shell money is hanging on Amoko's wall. Suddenly I am aware of this as a Laulasi man would see it: invested with a power, like a pile of banknotes, but much more.

After providing for your daily needs in Laulasi you join with the people of the lagoon in fashioning these objects of intrinsic beauty, a shell bead game, which requires much labour and involves everyone. As a man with a son you must arrange a good marriage for him. You must amass sufficient shell money to pay for a girl who embodies the virtues which the people of your village value most in a woman.

Meanwhile your son conforms to the social and sexual code because if he breaks it, a shark may attack him while diving in the lagoon. The girl will also observe the custom or lose protection of the guardian shark and value in the eyes of the village.

In this way the shell money system serves to reduce sexual competition among village males and may regulate the birthrate. Since the old people play a very important part in the production of shell money, when you get old you still have a vital role in the village. Even when you die your spirit will be venerated for guidance of the lives of your children.

If you have all daughters you are a really wealthy man. Aided by them you can devote all your extra time to producing shell money for others, trading beyond the lagoon with villages which do not produce shell money but which observe the same bride price system. In turn, these villages, having obtained sufficient food for their own needs, put extra effort into producing commodities of value for trade with Laulasi mint.

How family-proud a girl must feel at her wedding, clasping the sprouting coconut as her husband's parents present her folks with belt after belt of precious shell money in recognition of the value in which she is held. They are physical bonds, perfect symbols of a social agreement, cool, tactile objects, which maintain a stable system for the village.

Besides its place in the bride price system, shell money can be seen to affect nearly every aspect of social life. Because of its transmission from generation to generation it relates directly to ancestor worship; because people dive for it in shark-infested waters, to the shark cult.

As a trade item shell money serves to redistribute commodities equitably through the system.

## PREPARING FOR THE FEAST

Poor Bosikoru! The task of selecting thirty passengers for our voyage to Honiara would ruin any politician for life. For the shark priest it is such a headache that he gives me all the names and counts himself out. This is a tremendous occasion for the village. Never have so many people left the island at one time. Bosikoru and all the priests pray for calm, fine weather and then just as they were all about to embark, *El Torito* falls silent. Darkness everywhere. The people on the island are scared.

In the engine room Walt finds the generator breakdown is serious: the impeller on the water coolant pump has failed. Dripping with sweat over the hot engine he toils to dismantle it. To his fury, the replacement part will not fit. It had not been fully machined at the factory. Walt sets up a jury rig, pumping water from the starboard engine through the generator.

As it turns out, the breakdown is fortunate. In the village, Georgi is out of favour with the other priests. He is leaving on the ship without appeasing some trouble with his ancestor spirit. If he leaves without doing this, and anything goes wrong in the village during his absence, it can be interpreted as a bad omen, casting a heavy spell over the whole feast. The generator blackout scares Georgi and he has time to put things right.

At midnight the thirty voyagers, including Bosikoru, troop aboard, laden with riches: yards of shell money and fine wooden carvings, which they will trade in Honiara for pigs and food.

Guided by radar *El Torito* rumbles down the lagoon, through Alite Pass and out across the sea. On deck people rest beneath an awning, within the yellow submarine, or up on the bow. Down below, four women sleep on the settees with their beautiful little babies. Terry sleeps there too, and says they never whimper once all night.

Thursday morning: I've just come on watch. The sea is calm now and the sky is still full of stars. We're cruising quietly towards Honiara past the southern end of Florida Island. In an hour the sun will rise over the mountains of Malaita astern. The old chief has just lain down again on the wheelhouse settee behind me. Five minutes ago he got up to check things out. We had a yarn about our position and he examined the trace on the radar screen. He had no trouble relating features on it to places he was familiar with on canoe trips.

A girl is asleep on a mattress beside me with her little child, both facing each other in perfect rest; up in the bows a huddle of men, two under the crane, others between the two crates which the Laulasi men built for us to bring back some steers for their feast. Under the awning we've rigged on the rear deck most of the people are sleeping or smoking quietly. Nixon is whistling in his sleep, perched above the stairwell beside the automatic pilot. That damned parrot is a menace: he craps on the chart table; he climbs up on to our heads and pulls our hair, he pokes his brush tongue into girls' ears and now he's been eating the beautiful model of *El Torito* which Paketi, little brother of James Batefula, made for us from the balsa-like sago palm.

We have an aquarium in the wheelhouse with four devilfish (flash-light fish) in it. They give out so much illumination from their light organs that when the generator broke down last night, we found it was possible to read a book with them.

On watch we must keep a close eye on the engine temperatures as with this jury rig, pumping the starboard engine water through the generator to cool it, things are running a bit hotter than normal. Every forty-five minutes I must go downstairs into the engine room roar, and peer into the generator with a torch to see if its temperature dial is okay. All the other engine dials are in front of the wheel here. Now there's a thin series of light streaks on the horizon behind us, and the jagged silhouette of Malaita ahead in the shadow, the loom of Guadalcanal. We'll be there around midday.

Honiara is dead ahead, a blazing sunrise astern over a red dappled sea. I've never seen so much fine weather in my life. It seems like four summer times since I've been here. People are stirring. Strolling around stretching their limbs.

Waiting for *El Torito* in Honiara is Hollywood film producer Robert Stabler and a Los Angeles film crew who have arrived to film the *maoma*. They join the ship and we spend a few days getting fresh supplies including some young steers as our contribution to the feast.

One afternoon Bob Stabler arrives on the wharf and hails the ship, anchored out in the roadway. The only person on deck is five-year-old Tommy, grandson of chief Georgi. For this nude child of a Stone Age village it is his first experience of civilisation. Without hesitating Tommy unties the small boat hanging astern, rows over to the wharf and brings the large, dapper, silver haired whiteman aboard. Tommy has never used oars before!

On our return to Laulasi, decks piled high with goods and passengers, the villagers go wild with excitement. The feast is another step nearer. Supplies of rice, tea, sugar, taro and pigs are unloaded first. Then the twelve ton crane is fired up and the two steer-wild crates are hoisted aloft and swung onto the island. Laulasi, with its stone walls, is a perfect dock.

In readiness for the steers the villagers have been told to build a corral. Over behind the *moonblood* hut it is constructed of coral stones, but so fragile that the steers escape in no time. Corrida!

They take off through the village with all the young men in pursuit, a hilarious scene of confusion straight from a Spanish village. When one steer charges through the *moonblood* hut and sets off across the low tide reef flats for the next island, the Laulasi people are horrified. "Those Christians in the village down there will eat it." So fifty men and boys set out to herd the beast back along the reef to the pen. Up until the feast the inhabitants of the *moonblood* hut will have frequent cause to give the alarm: "Bullamacow running away."

Before the feast, *El Torito* makes two more voyages to help the villagers get the necessary food. A two-day expedition is made over to Florida Island for pigs, and another along the Malaita coast to Kiu, where we load 2,000 coconuts. This will be the first pagan *maoma* in the area for a great many years. Bosikoru tells me that they are having trouble buying pigs. The people in the Christian villages surrounding them have been told not to sell their pigs to the Laulasi people for a devil-worshipping feast. So without the extra range *El Torito* gives them in obtaining food, the Pagans may well have had their wings clipped. Each day canoes arrive bringing more and more huge pigs to lie outside the huts trussed and resigned.

The men are beginning to rehearse the sacred *ausano* dance to the tune of bamboo pan pipes. If this dance, performed at the *maoma*, is not executed with perfection, death will come to the whole village. Besides this, the playing of pan pipes is taboo on Laulasi and may be practised only before a *maoma*. All rehearsals are done on a sand cay near by.

Early one morning we awake to learn that an important ceremony preliminary to the feast is to be held. Moses, the chief priest, has gone out through the pass in the big ceremonial Laulasi canoe. We hear the distant singing of many voices and the thump of paddles on a canoe hull. The canoe approaches the village, the chanting paddlers garlanded with green leaves and flowers. In the prow is a small figure holding a green tree. It is old Moses.

Jack explains that he is holding a branch of the sacred *alala* tree. The whole village has stopped work to watch. The canoe comes into the landing nearest the taboo ground. Moses, naked and wiry, is chanting prayers to the shark spirits. On the canoe landing an old woman stands. In one hand she holds out a string of white shell money. In her other hand, behind her back, she conceals some red shell money. She gives Moses the white shell money. This is a re-enactment of the founding of Laulasi. This legend tells the story of a man from an inland tribe who came down to the coast about 400 years ago. There, fishing with his bow at Alite Pass, he met a beautiful woman called *Avelaua* who had drifted in on a log. She showed him white shell money and told him that if he would bring his people down and build an island out on the reef crest she would show them how to make the shell money and her guardian sharks would protect them. If they came she had more precious things to show them — how to dive for the red shell money.

Moses now steps ashore at the sacred canoe landing and places the *alala* branch near the taboo huts where the weather sticks are. He fastens it erect with vines tied to heavy stones. He is renewing the power of the weather sticks. He then prays to the spirits of the four winds to bring good weather for the feast.

Now I really appreciate how this pagan village must affront the missionaries. Here, in an important ceremony, the chief priest stands in the raw before his whole village and they are moved to the core by it all. I try to imagine the Pope or the Archbishop of Canterbury in this state, devoid of all ceremonial robes. Shakespeare has it: "What is man, but a poor, bare, forked creature."

After the ceremony Moses comes down to the ship. He has stubbed three toes badly on the coral cobbles. I patch them up while he and Georgi have a cup of coffee at the table. In the afternoon he makes a ceremonial pig sacrifice within the circular shark altar behind Aniboni. He brings out the oldest of the skulls from his hut. Tomorrow they will all come out. For the first time in decades the villagers' leading ancestors will come out into daylight and participate in the *maoma*.

Before this important pre-feast ceremony takes place Walt thinks he has time to sneak in a bit more research on the sharks of Laulasi. Time is getting short and he still wants to experiment to see if they are more conditioned to men than other wild sharks.

The whole village is lined up along the wall stones when the crane fires up and hoists our yellow submarine over the side. The Laulasi people are eager to see the wet sub in action and not a soul misses it — except the women confined to the *moonblood* hut because they are menstruating.

When the sub is afloat Walt and Janice clamber aboard, close down the canopy and with a whirling propeller, slip beneath the green waters of the taboo passage, the quickest route through the barrier reef to the open sea. No woman must ever go through this pass as it is adjacent to the three taboo huts where the sacred skulls are housed. But Walt figures that the taboo will not apply if they are underwater where Janice can see only the back of his head.

He is right too. I see that the islanders show not the least concern at the yellow blur heading for the pass. Luckily, they will never know the drama that takes place when Walt enters the pass, or it will be taboo to subs forever.

Half an hour later the submarine comes back — limping slowly across the surface to *El Torito*. Walt tells me what happened.

As soon as he turned the sub into the waters of the pass, she began to lose power. He nursed it for a while but it soon became apparent that the batteries hadn't charged fully. Now they were in trouble — a dying submarine — and if he blew the ballast tanks with a girl aboard, they would be right in the middle of the taboo pass. A collision between modern technology and stone-age man. Walt knew that any violation of the taboo right before the feast would cast a heavy cloud over the whole occasion. The villagers would expect Janice to die. He jiggled the controls and porpoise swims the sub for a short distance with the last bit of energy in the batteries. Then Janice and he climbed out and began to tow it just above the bottom, finning with all their might against the falling tide. Eventually they were exhausted. There was nothing for it but to blow the tanks and hope they had cleared the pass. Up she came with a rush — narrowly missing a canoeload of shark priests! The divers had made it by the skin of their teeth.

All morning the older men are busy making bamboo fish traps to house the loose skulls of their ancestors in the three taboo houses. The cyclone jumbled many of them up and they lost track of identities. By early afternoon high priest Moses is ready to bring out the first two skulls. This is a ceremony performed only prior to special feasts and has not been done for at least twenty years at Laulasi. Behind each taboo hut, against the rear wall, a bamboo shelf has been constructed at waist height.

From a side door comes Moses with two fish traps. How small they look, are these just children's skulls? No, they have no jawbones — the most ancient skulls of all are believed to be around 400 years old.

He brings them to the rear of this taboo house, Aniboni, and puts them on the shelf on either side of a branch of the power tree, *alala*. Then he begins to speak to his ancestors, the shark spirits, asking them to help with the feast sacred to their memory and to accept the presence of cameras (and me) recording this ceremony for the first time. Moses prays and he waits, standing there without a stitch on his small, lean, wiry body. Ansiagallo and Batitolo, headmasters of the taboo huts on either side of *Aniboni*, begin to bring out their store of skulls too — all enclosed in fish traps. Walt and I are disappointed. Not a skull in sight — this isn't much to film. Then Moses brings out a couple of bare skulls; cameras whirr, shutters click. Now we have some real skulls. And there is an ancient bamboo betelnut holder and a goodies bag for the comfort of these ancestors, hanging from the shelf. By now Moses is having a bad time with the three stubbed toes that we've mended daily with sticking plaster and antibiotics on *El Torito*. All round this taboo ground are irregular cobbles of coral — devilish to walk on with shoes let alone barefoot with an armful of your ancestors' skulls.

The other two priests have it much easier — a smoother path and all their skulls were newly enclosed in fish traps — but nobody seems to have been ready to tackle the heap in Moses' hut. Next thing, Moses arrives with a piece of burlap sacking chockablock full of skulls — he tips them out on the coral rock shrine behind his hut and its shelf. Klock, klock, klock, klock — ancient, brown and black, they tumble out and roll on the ground, eye socket over vertebral hole, over fang and molar. Then Moses just stands staring at us, holding the bit of sack by one corner — the only man who could pose without looking as though he was posing.

One moonless night Walt calls us all on deck. A strange light is moving around the lagoon near the Laulasi wall stones, like a disembodied diver with a torch: phantasmagorical. Then Ramo rushes up with a throw net and hurls it at the glow. He pulls in scores of leaping black fishes, snubnosed, lights winking demoniacally, each about three inches long.

"*Bulbulu*," Ramo tells us, "source of light. In English we call it devilfish."

Each tiny fish has a light organ just beneath its eye — a horizontal oval, glowing with its own cool fire. Up in the library we search the books and find that this is a very rare fish, *Anomalops.*

The light organ consists of long, parallel mucous glands well supplied with blood vessels, in which symbiotic, luminous bacteria grow. The whole light organ is hinged so that it can be folded forward, illuminating the water in front of the fish's mouth. The light can be extinguished mechanically too: by rolling the organ over so that the light faces inward and only the black rear side shows.

I grab mask, snorkel and weights, and slip quietly into the warm black lagoon, right alongside the village, only ten feet from the huts. Underwater I can still hear voices talking. Then, toward me comes the weird phantasma: a dancing pattern of lights, weaving and sparkling within twelve inches of my mask. I get out, grab my Rolleimarin and shoot a roll of the devilfishes. Their lights are intermittent: on three seconds, off one second. I find I have to shoot at random focus, because if I turn on a torch, the fishes flee like mice to their refuges in the stone walls of the island.

From reference books in the ship's library we glean all the existing knowledge of *Anomalops*, which we find is rather skimpy. Probably nobody has studied and photographed them underwater before. "A remarkable instance of friendly parasitism, discovered by Max Weber in the East Indies" . . . "Fishermen of Banda cut out the luminescent organ and attach it to lines, just above the bait on their hooks."

Walt and I talk it over. Theory has it that the function of the light is to attract plankton to the fish's mouth like bait. Then why would the fishes swim in a fast-moving school or flash their lights off and on? We feel it was more likely that *Anomalops* uses its light organs to pursue planktonic organisms on moonless nights, the only time that it leaves its refuge. Their intermittent lights would serve to avoid making them targets for larger predators. We notice that the fishes prefer to feed beneath *El Torito's* broad hull, where not even the starlight could penetrate. Perhaps in such darkness they are better able to surprise prey with their lights, or their prey aggregate most densely in utter darkness. This is a new niche — a safe way to exploit the nighttime planktonic life on a reef. Why is it not more widespread? Why have other fishes not developed these light organs?

Simon the village carver fashioned me a model devilfish with nautilus shell lights, the first he had ever made. Laulasi people often eat them.

## DURING THE MOONGAMES

Snatching a little time from filming village activities, Walt, Janice, Terry and I whisk out to sea in the skiff. Walt wants to try out the new black cape that Janice had made for him to mask his shark-repellant zebra suit. We nearly die laughing at the weird figure who leaps from the skiff clad in a black cloak and a convict suit. At 160 feet he looks equally absurd. Air from his twin hose regulator collects in the cloak, so that it bells up in a dome above his back. In his hand he clutches a shark rattle — twenty coconut shell-halves threaded on a cane hoop. This, we understand, natives elsewhere in Malaita use to attract sharks to their hooks. The hunchback of Notre Dame crouches on the white coral sand madly shaking his rattle. Within my mask, tears roll down my cheeks. A shark comes racing in, takes one look at the monstrosity and disappears. The exhibitionist sequence has to await further trials before it is successfully filmed.

On our return to the ship we get a shock. A bunch of nude Laulasi kids appear to be committing ritual suicide. They have coral rocks tied to their backs. From the stern platform of *El Torito* and the stone wall of the island they are leaping into the lagoon.

"Eiho Captain!" Splash. "Eiho Terry!" Splash. "Here come Wadey!" Splash. We watch in mild horror to see how on earth they can make it to the surface with great rocks harnessed on their backs. Fortunately they are virtually aquatic from infancy so twenty pounds of rock around their necks is a new game, not suicide. We jump in and film them striding over the bottom, grinning with delight. After seeing us dive from the ship using scuba, the children have invented their own version, the "rockalung." They often mimic our activities with toy movie and still cameras, guitars and models of our submarine, the ship and the skiff.

I scuba dive for some more fish photos on the lagoon flanks of the island. It seems crazy, taking pictures on the murky village rubbish heap, near a reef passage where sharks come to be fed. But every kid on the island swims there all day long. Occasionally one will dive down to where I am stalking fish and grin bubbles at me. Because it is a specialised habitat, there are many fish species that I have never seen in clear, open reef situations.

Some days ago a pair of Japanese cameramen arrived to film the feast. The Laulasi people were not too keen at first, but decided to give them a hut in the village for $100 a week. We approach them in a friendly manner but, while one is pleasant and willing to rap, the bossman cuts him dead. It is a very formal set up. The Japanese maintain an aloofness from the villagers, refusing to join in any games or other activities. One day we see the Japanese recording and filming the Laulasi kids singing. They have no idea what the song is about that they are recording for Japanese television audiences. I hope they never do. It is a song called "Japani Haha." In pidgin English it describes the derisive attitude of the Solomons people to their invaders during the last war: "Japani come down long high parachute. Me laugh long you Japani Haha."

Every day out here on the lagoon is so sweet, calm and perfect — and the evenings could not be more delectable anywhere on Earth. I've been studying the meteorological records: there is virtually no seasonal variation and a very even rainfall. No wonder these people have little sense of time and often, no idea how old they are. There is nothing to mark the passage of a year. The most important cyclical event is the full moon.

Outside a hut a tiny girl lies in her mother's lap, head cradled in one arm, passive and trusting while her mother engraves a design on her skin. From about the age of two months Laulasi children may receive an unpigmented facial tattoo. With a bamboo tool the mother is inscribing the pattern, following an outline previously drawn on the child's cheeks with a piece of sharp wood. As she scarifies the skin the tool is dipped into a coconut shell holding a mixture of burnt coral lime and the reddish juice of a young coconut. This solution produces a pale, lightly pigmented pattern on the skin. Traditional, the designs are varied but motifs include symbols of duality, *ger-oi-oi* (hot/cold; love/hate); unity, *lu-lu-da* (all-in-one); and source of shining light, *bulbulu.*

It is explained that these patterns are placed on the body by the hands of your parents to show their love for you all your life and when they were gone. They are sorry for us, that our parents showed no such love. Terry volunteers and has all three of the above symbols engraved on the back of his hand. Walt asks the wife of Bosikoru to place on his arm a pigmented tattoo, the beautiful traditional motif of a double frigate bird. Chicken, I remain satisfied with my smallpox scar. "Wadey," I am asked by some kids, "Doesn't your mother love you? She gave you no tattoo...."

Many of the older men and women have holes in the tips of their noses in which they wear plugs of black wood. Older women have pierced nose septums in which they can insert decorative sticks on special occasions. Their ears are pierced and hang droopily, an elongated hole you could stick two fingers in. This is for holding special ornaments.

This evening the sun disappears in the sea beyond the reef over towards Honiara, sixty miles to the west. As it declines it shines on the blue clouds above the mountains of Malaita about ten miles east of us. Streaks of orange and mauve coil amongst the blue with, in the foreground, the green forests of the mainland coast a mile over the lagoon from Laulasi. Canoes slip gently over the calm lagoon that reflects all the sky colours. As the sun vanishes, a huge full moon climbs over those same mountains and dances a silver path across the lagoon to the coral stone walls of Laulasi. Canoes cross its path in silhouette, still bearing feast provisions to the village. We sit there with the villagers in the most profound non-verbal communication I have ever experienced.

Now that the skulls are out, all this material is stored in the skull houses. Each time a flotilla arrives, there is a great screaming and shouting and beating of sticks. This is to frighten off any evil spirits when the food is taken to the huts. Georgi is the only priest who can enter the taboo huts while the skulls are out, and only when this noisy ceremony is performed. Temporary huts have been built for all the unhoused priests. What a great way of preventing any suspicion of pilfering in the village.

All this while I am wandering round the village from group to group, received with warmth wherever I go. Jack Kamada takes me by the hand and we stroll towards the taboo ground, away from the hullabaloo of the village, the evening cooking fires and the grunts of captive pigs. We cross the invisible barrier into a timeless, peaceful world where old priests are communing with the spirits, quiet mumblings in the darkness amidst the wind sticks, shark altars, skulls, and sacred trees. Jack tells me how pleased the villagers are that we keep all their laws and customs. He says that, while the Laulasi people observe European laws, their custom laws come first. "If a man uses one of our girls, without asking her father, we kill him." He explains the marriage customs and magical healing practices. He gives me a detailed description of how, at the death of an important man, his head is removed by one of his sons for storage in one of the taboo houses according to which lineage or totem group he belonged to.

Then I sit among the old men by the twilit taboo houses. Old priests are bathing themselves in the sea by the stone walls. Small boys sit in the shadows, listening to stories. No generation gap here: age seems nothing more than a condition like having blue eyes or being tall. They chat, smoke, chew betel and enjoy the evening after a heavy day working around the taboo huts in communal labour that brought them no income but was far more meaningful to them than breadwinning.

Outside *Aniboni* I meet Georgi, with a group of small boys, staring out towards the mainland coast at a sunlit hillside. Georgi explains that over there was Firtala, their ancestral home where yesterday in a Malaitan Court session the Laulasi people succeeded in winning a long-fought land claim, a strongly contested battle against claims from a bush people's village. Laulasi people are overjoyed but don't crow over their success. Georgi says Laulasi means, "stay here forever."

Along a passageway between the huts Amoko comes up. He says he has a gift for me and asks me to follow. He hobbles off with his long pole. A widower, living in a hut by himself, he is far from lonely. His hut is used by any young, single men in need of a crash pad, visitors or men just sleeping about generally; nobody seems to live anywhere in particular other than at

Laulasi or in this general area of the lagoon. In huts right next to Amoko he has married daughters and grandchildren living. Today the girls have put a new floor down in his hut, clean white coral rubble from the seaward side of a nearby sand cay. The girls load their canoes to the very verge of foundering. They paddle them tenderly home, load up saucepans, basins and buckets with tinkling coral rubble and bear it to the huts on their heads and shoulders. In the past week a bevy of village girls has done every hut in the village. They work at it as if it were a game; their bodies still have a grace and femininity even though their limbs are heavily muscled.

The children here have perfectly proportioned, Greek-statuesque bodies. As they mature they just thicken with muscular growth into husky young men and solid but attractive girls. After the first child, for some reason I can't explain, the girls' breasts sag into pawpaws. The old women are rarely fat and very lithe — full of energy. I've not yet seen a decrepit person here. They must live to eighty or more and die while still in good shape. Obesity, the Polynesian problem, is uncommon. I've not seen a paunchy man yet, although the diet is very starchy and these people have a strong Polynesian or Micronesian influence in their faces, their general appearance and manners. The gift Amoko has for me is an exquisite shell money bracelet. I am staggered!

In the open square, *moongames* are in progress. Tonight, with the full moon, the game bug bites the Laulasi people. They play until three, then resume as soon as they awake. The big boys, eighteen-year-olds, lead them off into one new game after another, like so many magic uncles on visits.

Two nights in a row Terry and I join in the games. They are big ring games involving chasing, eluding, patterns of courtship, hunting and observation training. Nobody wins. We find that after a certain length of time the attention span of the Western mind reaches its limit. Boredom creeps in.

Then we notice that everybody else is still enjoying themselves immensely, all these moonlit individuals. Sustained by this we carry on through the cultural barrier until we find ourselves in a timeless state of awareness — a tremendous contact high: every person under that magical moon is in tune with the whole group: sparkling eyes, ripples of feeling, squeezing of hands. Children of all ages from six to sixty participate. Ramo, champion bread-winner of the village, their Howard Hughes, is a foremost games player and several older women really throw themselves into it.

Then Terry and I get one helluva shock: three robed figures walk out into the square from among the huts. One carries a lantern, another a palm frond, the third, hand to forehead, is searching the sky for a star that can't be found. Then a very pregnant nun comes prancing out into the open. It is Stanley. Two boys beat him up with mock brutality. Then the Pope appears, fully rigged out with palm leaf mitre and all the symbols of office. With great dignity he marries Stanley to one of the wise men. These are pagans with a vengeance: they bite back.

The deck of our ship is always full of these happy, good-looking kids. I've not yet seen one smacked or misbehave. At the least chance the boys dance like crazy — little nude figures twisting, bumping and grinding and singing their heads off. I've never seen a child crawl, suck its thumb or cling to any doll-type object. They must be getting sufficient touch affection from their families. There's no one-upmanship, showing off or jealousy among them, just a joyful, romping mob who miraculously never seem to do any harm although they have the freedom of the ship. They still love to sluice the decks with water and slide on it with their bare bodies. Great fun but no good with pants on. They flock into the wheelhouse but only come downstairs when invited. We've been making them swags of orange ice cubes which really blow their minds. Never having seen ice, they go mad with delight, squealing home with bits to show their folks. But it has vanished.

When Nixon the parrot eats the perfect model of *El Torito* made by Paketi, the ten-year-old craftsman shows no sign of emotion — he just goes off and starts to make another, surrounded by a group of admiring boys.

As the children paddle their canoes across the lagoon they sing happily. If a canoe is flooded, they just kick their legs to splash the water out and then bail. They seem to have a much lower threshold of pain. When we put iodine on their cuts they never even whimper. We often take photos of them and Janice processes these in the darkroom and hands them around. This is greatly appreciated — one gesture we can make in return for their unstinting helpfulness towards us.

*El Torito* is running low on fresh fruit and vegetables. Ramo the breadwinner and James Batefula the fisherman, offer to help us buy some supplies from villages around the lagoon. Terry and I set out on a long day's voyage, which neither of us will ever forget. At the outset, cruising over the glassy lagoon the two Laulasi men offer us their customary betelnut to chew. The small, white palm nut is bitter and as tough as a cotton reel. But gradually we become aware *it is changing our consciousness*. We spend that mellow day in an altered state. At each stopping place the nut chewing is shared with those we visit. Often there are long periods of profound, non-verbal communication with people who no longer seem like strangers. Terry and I feel afterwards we have truly entered the local culture and been accepted. We had no idea betel was such a psychedelic. This truly is a stoned age society!

The outboard slides over the lagoon so effortlessly, there's almost no wake. We glide into mainland villages amidst trees and flowers and up to island villages built out on stilts from the shores of tiny cays. With motor stopped we waft to the wall stones, purring forward until we knock gently on the coral rocks.

In quest of pineapples, we visit a Seventh Day Adventist village on the coast. Near the jetty, women are working in the mangrove mud levering out coral lumps from the gluck for building hut foundations. Further inland we come upon a concrete block church in the final stages: a filigree concrete tower, utterly alien to any Solomons motif, with ten men toiling around a petrol-driven concrete mixer.

Next we visit Talolo village, an artificial island, which we sighted when searching for the sunken canoe. There we meet relatives of both Ramo and James who welcome us to lunch while two girls paddle over to mainland gardens to get supplies for us. On this tiny island there are only about ten huts, beautifully built, each raised three feet off the ground with wooden floors, woven palm leaf walls, shutters, doors, rooms and furniture. Each has a verandah overhanging the sea. Much nicer to live in than the concrete boxes with "authentically" thatched tin roofs that you find in most tourist resorts around the Pacific. Directly below, bright coloured parrotfishes are grazing at the flanks of the island.

Over lunch of baked fish and taro I ask Ramo why Laulasi huts are built on ground level with coral rubble floors while elsewhere huts are elevated like these.

James says it is because the taboo forbids building anything higher than the taboo huts unless you sacrifice two pigs, one at the Laulasi taboo house and one at Lalanga. There are three raised huts at Laulasi but no women can sleep in them.

James tells us the strange story of Silesi, who decided to build a high house on the outskirts of Lalanga.* Silesi had four sons and one eight-year-old daughter, his youngest child, whom he valued highly. He built his house on stilts with a steep pitched roof and a wide verandah. But Silesi had "modern" (read: Christian) ideas and made no sacrifices. He claimed he was not afraid of the spirits. Just as he completed his house and was on the verge of moving in, his little daughter was found dead, her body horribly sprawled among the twisted mangroves in a channel behind the house. James says that she was possessed by the spirit that lives in the area and leapt to her death from her canoe. Inconsolable in his grief, Silesi pulled her little canoe on to the bank of the channel and hacked into its side with savage cuts of a bush knife, rendering it useless. On our home journey we see the forsaken canoe, beached, upside down and gape-sided, the mangrove thicket where the devil lurks for those who break the custom and Silesi's new house, which has *never been inhabited*. Each day at the door a fresh sprig of leaves is fastened. Silesi lives at Laulasi now, a quiet and gentle custom man.

[*Note: On the coast adjacent to Laulasi, this village was the home of the islanders before they constructed their island. Following the cyclonic erosion of Laulasi, many people had to resettle there.]

James shows us a place in the lagoon where they set their nets. Good sharks chase the fishes into the nets for them. Then James tells us about Johnny who has a shark problem. He flirted with a Christian girl. He has not made the proper sacrifice of a pig to the shark spirits.

He first becomes aware of his problem when spearfishing with two other Laulasi men. He is wearing a shirt. James tells us: "And then shark say, 'You don't give me a pig, eh. You don't make me any sacrifice. I'll show you,' and he bite Johnny in his back and just pull his shirt out. Still Johnny doesn't make any sacrifice. Then, over at Ngella he jumps out of the canoe into water. He dive down to the bottom of the reef. He have a fish in his hand. Shark come and bite his arm. Now Johnny gets a pig to give to Bosikoru for sacrifice. He gonna fix up the trouble with the shark. Custom says, shark won't eat you for nothing."

James explains that even if he has a shark problem, no shark will ever attack a Laulasi man anywhere within Langalanga Lagoon because of the many years during which the people have worshipped the sharks there.

In the lagoon and within fifty miles radius of Laulasi, with the advent of the *maoma,* the trade in pigs is becoming very difficult. Nobody will accept anything but shell money for a pig, knowing the Laulasi people's need and their shell money wealth. But the canny Laulasi people are trying to buy pigs with Australian currency whenever possible. As James says: "Australian dollar easy to get: one hundred dollar, two thousand dollar, no trouble. We can spend them all in two weeks' time. Shell money stays with us for so long as we live. Hard to make and hard to spend. Australian money is round. I mean, twenty cents, fifty cents, ten cents. It couldn't stay with us for long. Because it's round like a world it's going to pass around the world. That's why they make it round. Shell money goes on your neck and it isn't round like a moon or like a world."

That night, there being no moon, I stroll down to the taboo ground with Ramo to see if there are any more devilfishes around. From the middle taboo hut I hear a high-pitched crooning: old Moses crouching alone in *Aniboni*, in the shadows by the embers of his fire, close to the skulls of his ancestors and the priests he once chewed betelnut with, knowing his own skull would soon join them on the pile. His voice rises and falls, communing with their spirits. We search and see a few devilfishes. I reflect that on Laulasi the old people would have little fear of death.

Returning, Ramo and I sit by the wall stones with Bosikoru's family, his wife, two sons and pretty fifteen-year-old daughter. We hear the BBC news from Melbourne: news of Arab terrorists; one million Soviet troops along the Sino-Russian border; fallout shelters in Peking, each to house 10,000 people.

I ask Ramo if he ever plans to buy an outboard.

"No," he grins, "Not ever."

## FOOD FOR THE FEAST

For two nights before the feast nobody sleeps. Until dawn the whole village is busily preparing *fola,* traditional tapioca puddings to eat with the sacrificial pigs. This, like shell money manufacture, involves a whole range of activities, broken down among various groups. One set grates the tapioca roots; another removes the meat from the 2,000 coconuts and grates it finely. Wrapped in a piece of cloth this is put in a wooden press. A pole fitted into a grooved fulcrum point is levered down by two men. Pressed out of the coconut mince, the milk flows into a bucket. This milk is then separated by placing in it hot stones. Removed from the fire with bamboo tongs, the stones are washed in a saucepan then plunged into the milk. This is repeated until a thick cream forms on the top with a thin watery fluid beneath. The water is kneaded with the grated tapioca into a doughy mixture; the thick coconut cream is pasted around it and the whole wrapped in banana leaves ready for baking in the *motu* or pile of hot stones, leaves and sacks. There is no apparent organisation but everybody is busy chopping wood, building fires, heating stones, grating, pounding, pressing, separating, cooking and stacking puddings. Men are involved equally with this food preparation but the grating work is done only by the women.

Ramo has a special task: he is making bark loincloths, *rala*, by beating the pithy inner bark of a tree, about six inches in diameter, until it spreads and thins to form a two-foot wide, five-foot long piece of bark cloth.

Walt helps by having cables strung from the ship on the tall palm trees to light the village. All through the night I never see any signs or expressions of fatigue. The entire series of tasks are approached in a carnival atmosphere of laughter and singing.

The day before the feast, preparations are made to stake out the ninety pigs that have been gathered in front of the taboo houses to be slung on poles in their palm leaf strait jackets. Parallel rows of poles are placed exactly six feet apart and staked to the ground. This traditional spacing is a carryover from the days of human sacrifices when captive bushmen would have been used instead of pigs.

At sunrise flotillas of canoes from every part of Langalanga Lagoon gaily converge on Laulasi. The sky is as blue as the sea. The tiny island is ajostle with people and pigs, drums and wooden gongs, shell money and flowers.

To heat the cooking stones, all the readied fires, *umafa,* are lit; mingling with the crowds is the scent of wood smoke, singing, laughter and the squeals of doomed animals.

To commence the ceremony the *ausano* dancers arrive: in two rows on the taboo ground forty fit Laulasi men from sixteen to sixty. All our friends are there, young Wale, powerful Jack, lithe James, Ramo in his new bark cloth. Prior to dancing, a green coconut is passed around ceremonially. Each man sips to reinforce his memory. Each dancer holds a quiver stick, a piece of bamboo multi-slivered at each end towards the central hand grip, and a wooden club to strike it on. To accentuate the stamping of feet each leg wears a *ra*, an anklet of dry seed shells.

Facing one another in the middle of the ranks, five old priests bow their heads together and begin to blow the sacred pan pipes; a raspy, hoarse harmony of notes that establishes the rhythmic patterns of the dance, patterns so hallowed that any mistake, the dancers believe, will bring disaster on the village. Twisting, gyrating, waving their arms the *ausano* dancers drive away the evil spirits from the taboo ground.

The ritual pig slaughter can start. With prayers from Bosikoru and the shark priests, pig snouts are noosed and bound. Squeals turn to muffled gasps. The dead pigs are singed and scraped. A scene of fantastic carnage, a bloody shambles, but nobody is the least disturbed as they busy themselves butchering the pigs, removing rib cages and legs, opening the carcases out into flat sheets of meat, collecting all the blood in bamboo tubes to be baked on the fires.

To carry the butchered pigs some men wear them on their backs like coats, arms through the legholes. Our film of this pig slaughter produces strong reactions in audiences. In the Western world man is sickened by the sight of blood, shielded from the daily operations of abattoirs, and yet he can condone high-altitude bombing of civilian populations.

Shortly after the slaughter begins we notice that about a dozen black-tip sharks have gathered by the seawall. At this point nothing has been placed in the water. We have not seen sharks there since the preliminary sacrifices some weeks earlier.

Walt dons his diving gear and swims down underwater from the ship to film them. He notices that he can hear the noise of the crowd from below. Perhaps this sound has attracted the sharks? When the pig entrails are thrown into the water, the children join Walt, swimming out to play games with the guts, tossing them to each other like streamers, inflating bladders, screaming, laughing and playing water polo. In spite of all this the sharks stay away from the children.

While the sacrificial pigs are cooking, the *maoma* celebration begins. On the village square in full costume, all the men, women and older children of Laulasi dance and sing for hours today, performing the traditional patterns of movement, tunes and words they have been rehearsing for weeks, patterns passed on from their ancestors by Bosikoru, Amoko, Kulani and the other elders, all combining to affirm powerfully their beliefs in ancestor worship and the shark cult. And Stanley clowns in their midst. Dressed as a buxom woman he lampoons every action, grimacing and writhing, contorting his body impossibly, rolling his eyes, his tongue protruding, a madcap, antic buffoon, a finger at the nose of self-righteousness and religious awe which has no part, we noticed, in any Laulasi ceremony.

In the dance twenty-six men in two files move with intricate arm actions and reversings to the voices and drumbeats of Amoko and his custom singers. Then dance leader Bosikoru leads out a troupe of Laulasi virgins; bare breasted, grass skirted girls from eight to fifteen, they sing and dance songs of love, canoe trips over to the Florida Group, the Japanese-American conflict, happy exchanges, stories of "black birding" (kidnap by sailing ships for endentured labour in Queensland or Peru) and exiles.

"My heart is in Laulasi and at the feast time, I will return there." Only one song is of recent origin: composed after the war, it tells of the great destruction caused by the American bomb that hit their village and the loss of their heirlooms and finery so that on this feast day, they cannot be as beautiful as in olden times.

Another action song is the story of an orphan: "Although I have no parents I am still happy because I can dance like this, and like this, and like this."

Kulani leads another troupe of Laulasi women of all ages, very expert in their movements. An exciting feature of this *maoma*, a masterly innovation, is the presence, by special invitation, of a group of Waitolo bushmen from Fiu, West Kwara'ae district, beyond Auki. These fine-limbed mountain men performed their own tribal dances, quite different from the Laulasi ones, each man carrying a totem stick depicting his lineage: a snake, a bird or a fish. Then Johnson Olisokulu speaks to them in pidgin English, their only means of communication. He thanks them for coming to Laulasi. He says that although the saltwater people have long been at enmity with the bushmen, this is all over now. Laulasi people must join hands with the Waitolo people, because both peoples still hold to their custom ways; they still worship their ancestors and reject all other religions. Laurence, the Waitolo leader, replies in a similar vein: "Both pagan villages, let us join forces," and everyone looks very happy — a shot in the arm for their beleaguered cultures.

I learn afterwards how Laulasi solved a diplomatic crisis. The Waitolo men indicated that they could not partake of any pig that had been sacrificed to the ancestors of the Laulasi people. But there are the steers *El Torito* has given to the village. How the Laulasi people must have savoured the thought of eating that beef — a treat as rare to them as caviar. They put tremendous effort into maintaining the animals on the grassless, waterless island. Now they decided to give all the steer meat to their guests, the Waitolo men, their former enemies.

A picture flashes through my mind: the skeleton of a bushman buried along with the taboo hut support pole through his chest.

As the canoes depart with loads of ritually prepared pork we realise that a *maoma* is not a feast in our sense: an occasion for consuming great quantities of food, for wine, women and song. Their very use of the word "feast" is just a linguistic attempt to find us an equivalent for something which defies translation. So our preconceptions are wrong and we are left to think anew.

The significance of the *maoma* seems to be as much in the preparation for the event as in the feast day itself. All the preliminary rituals and ceremonies, the group efforts, special tasks and rehearsals have revived interest in traditional forms and given the village a refreshed image of itself as an entity.

We are deeply moved by it all. At heart Western men may have an intuitive rapport with stone-age man, a kinship with ancient civilisation and traditions, stemming perhaps from deep-seated racial memories.

I see Amoko as a guide, taking the people of Laulasi on a voyage through their past. I see Kulani as the shaman, moving the village to action. I see Bosikoru accepting his role as chief shark priest, a position for which he once felt unworthy, tugged by influences alien to Laulasi — his earlier contact with the churches.

Without a powerful shark priest Laulasi has been weakened. Johnny has been bitten twice by sharks and there has been no high shark priest to whom he could make his sacrifice. The island has been severely hit by the cyclone, forcing many Laulasi people to shift to the mainland. Others are being influenced by surrounding religions. Those who seek schooling for their children see them move away from custom ways. Five Laulasi kids attending a Catholic boarding school at Buma ten miles away have been unable to see what was the biggest cultural event in their village history for several decades. I did see a nun at the *maoma*. (Of all the churches, the Catholics and Anglicans seem to be the most tolerant of village traditions.)

The *maoma* is not a regular event. It is celebrated only when there is need. A consensus arose that the shark cult needed reinforcing. The Laulasi culture has the rituals and traditions to strengthen belief and bond its inhabitants in the face of adversity, whether cyclonic or from alien culture. For Laulasi, the *maoma* is, in the words of R. D. Laing: "a built-in technique for maintaining its own inner balance."

In this stable, stone age social system, through the *maoma*, belief has been sustained in a preliterate culture, a culture wherein knowledge is transmitted, by deed and word among the living, and by spirit, beyond death. This cultural transmission is paralleled by shell money heritage: intrinsically beautiful objects passed along and contributed to by their diving in the realm of *Baekwa*, the shark. A system of beliefs, which at once ensures the transmission of knowledge through ancestor worship and gives mental support to these saltwater people when involved in a dangerous activity.

The shark cult was once widespread in the Solomon Islands and is thought to have been part of the culture of migrant people who came from the Indonesian islands and eventually moved on to Polynesia. The pattern of belief in the cult varied considerably in different parts of the Solomons and it extended from Indonesia to Hawaii and the southern coast of Fiji. As Bosikoru put it to me simply: "When a man dies we can still speak to him as a shark spirit: 'Sautehi i matawa. Mananga sau ou ou.'"

## LIFE AND DEATH AMONG THE SHARK CULTISTS

During our stay with the Laulasi people I made an effort to learn all I could of their ancestor-worshipping culture. While it is by no means pure and uninfluenced by Western contact, there still remains an unusually strong adherence to the original patterns of living. This is very rare in the Pacific nowadays.

I asked Wale many questions about taboos. Each day the sixteen-year-old boy came to me with fresh information. I found that he was conversing each evening with Kulani. who took delight in the boy's curiosity and explained many more customs to him than Wale originally knew.

Wale told me that within the family it is taboo for a sister to wash her brother's clothes or to sew them. If his clothes are drying outside and it is raining, she must not touch them, even with a pole. This taboo extends to a cousin or a sister-in-law.

It is equally taboo for a sister to step over her brother's legs at any time (or vice versa). If a brother wishes to forbid his sister from doing something such as going to the town, he says "I'll step over your legs if you do that." Then she knows she can never do it.

There are many taboos related to travelling by canoe over the sea, since this is the realm of *Baekwa*, the shark spirits. You must never weep in a canoe, for this means a shark has bitten you; you must never lie down; you must never use a paddle as a roller, for this would offend the shark. You must never haul a canoe onto a landing bow first, for a spirit shark following the canoe may then swim out of the water. It is forbidden to put your legs overboard while travelling in a canoe, because this really means you have been bitten by a shark and you are keeping blood out of the canoe.

It is forbidden to stand up in a canoe while it is travelling because if a man disappears at sea eaten by a wild shark, the shark priest, Tofi, must hunt for him. He would stand up in the canoe and search for him according to special customs. So an ordinary person must not do this.

If a canoe sinks, there is lots of flotsam. You must not pick this up for yourself or a shark would get you one day. It must be taken to Tofi and purged. If a canoe is lost at sea, a shark will circle in the area, playing around with the flotsam on the surface.

Wale told me how the spirit of his grandfather Jack protects him on long canoe voyages.

"If I have to go across to Florida Island (thirty miles away), I can be sure that the spirit of my grandfather is with me. The evening before I set out I put a sacrifice in my travelling sack: a mango, a coconut, or some taro. I must not step over it, because that is taboo. I place it on the wall behind my bed. Then, if it is raining and blowing that night, in the morning it will be fine and calm. I place the bag in the bow of the canoe. Then the sea will be flat like a table. The day will be bright and sunny. I must say: 'Grandfather, now I am leaving Laulasi. Be with me. We go now.' When I return I must take that sacrifice to the priest at the taboo house. The sharks can't control the wind. It is Moses who looks after that. The priest makes a prayer for my grandfather.

"Before he died my grandfather Jack — an old, naked, bearded man — took me to the taboo house. I was fourteen years old and I was very frightened to go in there for the first time. He made some prayers, and he told me, 'I will be with you forever, Wale.'"

A canoe builder told me: "When I make a canoe I know my grandfather is beside me. I can hear his voice in my ears, telling me just how to choose the tree in the forest. He tells me how to use the wood and shape it into my canoe. With my grandfather helping me, the work is easy. Down at Buma village the church gives them machines. They make furniture for the church to sell and they get eight dollars a week. That work is very hard for them."

When in need of help, Jack Kamada told me, you pray to your father. In a dream, speaking with his father, Jack recalled an old dance for use at the feast. For the shark worshippers, Wale explained, certain foods are taboo because of their relationship with the shark. It is taboo to eat a bonito, or any other fish bitten by a shark, unless a priest has purged it.

It is taboo to eat the octopus because the spirit of the octopus means famine. The octopus does not move like a fish — it stays in one place on the reef. Just as the octopus hides, waiting to snatch food, so the spirit of famine is always waiting to take food from the people. If an evil man wished to poison the food supply of a tribe, he would tell an octopus spirit to bring famine on them, in the same way as an octopus is always waiting to snatch up food.

"If a man is being chased by an enemy in a canoe, he can speak to the spirit of the octopus and make his assailant slow down just as an octopus grabs a man. This happened when a Laulasi raiding party was escaping the bushmen. No matter how they tried, the bushmen could not gain speed. So we do not eat the octopus. A shark can help you in the same way. We never kill the shark."

Another sea food that is taboo is the giant clam. When the Laulasi people still lived on the mainland coast, at Langalanga, there was a special pool, which was sacred to *Avelaua*, who had led them down from the mountain village and showed them how to make shell money. *Avelaua* had spoken "in a magic way" and put a spell on this pool. Sacrifices were thrown into it in reverence to Avelaua the shark lady. It was taboo for any women to enter this pool. But one day a woman called Kakado broke the custom. She was too proud to believe the taboo, and she entered the pool. Kakado gave birth to a baby shark. She kept it in the shell of the giant clam like an aquarium and there she fed it. Because the shark lived in the clam shell, Laulasi people must not eat clam meat. Interestingly, the flesh of the clam has been found in recent experiments to be repugnant to reef sharks. I also recalled having been painfully poisoned from eating these clams: marooned on a New Caledonian island by a hurricane, we ate them guts and all! Besides this, white shell money is made from the clam shell.

Dogs and cats are forbidden on Laulasi. Your spirit can go into a dog, because it is black like the shark. For Tofi and those of the shark totem or lineage, the colour red is taboo.

For Bosikoru and those of the ray totem, the taboo colour is black. So things which are predominantly these colours are forbidden on Laulasi. Otherwise the people fear they would lose the ability to find good fishing and to control the weather, the art of making shell money would be taken from them.

Around each cooking fire there is a small circle of stones. It is taboo for a woman to step within this circle, and she must handle all food with bamboo tongs. She must not prepare food for men while she is menstruating. At that time she must live in the *moon-blood* hut, where no man can enter. While there, she can make shell money.

Around the village on the mainland it is taboo to cut down trees other than secondary growth in special gardening areas.

One of their favourite foods is *koa*, a dish made from grated mangrove seeds, fish, coconut, and onions. These particular mangrove seeds are shaped like cigars and come from a very tall tree which grows some distance upstream from the sea.

Shark priests cannot eat it as the women prepare it by shredding the seed pods with cockle shells, into a pot held between their legs.

It is taboo for boys to fight in front of a taboo house. If they are sparring and one boy runs there, the assailant cannot fight him. That means death. It is taboo even to pretend to fight, or jump around there.

Reflecting on it all, it seems to me that the main structure of the taboo system revolves around the axis of the shark/ancestor cult. Those taboos of which I am able to gain understanding derive their moralistic force from these central ideas. Infringement of the taboo code endangers success in the food quest and shell money manufacture, or it results in illness, affliction, death, or natural disaster.

## LEAVING

Straight after the feast, *El Torito* had to leave Laulasi. The departure scene was such an emotional tumult for us that it was all we could do to handle it. To maintain self-control I found myself exposing roll after roll of film of the island receding from the ship, every villager crowded along the wall stones waving and a huge flotilla of canoes trailing from our skiff under tow astern. It was almost sinking with the weight of little nude saltwater kids all waving and singing. A half mile from their island they started to leap off and swim home along our wake — a forest of swaying arms on the lagoon surface with the palms of Laulasi getting smaller and smaller until all we had was the presents they had bestowed upon us: shell money belts and bracelets, grass skirts, tapa loincloths, carvings — and wet eyes.

We stayed overnight at Auki town at the western end of Langalanga Lagoon to tidy up our affairs.

When *El Torito* left Malaita, its early morning mountains were etched black against a faint dawning sky; the new moon a fingernail paring and the old moon a pale disc held in its curve, fish skittering over the glassy lagoon. Part of me has never left that lagoon.

In the wheelhouse we talked it all over, considering the function of *El Torito* in enabling us to make rich, cross-cultural contacts with villages such as Laulasi. On this ship we are privileged beyond the average Westerner who goes there to assume a traditional role already long established. From our last night yarns with people at the Auki Club it was clear to us that even after years of residence Westerners cannot easily reach the level of acquaintance we had enjoyed with the island people. We have no established roles and our unconventional appearance divorces us from precedents. We can share our ship world with theirs. Yesterday one artificial island "up anchored" and left another. Two communities of saltwater people parted.

For Melanesians, Europeans are usually an employer class. The resultant culture clashes may leave them with a low opinion of each other. At clubs and bars we heard many stories from Europeans of the inadequacies of islanders who were said to have fouled up various jobs of which they probably did not have an overall appreciation. The maddening situations that arise, understandably enough, can be quite tragic. Europeans either build up a conviction that these people are congenitally inferior, or, while secretly realising that in time the islanders will be able to cope, they give them an inferiority complex: "We aren't as clever as whites," which can result in a self-confirming prophecy about their inadequacy.

Not even the most outlying Solomon's inhabitants can avoid Western influences in a shrinking world. With only 179,000 people, at independence they stand a good chance for the future.

We hope that to balance the effects of modern medicine they will stabilise their population with a birth control programme at all costs — even universal advanced schooling; though with today's syllabus this really only fits their children for employment within a Western society where jobs are scarce and hopes are raised fruitlessly while denying them their own culture to turn to in their frustration. Since these islands have no real wealth or resources, foreign development and exploitation can only lead to disappointment. The Solomons group will remain a happier place than most on Earth if it retains its communal patterns of living.

On my way home through the New Hebrides (now Vanuatu) and Fiji I was to see the alternative: through foreign exploitation, communal life is breaking up in Fiji. Displacing the locals, multinational development companies are setting up large-scale tourist resorts and real estate parks for the jet set in all the islands' loveliest spots, turning the people into a nation of waiters and cheap labourers dwelling in tin shacks and suburban squalor. As a Solomons friend remarked: "A black man's home is a white man's paradise."

Gangs of young toughs roam the busy streets of Suva, resentful of all authority now that their village system has been disrupted. With understandable bitterness they know that a few of the chiefs who once led them have sold land to the developers and own mansions in the white elite suburbs. In these areas Europeans pay nightwatchmen with guard dogs to punch time clocks five times each night, fearful of the savage attacks of housebreakers. I have never seen so many Alsatian dogs or heard so much talk of violence as during my stopover with friends at Suva on my return journey to New Zealand.

Somehow, I got the feeling that the Solomons people, never really colonised, are going to handle their independence pretty much in their own way. The educated people who will take over the administrative posts are mostly young, and those we met had a strong desire to retain their own cultural identity and to revive respect for custom ways. The older generation, although often caught up in Western religions, and sometimes a bit cowed from Western arrogance, are not too far removed from their roots to get it on again.

Since I had pressing needs to get home to my family in New Zealand, I booked a passage on the cruise ship *Himalaya*, just about to sail. In a mood of bitter revulsion I watched the drunks tumble on board; listened to empty, worn-out conversations; studied the over-fed matrons as they jerked frantically at the handles of the poker machines lining the bar walls.

What, I wondered, is my Laulasi friend doing now to enjoy life? Talking by firelight at the sea's edge as a huge moon wobbles up from the Malaitan hills and beams a dancing golden pathway over the lagoon from the dark coast to the moonglow island. He is eating his mangrove seed *koa*, with fish and coconut cream, and baked taro. Soon he will go and play moongames with the village children. Ramo, the richest man I've ever met — master of his whole world — an eternity away from this.

In the streets of Honiara, some weeks after I left, Walt ran into Johnson Olisokulu from Laulasi. He told Walt that shortly after our departure, for the first time in living memory, he had seen a priest pray to the sharks and the sharks actually appeared with no previous bait or anything in the water. From the hands of Bosikoru, the fully ordained chief shark priest, they came and took an offering.

[Note: for an Epilogue, see Appendix I.]

# PART THREE

## ATOLL DWELLERS' WORLD

December 1974: On my second *El Torito* voyage, a long cherished dream comes true — my wife, Jan, our children Brady (11) and Karla (9), are with me, visiting Melanesian islands in Vanuatu and the Solomons and living with the Polynesian inhabitants of a remote atoll in lonely seas.

The lively and inventive marine biologist Dr. Walter Starck, owner-captain of the research vessel *El Torito*, and his wife Janice are very much part of our extended family, as are the American student Cliff Enger and seventeen-year-old Rebbekah Lee, discovering a new world in an interlude from studies. We have met the sea snake dancers of Mota Lava, revisited the shark callers of Laulasi, discovered ancient creatures deep in a limestone cave system, and traced rock carvings thousands of years old. I have found the shrines of headhunters at Simbo Island, searched for ghosts on the haunted and deserted island of St Jorge and now I will talk to an atoll medium about psychic healing.

This is a story of communication — between the friendly and unconventional *El Torito* family and atoll dwellers whose stone-age culture has survived in a steady state for eight centuries. And through it runs the teasing question: who are best fitted to endure in a world that seems intent on spending its resources with little thought for the present and future?

## LIFE AMONG THE GALLON TREES

Jan's diary gives her impressions of our arrival at Ontong Java:

"As we munch chocolate-coated almonds in our little cabin and the ocean swells flex against *El Torito*'s porthole, we are thinking what a very different and exciting Christmas this is going to be. In the wheelhouse Walt is poring over the chart, choosing a safe pass to enter the atoll lagoon and Janice is sunbathing on the skiff bow.

"Wade has been on watch since midnight and I relieve him at first light. After three days of open ocean this is the beginning of an exciting day for us. Not only is it Christmas, but also it is the day we are to arrive at Ontong Java. When I come off watch the whole family sits together in the cabin and we open Christmas presents from Janice and Rebbekah and those we have made for each other.

"*El Torito*'s motors slow and we all rush up on deck to find we are entering the pass to the lagoon of Ontong Java Atoll.

"Named by Abel Tasman (on his 1642-3 voyage), Ontong Java is a necklace of 110 tiny islands, arranged around an oval lagoon measuring 70km by 26km and forming probably the third largest coral atoll in the world. Each island is only a few feet above sea level. The atoll is divided into two territorial units with villages at opposite ends of the lagoon on the islands of Luaniua and Pelau. It has been inhabited for about 1,000 years. The narrow, curving island where *El Torito* drops anchor is Luaniua. From an outrigger, Henry Manuhea, whom we have met in Honiara, comes aboard with six other men to look over the ship and to invite us to his village.

"After a hurried breakfast we all go ashore in the skiff. As we approach, dozens and dozens of Polynesian children, mostly nude, some with bits of calico wrapped round their middles, come running from all directions. They gather round us, staring and unsure. Some of the tiny ones run crying off to Mum if you glance in their direction. What fine healthy-looking kids with their light brown skin and hair colouring ranging from black to brown, and some blondish on top looking as though it had been bleached by the sun. We are met by some of the men who speak English; others, especially the women, stand shyly at a distance wearing only a piece of calico around their waists. It isn't long before the *El Torito* group is split up and we are shown over the village. Wade and I meet a young part Australian called Frank Mulvey who is married to an Ontong Javan girl and hadn't been back to Australia for 13 years. His grandfather, H.A. Markham, was the first Englishman to arrive after German possession ended; an early windjammer trader from Liverpool, he married an Ontong Javan girl, Frank's grandmother, and lived there from 1907 until 1923. Quite a bit of Mr. Markham's writings on Ontong Java can be found in anthropological notes.

"Frank very kindly offers to show us all over the village and since we've primed ourselves on most of the existing literature, we ask him many questions about life in the village and which traditional ways still exist. He is a tremendous help to us.

"We start down one end of the island where there is a cemetery, one of four on the island. It has a strange and silent beauty: rows and rows of coral slab tombstones on white sand mounds, fringed with frangipani and coconut trees. Some of the tombstones have interesting carvings on them of tuna, sharks, turtles, and human spirits. The more recent graves are marked with crosses and some with a combination of crosses and fish. Each family has a section and every member belonging to that family will eventually be buried here.

"You just dig down until you hit some bones," Frank explained. The best way to bury anybody on an atoll is to cover him with sand from the beaches. This must save a lot of scarce space and it means that all the relatives are close together. Burials nowadays are part Christian, part custom. They still believe that if a man has a violent death his spirit continues to wander around and a memorial is placed in front of his house.

"Everywhere we go we have crowds of little brown bodies running ahead and behind us laughing and talking, repeating any word they can pick up when we speak. There don't seem to be taboos about walking on graves. The kids run freely all over them without fear.

"Then we strolled through Luaniua village and I am very impressed with it. With around 800 inhabitants, and 160 huts arranged in a rectangular pattern of 'streets,' it is the biggest and cleanest I have visited. There's not a trace of litter anywhere. Frank takes us into his hut where he lives with wife and two children — a boy and a girl — and his wife's three cousins. Two of his wife's other sisters are married and they live with their husbands all in this same hut, occupying a corner each. Papesi, the youngest sister, 17 years old, is not yet married. When she eventually marries, her husband will come and live in the hut too. This is the custom, Frank says. This is why daughters are well looked after in the family because when they grow up they marry and bring another provider, a fisherman, to feed and look after the family. So it is important that the girl is well trained and brought up so that she will be able to catch a fit and capable man.

"The huts are built completely from materials grown on the atoll. The large foundation logs and uprights are made from a species of pandanus tree. The roof is thatched with coconut palms. The walls are made up of woven pandanus leaves. Men and single girls make the roofs; married women are not allowed as they are considered too heavy to work on the roof. Girls and women weave the mats and walls. There is a door at each end to provide a good flow of fresh air. In the front section of the hut there is a large split-level floor above the door on which they stack all the coconut husks to keep for firewood. In the centre is a suspended food platform specially designed to prevent rats coming down from the roof. There are shelves all round the walls with articles stored on them to keep them off the ground. In one corner there is a pile of special black cooking stones brought all the way from far away Guadalcanal. Later we notice that not everyone has these good cooking stones. Most have to make do with the coral rubble or have little fires outside. There are no stones on this island, only coral rock, which breaks up when heated. About two feet in from the entrance of the doorway *umu*, or cooking fire, is set into the earth floor, lined with cooking stones. On these stones sit several cooked taro puddings wrapped in taro leaves and whenever someone is hungry he slices off a piece.

"The only things on the floor of the hut during the day are hand-carved wooden stools. The people sit and sleep on pandanus mats which, when not in use, are rolled up in neat bundles and hung from the roof.

"Pandanus mats are made by heating fresh-cut green pandanus leaves over the fire, then, after being soaked in sea water, they are laid out to dry on the sand. They are then stored in coils ready for when a mat is to be woven.

"Every day the bedding and mats are put out to air in the sun. Nothing is ever left to get damp or musty on the floor for any length of time. On the shelves are many woven baskets, some filled to the top with dried *copra* (dried coconut kernels from which oil is obtained), large hand-carved wooden bowls and other eating and cooking utensils, coils of coconut rope and calico for the only clothing they wear, a piece just wrapped around the waist.

"Frank shows us his coconut toddy or wine sitting in two large glass Japanese fish floats, bubbling away. He gives some to Wade to try. I am not allowed any because it isn't meant for women.

"In the middle of the village we come to a deep stone-lined well, 15 feet across. Formerly fenced off, it used to provide the drinking water for the people. Children caught in the well enclosure were punished and their parents had to pay a fine. The well water is not for drinking now so the children are allowed to play in it. They have two new wells, which pump water through pipes to taps all over the village. The pump, driven by a windmill, is now broken and the people are very short of water, but there are plenty of coconuts, and nobody is concerned.

"We pass the twelve-year-old tin-roofed courthouse. When it is used, which is not very often, it is mainly for land disputes among relatives.

"Next we visit the clinic and meet Samuel the Melanesian medical orderly. The clinic seems to be well equipped for a very remote atoll. I notice a portable autoclave in one corner: bedpan, urinal, scales for weighing babies, a fridge, and plenty of stocks on the shelves. Samuel says that they get short of dressings and band aids because they use them more than anything else. [Note: Jan is an experienced nurse.]

"I mention to Samuel that the children and people look very healthy and fit and ask if there are any diseases causing problems. He says they have no boils, but there are sores caused from pierced ears becoming infected. The main problem seems to be chest complaints from too much smoking of the coarse stick tobacco. The population in Ontong Java in 1900 is estimated to have been between 3,000 and 5,500. After the white man came and introduced diseases the population dropped to 588 in July 1939. Now things are very much improved. Malaria and tuberculosis have been virtually wiped out. The population is rising. A wall chart in the dispensary shows: Luaniua, 827 people with 158 homes; Pelau, 207 people with 53 homes. All children are vaccinated against tuberculosis, polio, and tetanus. Twice a week the clinic has days for giving these vaccines; no one is left out.

"The average family nowadays is six to eight children, whereas it used to be four to five. The boy/girl ratio is about 50/50. The infant and maternal mortality rate is very low now with improvements at childbirth.

"In the old days when a baby was born it was placed beside the mother and the umbilical cord was not tied and cut until the placenta had come away. This must have been the cause of many babies dying, but it favoured survival of the mother. The women still prefer to have their babies in their huts but they may receive injections from a midwife or medical attendant and if the baby or mother appears to have anything wrong they are sent to the clinic in Auki, Malaita. Frank tells us that when a baby is born, they still practise the custom whereby the umbilical cord of a boy is taken out and put on a hook for bait. It will bring good luck for fishing. If the baby is a girl the umbilical cord is taken down to the taro garden and buried there for good crops.

"The taro gardens are owned and looked after by the women and girls. Men are not allowed to go to the taro gardens unless the women are sick or there is no one else available in the family. There are two days in the week for going to the taro gardens, Tuesdays and Fridays. Fish, taro and coconuts are the main items in the people's diets.

"Village hygiene has been improved with a good water supply. All food scraps are buried in holes on the beach and everyone must go to the toilet in the sea. Young children are taught at a very early age good toilet habits. If they can't walk they are carried down to the sea. If they have an accident in the house a gentle cuff reminds them not to do it next time. At first impression, these people seem more aggressive than Melanesians and children get prodded or cuffed regularly if they are not behaving, but as I spend more time among them I realise that this is just their way of bringing up children; they are very concerned that they are well behaved. The cuffing and prodding is never more than gentle, along with a sound telling off. The children themselves, mimicking the adults, also seem to hit out at each other, especially the older girls. If we are walking along in a group and one of the boys tries to join in, he gets chased off and cuffed by the girls. One or two of the girls are very possessive and want to keep us all for themselves.

"Frank tells us that a fight might spring up between two men or two women just out of the blue, but they never hold grudges and the next day all is forgotten. Fights mainly occur when young unmarried men have been drinking toddy. It is rare for a married man to get into such a fight. They soon learn how to handle alcohol, which is freely available.

"In the middle of the village stands a makeshift church of corrugated iron sheets. The village church had been blown down in a hurricane a few years ago. Frank says that the village is divided. One half is religious and the other half holds to what is left of their traditional customs. The church is the dividing line. The non-religious call the religious half 'South Vietnamese' and the girls, whenever they fight, call the religious side 'germs.' We ask him which is the stronger and he says that there is a growing tendency for the people to prefer the old traditional way, but most of it has been lost.

"We pass a large area, which used to be the *malai*, just as the Maoris have a *marae*. They used to have big *sanga* celebrations here every year in December, which went on for 30 days. All the people came from the other islands fringing the atoll and even from other atolls far away. There used to be a big ceremonial hut, which held all the carvings and idols. The priests were the only ones allowed in this building.

"It is said that the structure was destroyed after the missionaries came and, on their orders, all the carvings were dumped in the sea.

"They then lost interest in wood carving since it no longer had any meaning. Their traditional priests once made prayers to all the gods for fishing, weather, fighting, growing taro and so on. At the time of the *sanga* festival, there was a running race the length of the island *in the lagoon water*, followed by the parade of nude virgins from whom the winner would choose a wife. Men spent a year in training and strict diet to prepare for the race.* With such a prize, competitors navigated outriggers from distant atolls, bringing Luaniua new fishing knowledge and fresh genes. They also had sail and paddle races and there was dancing and celebrating for the whole 30 days.

*[Wade's diary: "I met one of the last men to win this contest before Christianity terminated it. I took pictures of him with his handsome, strong family. I saw it as a folkway to attract well selected genes to the atoll from abroad as well as new fishing techniques. 'The men these days...' some village matrons told Jan. And they spat on the ground!"]

"On a log perch beyond the reach of small children, a pet frigate bird is huddled. For our cameras, Walt tries to get the bird to balance on his forearm. It hates his shiny wristwatch and pecks viciously at the glass. Then it solves the problem by roosting on his arm but leaves his fingers bleeding. December is the time of the year, Frank tells us, when the men sail to the other islands to catch baby frigate birds for pets. They tie strips of coloured calico to their wings and legs. When they fly in from the sea at night the people know who each bird belongs to by the colour of calico streaming out behind.

"Some seabirds are eaten, especially the booby and the tropic bird. The latter is particularly popular roasted on a spit. Frigate birds are not very palatable although some people eat them. Caught and tamed before they can fly, the frigate birds stay around the village for two or three years, going off hunting each day. Then, Frank says, they disappear — possibly at maturity.

"An adult frigate bird has a wing span of up to eight feet. In earlier times when long canoe voyages were made, the birds were used for message-carrying and locating land. The missionary George Turner, at Funafuti in 1876, saw a frigate bird arrive from Nukufetuu carrying a message. The note was placed in a light piece of reed, plugged with cloth and fixed to the bird's wing. Formerly the natives had sent pearl fish hooks from island to island by these birds.* There were perches on most islands and the birds were treated as pets and fed with fish. There is a well-authenticated record of a frigate bird covering the 160 miles between Nauru and Banaba in two hours.

*[Note: A pearl fish hook was a man's signature; each made his own. Arriving on a bird it signified the canoe voyager had arrived safely at his destination and could be expected to return when the winds were favourable.]

"By the time we have looked over the whole village we are hot and thirsty. Back on the lagoon beach near the row of six men's club houses we meet Walter Hemoku who speaks English very well. He has chosen to come back to Ontong Java from a good job as an agricultural officer in Honiara to be with his people. When his wife's folks died she needed to come home and assume land ownership. Land is a responsibility. Walter, who is president of the village council, tells us about land ownership. In the Luaniua territory, ownership of land goes to the oldest girl in the family. Taro gardens are also owned by girls. In most cases when a couple get married the boy lives with the girl and her people. In some cases if the boy is wealthier, then the girl will live with the boy in his family's house. In the Pelau territory, ownership of land goes to the oldest boy.

"Wade is invited to join Walter in his clubhouse; his club is called *Australia* or *Papii*. They have names for all six of them: women aren't allowed there so Karla and I go for a swim in the lagoon. In no time dozens of little children are all around us in the water. We make a move to grab them and they yell and dive under to get away, coming up laughing with looks of mock fright on their faces as they swim away only to come back, daring us to try and catch them again."

An impression from Karla:

"Yesterday we arrived at Ontong. I went ashore along with everybody else and I played with all the little children. I noticed that these Polynesian children fought each other whereas Melanesian children hardly ever fight. We saw a tame frigate bird on the island and naughty little Walt Starck got pecked when he tried to pick it up ... All the little girls decorated our hair with flowers. I made friends with three girls called Aora, Gior, and Lingo, and I spent most of my time playing with them in the lagoon. They were all smiling and laughing because they were shy. We dived down holding hands and we did handstands underwater and we made up a whole lot of different methods of splashing each other."

## THE ATOLL FISHERMEN

Wade: Frank and I join the Christmas Day toddy drinkers in *Australia*. Wearing garlands and necklaces, the clubmen are passing around tins of scented powder, dusting their necks and daubing it on cheeks and foreheads. "May as well look like a clown if you're going to act like one," Frank grins. In *Malaita*, the next club house, Walter Hemoku introduces me to their toddy brew. Wall, from the grin on his face, is already into it. Edwin comes up with a glass fishfloat full. He upends it into a huge tin kettle. It gurgles and geysers until the last drop of fermented nectar leaves the glass sphere. A pickle jarfull was passed to me. Ukeleles strum, the men sing and on the sand between the club and their lined up outriggers, the fishermen dance. With Walter, the president, Henry and Edwin and I join in, whirling and spinning under the toddy-bearing "gallon trees." (Called so because some coconut trees produce a gallon of nectar for fermentation into toddy each day.)

For Luaniuans fishing is a very personal thing and there are many closely kept secrets, but when we get to know the men we are able to accompany them on fishing expeditions, to join in the chase and record the action on film and tape.

Through his bamboo diving goggles Akai watches, head over the side of his canoe, for the fish to gather. The boy beside him tosses out live bait-fishes. Alfred paddles in the stern to keep their outrigger in the middle of the lagoon passage. A baitfish twitches on his hook and Akai whips a big fish aboard with a graceful springing action of his fishing cane and returns for another. More live bait pepper the surface. Jacks, rainbow runners and needle-fishes flash into the air and rain into the canoe.

We have heard that Luaniuans fish for tuna and bonito using live bait to chum their quarry. So here we are, close by with the skiff and all our film gear. A camera shooting on the bow, Janice and I have to paddle the half-ton skiff hard to keep within range of the outrigger. We cannot use the motor for fear of frightening off the fish, which are attracted to the live bait. While the camera hums we slave against the wind and the current sliding out from the atoll lagoon into the open ocean. Then Walt dons scuba and slips over the side for some underwater sequences of the action.

At last my chance comes and I leap in with snorkel to see what is happening. Through the mirror of the surface the tiny bait-fishes bounce and hightail it for the bottom 60 feet below. They have to run a gauntlet of snapping jaws and silvery fins, for the big jacks are wheeling around in a dense cloud, fighting like seagulls over every fugitive bait-fish. Below them, hovering just above the coral sand, a group of trumpet-fishes with mouths like vacuum cleaners wait to engulf any fish fortunate enough to escape the *melée* above.

On the outskirts, other less agile species cruise, hopeful of a stray crumb. I dive down amongst them to watch the feeding frenzy more closely, observing what happens each time the baited hook descends into the fish swarm — how it matches the bait-fish so exactly that they are duped and whisked up into the sky. I see three grey sharks prowling over the bottom: 30 feet above their snouts a jack is hooked. As it rises, spiralling upward right in front of my mask, two greys rocket up, closing on it in a double helix of writhing bodies, fins, and jaws, as they try to snap the silver spindle from the line. The third grey zooms into the fray but the fish has disappeared into the canoe. Only 20 feet away I suddenly become aware that I am more than just an observer — I'm an alternative target! But fresh bait-fish shower down and the "bun rush" continues without including me. I recall the islanders telling me their technique for repelling grey sharks if bothered by them while baitfishing or spearfishing. It was after they had seen our underwater movies aboard *El Torito*. With magnetic concentration they watched Walt swimming among greys with impunity in his zebra-striped anti-shark suit. "With that shark you just catch one and cut open the belly. You leave him hanging from the canoe while you spearfish. All the other sharks stay away."

Walt and the rest of us aboard *El Torito* soon realise there is plenty to learn from these Polynesian fishermen. After centuries of fishing the same waters, living on a diet almost entirely of fish, coconut and taro, the people of Luaniua village can still go out any day and catch loads of fish — either in the lagoon or on the ocean side of their tiny island and within as little as half a mile range. We are trying to establish how this can be. The villagers have superb physiques and are amazingly healthy on their plain diet, but they eat great quantities of fresh fish, and with the few vegetables they manage to grow, beside the prolific yield from their taro swamp and their abundant coconut, they get all the necessary vitamins and trace elements.

Western fishing methods are adapted to temperate waters where there are few varieties of fishes although these may occur in great abundance — like the former Atlantic cod fisheries. In the tropics there is an enormous variety of species but each type occurs in relatively small numbers. When Western style fishing techniques are introduced to tropical waters all too often the result is over-exploitation and serious depletion of fishing stocks. In many of the Pacific islands the European influence on fishing techniques has been disastrous for the reef-fish communities and many island people these days are changing their diet from fresh fish to canned "peasoupo" — imported corned beef.

For the present the Polynesians of Luaniua have the answer. With their variety of traditional fishing techniques they are exploiting the diversity of the coral reef without upsetting the ecological balance. On an atoll, survival of living things depends on an interdependent, closed system, much like a long range space-ship. The lessons of atoll survival could be equally well applied to spaceship Earth.

Earlier this morning we set out with Akai and his crew to see how they catch their live bait-fishes. Wherever in the world this chumming technique is used, getting the bait is quite a problem. With a gay sail of patchwork pareo cloths, their outrigger skims across the sparkling blue of the lagoon to a spot near the reef pass, a shallow tidal fan, where ocean water spills across the reef. A net would be useless in such an area, becoming snagged on small coral outcrops. Instead they simply use a 200-foot length of palm leaves tied together in a continuous screen. Closely directed by Akai in the middle, with one man on each end they walk in a big arc, gradually closing into an oval, encircling hundreds of tiny fishes. As the sides draw closer and closer the boy fetches from the canoe a pair of poles between which white calico is stretched, like a sail. This is placed at the belly of the enclosure, the edges weighted down with lumps of coral. Then the bait-fish are easily chased in, the poles raised and the catch transferred to a long basket lashed alongside the canoe at water level. After four such hauls their live bait "well" is seething with bait. Since these tiny fishes abound on the reefs, those captured will be rapidly replenished from surrounding rocky areas where they can't be taken.

Day after day we go out fishing with the villagers and every time, according to the weather conditions and their own whims, they choose a different technique. Each family group has its own special fishing arts, passed on down the male line and jealously guarded. These people dislike repetitive, routine work and look on fishing more as a game, with tasty spinoffs, than a means of earning a living.

We became more aware of this during a spell of very calm weather. A fever to catch the oilfish, *Ruvettus pretiosus,* seizes the village men. When the weather is calm and there is no wind or current it is possible to go out onto the open ocean and drift all night, miles from the atoll, with a 12-inch baited wooden hook and a five-pound weight trailing 1,000 feet below the canoe over the abyss. In the darkness great *bathypelagic* fishes come up from the depths, and among them, the oilfish.

At Luaniua, competition among the men is intense to see which family is the most successful at catching the oilfish. It is a feat of strength and stamina that demands the utmost in fishing skill of each man. The oilfish itself is no gastronomical delight: very oily, its flesh acts as a severe purgative. That doesn't deter the fishermen — it's all in the game. However, in the course of the night's fishing they may catch several species of fine, deep water fish. The sportsmen made no mention of these. They enjoy the champion's discomfort, as he has to make frequent sorties into the sea to evacuate.

More than 1.50 metres in length and weighing 50 to 60 kilos, the oilfish, with its jutting lower jaws and fearsome vomerine teeth, belongs to the snake mackerel or family Gemphylidae. When first pulled out of the water its body is brilliant orange-yellow or pink, but this fades rapidly on death. A deep water carnivore, it is found throughout the tropical Indo-Pacific at depths of 200–300 metres.

One morning Walter Hemoku comes in from a night out on the ocean. Over coffee in the cabin he tells us the current has been bad, causing his line to stream out. In his canoe he has only one big oilfish, but beside it I saw a 15-pound queen snapper (a bathypelagic lutjanid, genus *Etyli*) with large eyes and a filamentous tail, and a ten-pound deep water scombrid with big teeth.

With Patteson and two brothers we set out one night to film spearfishing in the lagoon. The skiff crosses a mirror calm atoll bowl, radiant under a three-quarter moon, even the stars casting their paths in the water. While our floodlight generator rumbles, Walt films them underwater and topside from the skiff. With torches and handspears the divers skewer 40 reef fishes sleeping in the coral — all within very easy reach of the village.

On the beach beside Malaita club house, Komilo demonstrates for us his fishing technique. Respected as the tuna fisherman who had taught Akai, we sense he has been a little piqued that we had filmed Akai instead of him. Now, with a big audience gathering he tells us that he has special chants for tuna fishing but these are too secret to tell us. However he goes and fetches a short 14-inch stick to which two trochus shell hooks are attached on short lines. With this little rod he hooks rainbow runners, after chumming up these beautiful pelagics with bait-fishes and special prayers to the ancestors. He demonstrates using coconut shells for *pretend* fish. He uses one hook at a time, keeping the other line in reserve. Having no barb the catch falls off quickly into the canoe and he can soon fill it with fish in this way.

When the moon is almost full the men go turtle fishing. Across eel-grass beds on the reef flats, they link four nine-inch mesh nets. Then they drive turtles into their nets. Shifting from island to island they may spend two or three nights out at a time and would once have caught 20 to 30 turtles of all sizes.

The traditional method for catching them is to dive down to the coral caves where they sleep and plant a three-barbed hook in their necks. The netting technique, I was told, the master fisherman Komilo introduced from the Mortlock Islands in 1927. The turtle population now shows serious signs of depletion. An expedition while we are there yields only six small turtles. From the importance of the turtle motif on tattoos and tombstones it must have once contributed much more to the atoll dwellers' diet.

*El Torito* accompanies the villagers when they hunt fish for a wedding feast. Eight outriggers sail across the lagoon to the southern rim of the atoll. With the skiff and our diving gear we join in the chase. Chest deep out on the reef flat, a circle of 30 young men, relatives of the groom, form a human net. Each holds a canoe paddle at right angles to his body. Gradually our circle tightens around a swarm of reef fish, mainly rabbit fishes or siganids. There is no splashing or disturbance as this will cause the fish to panic and dash through the ring. The excitement of such a group activity is intense — especially when we notice we have a shark in with the fish.

The circle is reduced to 50 feet diameter and the shark makes a rush for deep water. A 30-foot net is placed at one point in the circumference. The fishes, sensing a gap in the circle of paddles and legs, head straight into the net and the mouths of the wedding guests.

A brisk wind has come up. Eight sails rise and the canoes fly over the choppy lagoon while *El Torito* races alongside them as close as we dare. Through a telephoto lens the action is incredible. The outrigger floats are clear of the water. We are doing seven knots and they surge past us, just a collection of logs, coconut fibre and calico. One man sits at the rear hugging the steering paddle. In the centre another holds the sail rope and acts as a counterweight, and a boy in the bow bails nonstop.

A traditional song of celebration, recorded by Hogbin in 1930, goes as follows:

> *The shadow of my canoe lies in the sea*
> *and the outrigger splashes up and down in the water.*
> *See — the outrigger flies like a bird.*

One canoe thrusts its bow deep into a wave. The crew lets the sail go slack while they stop to bail their fish-laden canoe. Even then *El Torito* has to make all speed to reach the village before this last canoe arrives. Walt drops anchor and we leap into the skiff to film them landing their catches. On the beach the men put all their fish into baskets and give them to two old women for the wedding. Then they get some coconuts and sit in the sea eating raw fish and coconut, laughing and joking together.

Just then a fierce squall hits the lagoon. *El Torito* begins to drag anchor. In the short time it takes Walt to get aboard, a really good sea builds up.

Beyond the reef, out on the open ocean, we watch two sails dipping to and fro, trolling for tuna in the atoll lee, with the squall tearing at them — a white cloud of birds overhead; and a lone man in a small canoe line-fishing. The rain blots them out from time to time. Then I glimpse the sails again — heading further out on the vast ocean. I can see clearly that the outrigger canoe is ideally adapted to the atoll situation — the dugouts and plank canoes of the Laulasi people could never sail like this.

Along the lagoon shore between the six club houses the outrigger canoes are hauled out after each voyage and covered with palm fronds to ward off the sun. They are hewn from driftwood or from the spicey smelling *pingipingi tree* which grows on the island. Up at the Pelau end of the atoll the currents bring in good-sized drift logs so they have better canoes there, I am told.

The outriggers have identical ends, the bow and stern being interchangeable, they can sail either end foremost, always keeping the outrigger to windward as a balance weight. Changing tack, the mast is raked towards the new bow, the sail swings around behind it and the steersman takes his paddle to the other end.

In the previous twelve months the villagers have started using outboards. Walter Hemoku encourages them to take sails along, knowing that on other Micronesian atolls when the outboard was introduced many more men were lost at sea. The villagers take very good care of their outboards, rinsing and treating them with anti-corrosion oil. They know nothing about mechanics and Walt does his usual good deeds but a bright boy is receiving training in Honiara.

For Walt life afloat is a constant series of maintenance jobs for which he needs all his ability and every tool in the workshop.

Today, for example, the port engine would not start and the battery charger fused so he started it with a jumper wire from the starboard batteries. Then, when the squall hit we had trouble raising anchor, the winch switch had seized up.

## TO RONCADOR ATOLL

Wanting to gain a more intimate view of these Polynesians and their fishing methods, Walt offers to take a dozen fishermen and two canoes over to Roncador, 50 miles from Luaniua. It is a *young* atoll reef with no islands, just a moat of limestone barely exposed at high tide and enfolding a calm lagoon in mid-ocean. The grandfathers of Luaniuans used to fly down to Roncador in big seagoing outriggers. I've heard that these people with 10- to 15-metre canoes once thought nothing of making the 300-mile voyage to Honiara just to get tobacco. But the British administration actively discouraged inter-island canoe voyages and the big seagoing craft are no longer built. There is not much use for them just for atoll fishing.

Walter Hemoku has no trouble finding twelve men from *Australia* club house. We will have an excellent chance to study their fishing techniques, to swim with them underwater in exciting situations (the reef passes abound in sharks) and to gain a better understanding of their attitudes to life.

In the late afternoon *El Torito* enters the pass on the south side of Roncador and anchors on a pinnacle near a wreck. It is the *Fong Kuo No. 51*, a Taiwanese fishing vessel, sitting on the reef in eight feet of water. With the skiff and two outriggers we make an excursion there. The twelve Luaniuans swarm over the rusty hulk, prying loose nails and tiny floor tiles for their draught games in *Australia* club house. They gather up the birds' eggs and, once satisfied there is nothing left of value — the ship has been very well stripped — they pull down the 60-cent diving goggles from their foreheads and leap overboard. Patteson spears two surgeon-fish at once.

I look down the engine room hatch. There is Brady alone in the bowels of the ship, standing in silent thought while the Pacific rollers thud against the stern, causing the hull to resound like a drum. He's made it. After his frustration at Pocklington Atoll, when he could not board the big wreck we visited, he is now exploring a wreck. I wonder what is passing through his mind but decide to leave him alone with his dreams. Later, in his diary I read: "The ship was completely cleaned out — there was nothing left on it. I managed to get into the engine room. I was standing on a platform just above one of the engines. If I bent down I could see what would be a generator. While I was standing there I thought of the men who were working with the sweat pouring off them, keeping everything going when there was suddenly a hard jolt and they found themselves swimming in darkness."

Twenty divers aboard *El Torito*, and only Puggy, the ship's dog, stays high and dry.

Writes Jan:

"Everyone went in for a dive. Brady, Rebbekah and I had to wait until the others came up because there wasn't enough gear to go round. It was about 6:30 and getting dark but we could still see enough to have a terrific dive. The water was very clear and we went to 90 feet. There were huge clams everywhere. We had promised the men we would bring some up for them to take home. Rebbekah and I got the giggles as we watched Brady gathering clams and placing them in a pile near the anchor rope. They were so heavy that he would give a leap and fin madly, only to go crunch on to the bottom again. He looked so funny leaping along the bottom like a sandhopper. We saw a large leopard ray, which gracefully winged past us. When we struggled to the surface, our arms loaded with a huge clam each, there was great excitement. The men were pulling in fish after fish and we thought we had better get out because as soon as the sun went down the sharks would come with all the struggling fish and guts floating around. Sure enough an hour later they started catching grey sharks.

Brady: "When everyone came back I went for a scuba dive with mum and Rebbekah. The first thing I saw was a giant clam. We found out they were common. When we got halfway around the pinnacle we were diving on, we saw a leopard ray. It was six feet across and rippling along at a speed that never grew or diminished. We followed it to the anchor, and got some clams we had gathered for the men and went up. We found that they were all fishing like madmen and they were catching things too. By the time it was dark they had enough for a few days. When they finished they were just catching grey sharks and blacktips."

Writes Jan:

"What a breathtaking sunset. The men sitting out on their outriggers and on the stern of the *El Torito* looked splendid silhouetted against the blood red sky. They started to slit the sharks' stomachs open. They said that when the other sharks smell the stomachs of their own kind they get frightened and go away. It did seem to work because they stopped catching any.

"In the opposite direction, the moon rose out of the sea, just as spectacular as the sunset.

"The men filled a huge pot to the brim with the fish they had caught and boiled it for their dinner in salt water. They sat on deck eating it with taro pudding that their wives had prepared.

"Their method of fishing was interesting. They would bait a hook and tie coral stones on either side of the bait in such a manner that by jerking the line when it had reached the bottom the stones fell away. One of the men got a fish bone in his finger and his mate cut it out with a razor blade then dunked his finger in iodine and wrapped it up without a flinch.

"That night Walt showed them our two films, *The Wall of Mouths,* a coral drop-off film and the Laulasi shark worshippers film. They enjoyed them immensely and were very excited with the shots of fish they recognised under water.

"The next morning when we got up, the last day of 1974, the men had already caught a huge pot of fish for breakfast. Walt decided to shift to a different place on the ocean side of the atoll. As we were moving the men caught a huge dog-toothed tuna. We hove to near where we could see some wreckage from a ship. The men leapt overboard and swam through the surf, running over the coral reef with bare feet. They are so strong and fit looking, with wonderful physiques. When they came back they said that there was pile after pile of good rope on the wreck and they would like to get it to take home. It would be very useful in the village. So Walt went back through the lagoon pass and around on to the calm side of the reef so they could take the skiff close and load it all on. They spent all day at it and came back with ladders and steel pipe and as much rope as they could handle. Brady had been with them too and he was so exhausted trying to keep up with them that he fell asleep trying to write his diary.

"The rest of us spent the day diving and snorkelling around, enjoying the life on the reef. That night, New Year's Eve, we went up on deck. The men were all happily playing cards on the bow in the light of a full moon. We had the music playing from a tape recorder which we danced to. It was the most beautiful New Year's Eve I had spent because it was so different and in such a very remote place.

"At Roncador *El Torito* turned into a fish factory: the men kept catching great quantities of fish and cutting it all up to go in the deepfreeze to take home to their families. Every meal they cooked a huge pot. From time to time we would bake scones and cakes and rice for them and we kept the fresh water flowing because it was very thirsty work. There was such a happy atmosphere on the ship and very catching. Everyone was enjoying himself to the utmost.

"On the afternoon of the last day we moved to the pass. It was high tide and should be slack water. We all got in for a dive. I went with Wade to 100 feet. What a tremendous place and the fish were the thickest and biggest I'd seen anywhere on the whole trip; large schools of coral trout or grouper everywhere, Spanish mackerel and barracuda, myriads of colourful reef fish and gigantic coral formations.

"We found an eight-foot nurse shark lying under a plate coral. Wade took some photos of me right up close to it. We managed to get about three shots before the shark realized we were there, and moved off.

"Wade went to reload his camera. I still had 1,000 pounds of air left so I took Brady down because he would most likely never see anything like this in his life again. When we surfaced Wade had taken Karla in while waiting for us. I was so thrilled that the whole family had been able to see that pass. Soon the tide would turn and a fierce current would set in again so Wade and I quickly donned fresh tanks. We swam out to the drop-off and over the edge, down the sheer cliff to 150 feet. The water was so clear that when you leaned out you could see down another 100 feet or more. It is a funny feeling to lean out in mid-water over a cliff and not fall off, down, down, down.

"We were watching out for grey sharks. Walt had seen six out there. Wade had painted white stripes on a black umbrella and we wanted to see if the sharks were frightened when we opened it out. He also wanted to get some good photos of them. We didn't see any until we began to move back up the cliff face. One quite large one swam up past us about six feet away and when we looked down we saw one swimming away from us. A white-tip came cruising past and Wade managed to get some shots of him. To show the visual effect he took some of me with the striped umbrella beside a very beautiful outcrop of coral.

"We moved back over the reef marvelling at the huge 150-pound grouper that came right up close to us. There were six of these and they seemed to be in pairs. While we were decompressing under the boat looking at the never-ending hordes of fish streaming past, a tiny little grey about 18 inches long came to look at us. He was so cute, just like a puppy. Walt shot two grouper for tea. This brought two greys sweeping up over the reef darting about in a disturbed way but they didn't come close or get aggressive. The sharks must be too well fed here and weren't worried at all about our presence. We obviously weren't a threat to their food supplies so we couldn't really try out the umbrella. I had breathed two tanks and didn't even feel cold. I think I was just too excited and exalted over this fantastic dive to feel cold.

"The atoll men were terrific divers. Using only plastic goggles and no flippers Walter Hemoku dived down 50 feet and saw a turtle in a cave. He surfaced and got a line with a hook on the end, dived again, creeping up and lunging the hook into the turtle's neck. The guy above then hauled it up on the line. The hook is a special one used for turtle fishing with three barbed hooks on it.

"We had to wait there until midnight to leave for Ontong Java so that we would enter the lagoon in daylight. As the tide began to drop a ferocious current set in and with the wind springing up from the opposite direction it began to get rough. We realized how very fortunate we had been to dive in this area at all.

"A storm came up and we had a rough trip back. The men had to leap over the stern to bail out their swamped canoes all through the night. It rained so hard that the skiff carrying her heavy load of rope and junk off the wreck was getting very low in the water and Walt and the men had to leap in again and let the bungs out so the water would drain out as we were going along.

"When we got back the men were met by a very excited group. They had plenty to show and tell of their trip to Roncador and a good supply of fish for everyone. The man who found the ship's ladder was going to use it for a two-storey house he planned to build. They had days and days of untangling rope ahead of them but for them, doing it in a group was very pleasant."

Wade: As we slam and bash our way back to Luaniua through the night, I dream I am within a huge office building. Bombs are crashing all around and people are cowering in the hallways and beneath architraves, fearful of a direct hit.

Writing my diary up in the wheelhouse on watch, the radar screen image is obscured by dense thunderclouds and rain is smoking up over the bows, whirling in vortices around the crane and the deck gear and lashing the wheelhouse windows. All over the floor around me, and downstairs in the saloon, the Luaniuan men are sprawled in sleep.

Diving that virgin atoll pass at Roncador with Jan was a highlight of our trip. I felt a trancelike state induced by the strangeness of the scenery, the masses of fishes whirling around us and the eerie tranquillity of it all. It was like looking down the barrel of a huge gun, or watching a busy intersection the moment when all the traffic lights are red. An hour after we left the water the tide started to flow again, all the water from the lagoon, an avalanche sluicing over the great curving valleys and ridges and the ship tossing on the tidal waves as she strained at anchor. Below us all the great gorgonian fans would be folding over and all the fishes sheltering in caves and beneath ledges. Diving there at slack water we felt as if in a charmed state.

The development of coral was massive: great organ pipe corals, densely compacted by the water pressure; undulating hillsides of yellow soft corals, plains of coral rubble and the white snowflakes of the calcareous seaweed *Halimeda*. And beyond, the drop-off to infinity, with spills of coral sand cascading down chutes and piled in drifts on ledges — all evidence of the powerful water movement there. Eight hundred feet below I could visualize a talus on the reef slope — a great pile of sand and organic debris sloping on and on, far beyond the sun's rays, where a range of deep water predators cruised up along the reef slope before it tumbled off into the ocean abyss. Two thousand fathoms is the depth of the ocean floor in the part of the Pacific from which these atoll mountains rise — the "eternal hills" of the poets, their summits a coral-fringed lake in mid-ocean.

## SPIRIT ANCHORS

The social fabric of the Ontong Java people was last described in 1930 by anthropologist Ian Hogbin at a point when the atoll society appeared doomed having sustained a population decline of around 90% in the previous 30 years. While here, I am eager to see what has remained intact. During *El Torito*'s oceanic travels I have become increasingly intrigued with the healing practices of primitive societies which often use altered states of consciousness, termed hypnotic trance or "possession," to influence the mind of the sufferer. I wonder whether these altered states might provide some rational explanation for the effectiveness of such methods.

Alone one night I go ashore with the skiff to visit a spirit medium. My guide has arranged to meet me at the trade store: the hut belonging to the village cooperative society. On the beach I ask the kids who run up out of the darkness to lead me there. Instantly one clasps my hand and tugs me along while the others race ahead singing "soceetee, soceetee."

There I learn that the medium is involved in a special ceremony. Olau has composed a song of celebration, an *olioli*. His married son Ezekiel, who speaks good English, takes me along. Sounds of singing and drumming grow until on one of the sandy avenues that run between the huts I come upon a strange and unforgettable sight: more than 100 villagers sitting in a circular mandala pattern, all chanting to the beat of their bamboo tube drums. Around a space fifteen feet across sit twenty of the older men on carved stools. At the centre, an oil lantern is burning; the light of the lantern is flashing on the bamboo tubes and the leaflike blades of canoe paddles as the handles pound on the ground. Around them is a second circle of younger men and boys and then an assembly of women, girls and babies. In the first circle one man stands out. He is wearing a spikey crown of golden yellow pandanus leaves.

"Who is that, Ezekiel?"

"That man is my father, Olau. When Mr. Hogbin came here in 1927 my father was twenty years old. I think Mr. Hogbin attended his first marriage. His photo appears in Mr. Hogbin's book. My father is well known for making *olioli* about important things in the village life."

To the thump of his bamboo tube, Olau leads off his composition. The group responds, first the men and then the women taking up the song, pounding in unison the resonant coral ground, singing with a sliding assonance of evenly stressed vowel sounds: "Komai kakala vosili, ihakiha vosili..." The massed voices blend in a three-part harmony and the words of the chant are very repetitive giving a pleasant, lilting cadence. Some drummers only strike on every second beat. Kaboom, kaboom, kaboom, kaboom — a hypnotic, blood-pounding rhythm.

With a sudden shout of "honay!" each chant abruptly ends. A brief interval of laughter and excited chatter and another elder leads off, the men and women resuming their alternating responses. Rapt in the whole performance I push the tape recorder button and listen on the fringe of the group. There are twelve chants in each cycle. On completion the whole assembly arises, carrying their stools, tubes and paddles, and proceeds slowly along the dark avenues towards another part of the village, all chanting the same responses but with a measured dirge-like cadence — a replay of the previous performance at a slower speed. The pace is restrained by the ponderous hollow thump of an unusually thick bamboo tube.

During the chanting teenage girls circulate among the singers dowsing necks and shoulders with sweet-scented talcum. Everyone wears necklaces of pandanus nuts and headbands of bleached white leaves, long ribbons that catch in the light as they nod. Married women have on their broad marriage belts of multicoloured glass beads and saffron calicos. The girls look lovely in the lamplight, their breasts gleaming, lithe tattooed bodies and smiling faces. The lamplight flickers on the paddle blades and dances on the thatched walls of huts; it gleams on the bouncing bamboo tubes and all the clenched hands beating together. The hut fronts, made of woven mats, a series of overlapping rectangles, have a varied texture that catches the light and the shadows in a rich play. Above, the silvery coconut fronds, the thick scent of powder, the spicy smell of turmeric garlands and the smoke of taro cooking pits.

At the third station I tape some comments: "Shadows of tube drums dancing on the hut walls, pert breasts catching the light, girls still sprinkling powder, people laughing and smiling to each other as they sing. How good it must feel doing this with your neighbours on a fine night: another sort of moongame. Mothers sing holding their babies; all the little children are here. It's been going for two or three hours now. Nobody seems at all tired. This station has lasted longer than the second one. Now they're moving on again.

"This is the fourth corner of the rectangle they have moved around. They're settling down again. A little cramped here — the crowd seems to have grown. About half the village is here now, Ezekiel says. Everywhere I see happy Polynesian faces — for a moment I'm flying back in time to the traditional Maori society of my own country... I am finding the rhythmic pounding and the whole setting is altering my awareness. So this is what it is all about! On a sparse atoll there are no special plants. But virtually every culture finds some pathway towards reaching altered states. "Good for your head?" I ask Ezekiel. He grins and nods vigorously: "Yes, good for your head." Ezekiel tells me he is going to join in. How I wish I could too."

In a clockwise progression the atoll dwellers repeat their song cycle at seven different stations around the village. After the seventh they break off. A few people rise and go away, returning with bundles and mats which are placed in the centre of the group. There is no order or formality, but very casually and gradually something is happening.

On to the mats dozens of packets of stick tobacco are tossed. By this time I realize that the distinguished looking person alongside Olau, who has often led the singing and wields the thickest bamboo tube, is Father Caspar. Head of the Melanesian Mission church (Anglican) at Ontong Java, he has just returned from Pelau village at the far end of the atoll. In his honour Olau has composed this *olioli*, celebrating the mission school and recapitulating its history.

Now, it seems, Father Caspar is taking the lead role. Before him two young men, teachers at the school, kneel on the mats. They start breaking open the packets and stacking up the shiny tobacco sticks. Once done, the older men, all except Father Caspar and Olau, begin to come forward in turn, slowly and casually, each receiving a stick. Nobody is overeager — there is a lot of good-natured banter and laughter as various characters appear. Next it is the women's turn: first the teenagers, then the older women and finally all the very young girls, receive a stick of tobacco. When some of these were slow to respond Kamilo, the master fisherman, chastens them: "Come on, don't be bashful!"

Once everybody has collected a stick the whole sequence is repeated. Six times everybody comes forward and is given tobacco by the teachers. It is after midnight before this ceremony is completed. About five hours of intricate, rhythmic chanting and the tobacco distribution: I have watched an *olioli* ceremony.

In most Pacific islands Western churches have so entirely eradicated traditional ceremonies that the continuity of such oral traditions has been irretrievably broken. With the drastic population decline on the atoll, Father Caspar must have become aware of the consequences of such a culture loss and now I see him taking a lead role, adapting the pagan *olioli* to the religio-educational patterns of the west.

Aboard *El Torito* next morning, I tell the crew of the incredible ceremony I have witnessed. Then we recall a book in the ship's library: *Mind Games: A Guide to Inner Space,* a series of exercises which groups of people can follow to induce altered states of consciousness. In one game the authors, Robert Masters and Jean Houston, suggest an all-night session, out of doors, in a pleasant, private setting, with a fire as a focal point for concentration and prolonged listening to the beating of drums, dancing and chanting.

Perhaps this is why the *olioli* had such a pleasant effect on me. Even as a non-participant, I came away feeling exhilarated, very relaxed, and in touch with the people of the village.

On my second attempt to meet a spirit medium Jan and I go ashore at nine one night. Following our guide through the village at that hour is quite magical — a full moon silvering the children playing on the beach and the groups of people reclining on mats outside their huts; no dogs barking nor babies crying; a faint background music of crickets and quiet voices.

In their hut the medium and her husband sit along with three small children. An oil lamp throws shadows on the leaf walls and her tattoos etch the features of her expressive face in the soft glow.

Our guide explains to her that we have studied reports of anthropologist Ian Hogbin, who described the methods of mediums in this village 44 years earlier and that we wish to learn whether the practices are still maintained.

With graceful arm gestures and soft but deliberate tones she begins to answer my questions, this lean, vital woman of around fifty, with occasional nods and comments from her husband. I record on tape her replies to the questions put to her through our guide and translator, who speaks fluent English and has a warm relationship with the couple.

Q: "In his story Mr. Hogbin said that when somebody was sick the medium would lie down and the voice of the *kipua* (ancestors) would speak through her mouth. Is that still true?"

A: "The medium can hear *kipua* speak to her and she can also hear any ordinary man when she is in a trance. When the *kipua* speak through her mouth the tone of her voice changes and strange words come."

Q: "Does she remember what the *kipua* were saying when she comes out of the trance?"

A: "She does not know — just the listeners. When she is out of her trance she has to ask her husband or the listeners what the *kipua* is saying."

Q: "If some person in the village who keeps the custom gets sick tomorrow, would he come to her or would relatives bring that sick man to her house? Would she go into a trance and tell them which one of the *kipua* was causing that sickness so that person could get better?"

A: (This time the woman spoke at great length.) "She is telling us that before, when the mission came here, the first thing they did to her was force her to give up all the customs she possessed, tokens for the *kipua* and services to the *kipua.* Now she must neglect everything. Since 1969 she has to give up spiritual healing because of church pressure; all she is permitted to do now is massage and set broken limbs. She is skilled at this.

"She is sorry about what she has lost but fears the mission and must keep quiet. If there is a sick patient who requests her help, she can still do it but most people have now been persuaded not to come. If the patient comes to the medium's own house then her *kipua* can fight against the patient's *kipua* and help the patient recover. She will not take any food for quite a long period before the trance. The *kipua* can speak to her mind. For example: I am a *kipua* and I speak through her and I say 'You will be recovered tomorrow' and straight away the man starts to get well. If I say 'No, tomorrow you will die — that is it."

Q: "How did she become a medium?"

A: "Before she became a medium she was very sick and took no food for almost half a month. Her vision became very blurred. At night time things were very bright. She could see *kipua* at night. During daytime she could see only shadows. After that she found she could see *kipua* — she knew that they wanted her to be a medium. She tells us there are four women mediums in the village but one is in Honiara at this time. Another of them no longer practises. During a sickness lasting several weeks her dead father's *kipua* had opposed her mediumship although her dead mother's supported it.'"

Modern medicine and the human sciences acknowledge the influence of social factors on man's health, recognising that there is often a socially relevant cause to his misfortunes. In a primitive society the interdependence of its members is much more obvious than for us. Between the living and the dead, past and present generations, a strong sense of continuity exists so that ancestors and gods are seen to intervene in the affairs of their descendants.

In her case study of magical medicine among the Yorubas of Nigeria, Una McClean's words fit the Ontong Java ancestor cult as well as they would, with minor discrepancies, scores of other indigenous groups from the Eskimos to the ancient Greeks. The presence of ancestral spirits "permeates family compounds and sacred shrines and may at times descend upon living men and women who are in a suitably perceptive state of trance."

In such societies if somebody infringes the social code it is often believed his ancestors inflict disease on him.

"There is a very intimate connection between sickness and punishment," Hogbin says. "The people of Ontong Java believe that most of their illnesses are sent to them by the spirits as a punishment for having committed actions which are wrong."

With reference to the Yorubas, Una McClean wrote: "Much so-called neurotic illness is a way of reacting to personal difficulties and misfortunes. People in every culture are primarily involved in their relationship with the members of their immediate families and with those of other people in the community who can affect their happiness and prosperity. People worry over major decisions to be taken, they brood over the possible complications behind others' words and actions, they suspect ill will or lack of love from the people whom they depend on most. They are obsessed with domestic difficulties or caught up in long drawn-out struggles between the generations."

A doctor friend once told me of an experiment in which a patient was given the Mantoux test for tuberculosis (prior to a B.C.G. inoculation) in each arm. Placed in a hypnotic trance she was told that in one arm there would be no reaction. Normal swelling occurred on her other arm: lymphocytes from nodes in the armpit had been summoned to repel the invaders. But with the arm where hypnosis was used, there was no reaction. Examination of the tissue showed that not a single lymphocyte was present. It seems that the mind had interfered with the body's immuno-reaction. (Just as in well-authenticated laboratory situations, yogis in trance have demonstrated mental control of the body's autonomic nervous system, arresting the heart and the stomach, etc., once considered impossible.)

Should a man infringe upon the social code of his group, it may well be that his body's immunosystem becomes depressed, just as our other glands are triggered emotionally. Endemic organisms such as viruses lurking in his environment are then able to invade his body. But if he accepts the village code, making some sort of direct appeal to his ancestors, he may recover, his body's immunosystem successfully repelling the alien organism.

From my 1974 interview with the medium in Luaniua village it was clear she still believed that in a state of trance, ancestral spirits or *kipua* could speak through her mouth to the living and that her own *kipua* could intercede with those of a sick person for his recovery.

Forty-four years earlier Hogbin was able to describe the traditional culture in much detail. The Luaniuan believed that from the time he first crawls, a man has a spiritual entity, his *kipua*. Not normally visible, it resembles him exactly, and can move about freely in his vicinity. When he dies, his *kipua* lives on forever: the spirit of the original man. It is capable of exerting a powerful influence on his descendants: *kipua* are the cause of birth, success in fishing, changes in weather and many other everyday events. Most importantly all sickness is inflicted upon the living by the *kipua* of the dead, usually by those of his immediate dead relatives.

Such is the supernatural origin of illness. To counteract it there were two approaches. Ultimately each reinforces the tribe's social code. With some specific illnesses a man could seek the intervention of a specialist in that complaint who would perform the appropriate ceremony with a prayer to the patient's *kipua* for his recovery. Knowledge of such prayers and rituals belonged to the headmen of certain joint families whose services were repaid with gifts. Or the sick man might seek to find which of his ancestors wished him to die and which were favourable to him. For this there were three processes of divination: two involved questioning the *kipua* and then manipulating leaves or sticks, as one would cast dice, to determine negative or positive responses.

The third way was to seek the help of a *koulaiku* or spirit anchor: a man or woman who claimed powers as a medium.

Ian Hogbin wrote:

"If anyone is sick and it is thought advisable to seek the aid of the *koulaiku*, a member of the family first makes him a present of eight coconuts. If the sick man is able to be moved, and it is very rare that someone is so ill that his relatives are afraid to carry him, he is now borne to the house of the *koulaiku* and laid upon the bed mats there. The interior of the house of this person is the same as that of any other house except that in one corner are the paraphernalia of his calling. These consist first of a white coconut leaf split down the middle and tied to a rafter. Underneath this is a bottle of coconut oil and a bundle of dried pandanus leaves. The latter are known as *henua*, and are the choicest leaves available, bleached white, split open and then smeared with orange coloured turmeric. These *henua* represent *kipua* who are in the habit of using the *koulaiku* as a medium. As soon as a new one does so, which may be only a few hours after the death of the person to whom it originally belonged, the surviving relatives give the *koulaiku* a *henua* representing it, to add to his bundle.

"After nightfall the *koulaiku* prepares himself to be possessed. He smears himself with the oil and then lies down in the corner of the room under the *henua* bundle. The lights are extinguished, and all remains quiet for some minutes. Gathered round the sick man, of course, are his relatives and friends. Soon the *koulaiku* begins to writhe about, and may even become quite frantic and have to be pinned down by both arms and legs. Sometimes he screams and foams at the mouth, but at other times the possession is of a rather simple order, and all that passes over his body is a slight quiver. Then a low whistle is heard, the signal that a *kipua* has now dominated him. The assembled relatives of the sick man begin to ask questions, which it is believed the *kipua* itself, not the *koulaiku*, will answer. The questions are confined chiefly to inquiring which *kipua* is sending the disease, whether it wishes the man to die, and what are the reasons for the visitation. When it is desired that no more questions be asked of this spirit another whistle is heard, the signal that a new *kipua* is in possession of the *koulaiku*. These *kipua* are always dead relatives of the sick man. They do not speak in the natural voice of either the *koulaiku* or of any other living person, but in a shrill squeak.

"After all the *kipua* concerned have used him as a medium there is a much longer whistle than any of the others and the man returns to consciousness. He drinks copious draughts of water, but is otherwise unaffected by association with the forces which have been manifest in him. He is quite unaware of what has been going on, and has to ask in order to learn what words have passed his lips.

"There are usually some half-dozen *kipua* concerned; those of the mother and father, mother's brother, father's brother and any other dead relatives who have stood in an important relation to the man, his headman perhaps, or his grandfather, or brother. Sometimes half of them say they want the man to die, and the other half say they want him to live. The *kipua* of the mother and the mother's brother are nearly always favourable to the patient, while the members of the man's own joint family, his father and father's brother, usually wish him to die."

Hogbin gives an account of how one famous medium, Pipia'a, came to her powers (typically in an altered state of consciousness while ill):

"While she was a young girl she fell down in the street, and when picked up she was foaming at the mouth and all her limbs were twitching. She was carried home, and it would seem that for two days she was delirious. This was regarded as nothing more than a severe illness by both herself and other people. Then almost the same thing happened again — a fit and delirium. When she regained consciousness she announced that she had been possessed by the spirits of the dead, and that henceforth she was a *koulaiku*."

Hogbin was convinced that the two mediums he knew best, Pipia'a and Ke Ahua, were genuine and that from time to time they were mediums of the spirits: "I am also prepared to believe that they do not know what they are saying while they are possessed," the anthropologist wrote.

Having identified the *kipua* influencing the sick man the medium performed on him a complex public ritual to exorcise the ancestor spirits which have designs on his life. Called the *sau* or "spirit sweeping" ceremony, it meant that the sick man publicly demonstrated his acquiescence to the ancestor code in return for his health.

Consistent with the theory of a direct physiological response of the patient's body to the medium's message, I found it interesting that certain non-pathological complaints (excessive menstrual flow, dropsy, etc.) where such a response could not be expected, were specifically excluded from the medium's realm. These were ascribed to certain gods. Besides their recent ancestors, Luaniuans revered as gods and remembered in myths those ancestors who founded the atoll settlement. Sufferers from a certain misfortune consulted the headman of the joint family, tracing its descent from the god-ancestor held responsible. This headman performed on them a *sau* ritual to make the god undo the wrong he had done. Also ascribed to the gods were pestilences and epidemics, over which, no doubt, the medium would have had little influence.

A reading of Eric Schwimmer's 1966 book *The World of the Maori* shows the certain aspects of Luaniuan village life were shared with the culture of the Polynesians who settled New Zealand. Maori priests served the ancestor spirits (*atua*) as mediums and were called *whaka atua* — god canoes. When possessed "their eyes became suffused and staring, the face flushed, body and limbs twitched convulsively under the spirit's control. When the possessed medium spoke it was in a squeaky, high-pitched voice regarded as the voice of the *atua*." (cf. Kulani, shaman at Laulasi.) In this role the Maori priest or *tohunga* cured traditional diseases until the Tohunga Suppression Act of 1906 led to their decline.

In today's world, medicine is increasingly in the hands of a highly educated, overworked minority. Weighing this all up I feel there is good reason to believe that psychic medicine such as the Luaniuan mediums dispensed was often most appropriate, considering the social origins of much illness. Like acupuncture it is equally deserving of scientific investigation alongside current research into the pharmacological treatment of disease.

## THE ATOLL KIDS

One evening when Jan lands on the beach she is met by a bunch of kids.

She writes in her diary:

"I asked one of them where Wade was, and a little girl took my hand and led me to where Wade was sitting outside a hut on mats in the moonlight. He was talking to Patteson and his wife Merrilee, a Luaniuan couple about the same ages as ourselves. They have three children, Irene (9), young Patteson (11), and Lynda (3). Patteson is a teacher and has been to America and England. He wants his people to be taught a lot of the forgotten arts and customs in the schools.

"Merrilee brought us coffee. She sat down beside me and made me a turmeric lei, rubbing the perfume into it with coconut oil.

"It was pleasant and peaceful in the soft moonlight with a gentle hum of people's voices talking quietly. You could hear the crash of the waves on the reef so close by. On our way back to the beach we padded barefoot through the village without a sound, past people fast asleep on mats at the doors of their huts, the trees making soft shadows everywhere. Kids were still playing on the beach. There is no special time for them to go to bed. They just go to sleep when they want to. If they play late at night they sleep during the day, under trees, on the beach. One day we nearly walked on a couple of sand babies, both lying curled up together sound asleep covered in sand.

"Each day we go ashore and spend a lot of time wandering round the village watching what is going on, swimming with the children or sitting in the shade. As we sit around, the girls put flowers in our hair and clean our nails with little fine sticks. They even looked for lice in our hair, much to our amusement. Most of the children have their hair cut short and occasionally you see one or two delousing each other, but the medical officer said there isn't much problem with lice.

"While the others are filming I often find myself watching the village children from a distance. They are very happy and well behaved. Parents and older children soon put things right with a cuff or a poke if they misbehave. I never see any ganging up and meanness to any one child. When the children are all crowding round us I notice a pattern of behaviour that seems to take place only because we are here: we are something new. They all seem to want to be the one that is the closest or the one that can touch or hold your hand. We find then that they may become more aggressive: some girls are very possessive and want you all for themselves. If a child touches you or brushes you they will hit them hard or give them a push. Any boys trying to join the group get yelled at and chased along the beach. I feel that we are responsible because when we aren't with them none of this goes on. But I never saw this with the Melanesian children of Motalava, Simbo or Laulasi.

"I notice that the older children are very concerned if a younger one gets hurt and will run to his aid. Girls are often seen carrying a baby sister or brother around on their backs in a piece of calico, or perched on their hips. They play in the water most of the day when they are not doing odd jobs for their parents or sit under the trees playing skittles with a row of pandanus nuts stuck in the ground.

They use the centre of a perfectly round nut for the balls. This is the *Barringtonia* nut that drifts here from forested islands far away.

"At an early age they play ukeleles and sit harmonising together beautifully. They weave square *balls* out of coconut palm leaves. They make windmills that really work.

"The children seem to play mostly with those in the huts closest to their own and don't go too far away unless their parents are with them. As you move to a different area of the village you are joined by a fresh group of children who all tag along.

"While we are swimming the women are standing in the water, cleaning their pots and pans. First they sit on the water's edge using sand to get the black off; then they go out deeper and stand rinsing pots, washing themselves and combing their hair. Two women are standing up to their waists scaling and cleaning fish. I think what a pleasant way to do your housework.

"Women swim at all times, Frank tells us, even in the middle of the night. The men feel the cold and usually swim only when the sun is up. Frank says some girls are very good at swimming long distances under water but they can't dive down as deep as the men.

"When we have spent some time around the village, Wade and I go to see Frank again. Having read Ian Hogbin's 1930 account of village life we question Frank at length and later check with two other informants about the rearing of children nowadays.

"During the first three years the babies are looked after solely by their mothers and are breast fed all this time. If another baby is due then the first one must be weaned by adding more solids to its diet. Until the baby is six or seven months old the father is rarely permitted to hold it. Nowadays, if it is the first born, the father is secluded from both mother and baby for six months. The period used to be a year. With subsequent births this seclusion is only for two months. Frank tells us that every now and then the baby is brought by a close relative for the father to see and hold. The reason for this seclusion is said to be that it permits the mother to give undivided attention to her child. After that, fathers love to carry their children about; we saw this often in the village.

"Ideally the education of a boy is shared by his father and two uncles, one of the uncles being his father's brother and the other being his mother's brother. They take him and teach him the things they are most skilled in. When the boy grows up and gets married he moves in with his wife's family. While still young, therefore, he spends more and more time with his father's brother. He may even stay with him for long periods if his mother wishes. He is taught by these three people how to make nets, canoes and huts, fishing skills and the many other tasks that a man is expected to know. In this way he gets a much better education than if he were taught only by his father. Boys don't get married until they are around 21.

"Girls are brought up by their mothers. As there are usually two or three other women in the same hut as well as elder daughters they have many people to learn from. They are taught simple house cleaning duties; then, as they get older, they learn mat and basket weaving, cooking, tending taro gardens, husking, grating, and extracting milk and cream from coconuts.

"When a girl is 12 years old, tattooing begins. This goes on until she is married. By the time she is halfway through her first pregnancy the tattooing is completed. Nowadays they only tattoo from the knee to waist and even then some are not bothering because the church has told them to stop. Especially when large areas are done the girls can become sick, with painful festering sores. Tattooing is done with the juice from a berry which has been dried into a powder and mixed with coconut oil, or else with lampblack. The pigment is smeared on the skin and the design is made by jabbing a fishbone up and down on the skin. If the girl's father or grandfather has some particular skill such as catching turtles, this appears in the design. One girl had a row of tiny turtles leading up the leg and then back down to the knee. Some of the tattoos on the older women are very fine and intricate, all over their bodies and on their faces. I have copied a number of them in my drawing book. Men are also tattooed with spear and fish designs, but this is rare now.

"Girls get married at about 18. They still have arranged marriages but if a girl or boy doesn't want to go through with the marriage it can be put off. A boy and a girl may be betrothed as early as 13 or 14; from that time until the wedding, the families exchange gifts even though the boy and girl have hardly anything to do with each other. From the boy's side there are gifts of fish and from the girl's side taro puddings. Fish, because it is plentiful, is not considered as valuable as taro. So the boy will give many presents of fish during a week, with the girl giving perhaps two puddings. The puddings used to be four feet in length and six inches deep. They do not make them that size now.

"The girl looks for a man who is good looking, fit and strong. He must be very skillful at catching fish, not lazy and a good provider. Likewise a pretty girl will be sought after if she can be a good homemaker and is well trained.

"When the girl is married she is presented with a beautiful marriage belt by her mother-in-law, to be worn on special occasions. Frank showed us his wife's belt. It was made with very special glass beads woven into a wide pandanus belt. The beads were brought to Ontong Java by German traders in the 1880s and have been handed down through the family. He also shows us an old, very valuable square German gin bottle in which they keep oil. Wade takes photos of the beautiful Papesi with the belt and the bottle.

Frank points discreetly to a girl wearing a string of buttons barely visible under the white calico running round her hips. These buttons were also brought out by German traders and have been handed down ever since. They don't use just any buttons. These German buttons are regarded as valuable. The button belts are worn by virgins and are taken off when they marry. Morally they aren't so strict nowadays, just as in our society. If a girl is known to have 'played around' she still has a chance of getting married. In the old days if they were caught they were very hastily married off to save the girl's face, or they became prostitutes.

"In the old days the boy was allowed to visit his wife only at night until they had a baby. They weren't considered properly married until they had their first child. Now the husband lives with his wife as soon as they marry but the husband, if he wants to, may go to the *kalaniu* (a play area for single boys and girls) and his wife is not to complain or show any jealousy. There he may flirt and carry on with other girls. It is considered bad taste if a woman shows any jealousy. He can go there any time during married life, but married women are not allowed. It is very difficult for a man to get away with anything, though, because his sisters and cousins keep an eagle eye on him.

"When a woman becomes pregnant for the first time she is then considered her most beautiful and she is pampered and admired more than at any other time in her life. She doesn't have to do any work for the whole nine months and is waited on by the other women in the hut. After the baby is born she is to do nothing else but look after the baby."

[Wade: Note: The Luaniuans used to have an odd explanation for the cause of conception. They held that a woman could not conceive unless she wished; that casual sex did not produce babies. It took repeated sex by a husband to store up menstrual blood to make a child. Perhaps they got it wrong for the right reason. They had a low birth rate at first contact: 3.5 per family. I have reason to suspect that for atoll people conception was once a conscious decision; so may it be with dolphins and wolves. For apex animals, predators at the top of the food pyramid, over-population is not the way to go.]

## A VILLAGE OBSERVED

Brady: "This morning the lagoon was as flat as a millpond. From the bow of *El Torito* I could see everything underwater. I even saw a blacktip shark cruising around. Everybody else went ashore while Cliff, Rebbekah and I had a dive. Cliff caught a fish for Stabler, our pet booby bird. In the afternoon I went ashore in the rubber boat. When I got into the village there were yellow women with orange faces beating steel drums and an aeroplane wing with air-cracking rhythms."

Jan's diary at this time contains many glimpses of life on the atoll, and the children wrote interesting impressions from their own special viewpoints. For a while, then, Jan resumes the story with occasional interpolations from Brady and Karla.

Jan: "One day when we go ashore we hear a loud rhythmic sound. A couple are getting married. All the women are sitting round in a semicircle beating on drums and tins. They have on their custom dress. For any special function the women wear a mustard coloured calico pareo, hand dyed with turmeric powder, and their special bead belts. They cover their bodies with yellow powder ground from turmeric root. There is another kind of turmeric from which they get a bright orange powder. The orange powder being less plentiful is more valuable. This is put on round their necks and up the sides of their faces, forming a peak in the middle of the forehead with an orange line down the nose. The rest of the face has the yellow turmeric on it. They look very striking with their tattoos and yellow faces framed in orange. Round their necks they wear turmeric leis made by rubbing the long green leaves into ropes and tying them at the ends. Then they daub some turmeric powder in the palms of their hands together with coconut oil and rub this into the leis, creating a very delicate perfume. On their heads they wear garlands of the *palmou* tree. They boil the slender branches with leaves on before drying them on the hot white sand. The leaves and branches bleach and are joined together to form a halo. They also wear strings of brightly coloured beads. Women who have lost their husbands do not wear any form of decoration.

"The men are dancing and as they advance towards the women who are beating on the drums the women build up a frenzied tempo until the men are leaping about keeping time right in front of them.

"This continues all afternoon until a bell rings. The wedding is part religious and part custom. While the couple are getting married in the church the dancing and drumming has to stop. As soon as the ceremony is over all the relatives start laying out food on the mats: taro puddings from the bride's family and fish from the groom's side.

"Cabin biscuits, tea and sugar are supplied by both sides. The bride and bridesmaids wear white dresses and veils and the groom and his brothers wear suits. During the feast girls are walking round dousing everyone with powder and perfume.

"As soon as all have finished eating, everything is cleared quickly away and the ground swept, leaving no trace of rubbish so that they can get back to the dancing. We are amused to see how quickly the bride and groom shed their wedding clothes which are then strung out on a clothes-line to air. Later in the evening, we are told, the women will be playing ukeleles and dancing so we all go back to the boat to have dinner. When we return about nine o'clock everything is quiet. There are only a handful of women playing. When they see us arrive they strike up a beat and we say: 'Come on, let's dance.' This really gets things going. People start coming from all directions crowding round to watch. One or two women join in and Edwin begins to dance with Wade, matching every antic that Wade makes. Everyone is cheering and laughing. Within ten minutes everyone is back in full swing again. Walt is pleased as he wants to film it all and has gone to a lot of trouble bringing the generator and movie rig ashore. What excitement when the generator and bright lights go on! Most people have never seen lights like this in their life.

"Walt films Janice and me dancing with two of the men and Wade with Papesi. Even Karla gets up and dances. She looks lovely too and Walt films her as well.

"Then it is the women's turn to do their custom dances. Sitting on hand-carved stools among the ladies, we are presented with turmeric leis and head garlands and doused with powder and scent. One woman rubs some orange powder on my nose and cheeks. Because we are sitting so close and rubbing up against the person next to us we are soon covered in yellow turmeric powder too. In the middle of all those scented, hot bodies you really start to feel part of it with the music and singing and the dust rising from the dancers' feet. You have the feeling you want to go on and on. The women are all raving over Wade's dancing, running off and telling people to come and watch the man with the beard and all the hair. I join in the dance for married women only. It is quite easy to follow on behind and pick up the steps. Karla and I are presented with sticks of tobacco.

"It starts to rain and everyone runs for shelter. We sit in the little huts until the shower passes over. Everyone goes back to the boat except Wade and Karla and me.

"When we leave at midnight the party is still going strong. We have a shower to get all the turmeric off our bodies and hair. Even so in the morning our sheets are stained yellow and for days our skins seems to be oozing yellow onto everything we wear."

Karla: "Last night we went ashore for the dancing. All through the afternoon and into the evening the women beat tin drums while others danced. We danced to the music of some ukeleles and guitars for quite a long time. Dad did some really neat dancing with everybody. I danced with all the little girls till I was wet with sweat. After that we went and sat in Patteson's hut for a while. Next morning I woke up to find that my pillow and sheets were covered in yellow turmeric powder. My hands were yellow, my hair was yellow and my knees were yellow."

Jan: "The people living on this atoll are healthy and strong. There are no plump or skinny children. We don't know why this is but if we can find out it will be a great lesson for us. Their basic diet is coconuts, taro and fish. They swim in the sea every day. The men are always doing jobs that need strong muscles and so are the women. When there aren't enough boys in the family to catch the fish the girls are taught and they are just as good as the men."

Karla: "Yesterday we watched some men fishing on the reef. They were forming a big circle around their net and they would slowly close into a tight circle. They did that until they had enough fish. Then they put on the sails on their outriggers and sped back to their island. They went faster than *El Torito*."

Jan: "One day Karla and I are watching a group of women playing cards. One of them gets up and goes into her hut. She comes out with a coconut in each hand and says in a loud, clear voice: 'Here you are my friends, a present for you.'

"I am very grateful because we are thirsty and surprised too. I am not expecting anyone to speak English so clearly. We find that a lot of men spoke English but few women. Quite a few children and teenagers have learnt English at the little school.

“While we are ashore we come to realize just how important the coconut palm is to these people. It must be one of the most versatile plants in the world. We notice two girls pulling a long raft of coconuts down the shore in waist-deep water. We find out that they go along the coast to the coconut plantation and bring all the coconuts out of the bush to the water's edge. Then they tear a strip of husk down one side of each coconut and tie it to the next until all the nuts are joined together in a long line. As they float, all they have to do is walk along in the water pulling the line of nuts after them. In this way they can bring a huge number of coconuts down to the village. When they get to the village everyone helps carry the nuts to stack them outside their huts. Then the husking begins. They have a stake with a sharp pointed end at waist level. By driving the coconut down onto this stake they tear the husk off.

“Husks are very important to the people for firewood. They always have a stack of dried husks in their huts ready for lighting fires. Coconut rope is made from the husks also. The husks have to be soaked in seawater for a month until everything has been washed away leaving only fibres which are beaten to remove any remaining unwanted parts, rinsed again and left to dry in the sun. The fibre is then ready for plaiting into ropes.

“The coconuts are cut in half by women sitting in a group. The drier coconuts are piled together and spread by one of the men on wire netting racks if they are lucky enough to have wire netting. Otherwise they are put on large tables made of wooden slats to dry in the sun for copra. Copra is very valuable to these people. They get 12 cents a pound at the present time. This means the island would be earning $10,000 a month. As the nuts are cracked open some of the water from the nuts is collected in a large pot and the children hung round to eat the kernels or 'lolly' in the centre of some of the nuts as their mothers handed them out.

"The moister nuts are placed in baskets for extracting coconut milk. One woman sits astride a special grating stool which has a piece of wood that comes up between the legs with a grater on the end. She then grates all the flesh out of the coconut which falls into a bowl. The fibre they use for extracting the milk from the grated coconut is made by soaking the bark of a hibiscus tree in water, until all the resin washes out, leaving the fine flat fibres. They used to weave cloth and sails out of this special bark fibre in the old days but now they can buy calico and canvas. The grated coconut is gathered up in large handfuls and placed in this fibre which is then wrung and twisted until the milk runs out.

"Beside the women grating coconut sits a mother with her two-month-old baby. She is spoon-feeding her baby with pap made from the coconut water and the flesh of a green coconut which is very soft, all mixed together into a pulp.

"To extract the cream from the milk it is heated over the fire. A special black stone is heated until it is red hot and then dropped into the milk. This makes the coconut cream separate and float to the top. The milk and cream are used for making their taro puddings and for cooking fish.

"Coconut oil is used for combing into their hair and rubbing on their skin when it gets dry, scented with turmeric and other perfumes. They also use oil for lamps but find it cheaper to buy kerosene from the trading boats and save the coconuts for copra.

"As well as pandanus, the coconut fronds are used for mat-making. The coconut rope is very useful for binding and securing, especially in canoe and hut-making. Once the dried coconut is taken out of the shells and stored in huge baskets to await the copra boat, the shells are kept for firewood. Nothing is wasted. Besides the alcoholic beverage the men make from the nectar, the women reduce it to a syrup for use in cooking.

"There are also some medicinal uses. The husk is taken from a green coconut and the juice is squeezed out. Warmed over the fire, this is poured straight on to the cut and it stops bleeding. The wound is then bound with a wrapping of this same green coconut husk.

"It is a pleasure to watch a Luaniuan family working together. The warmth and companionship with everyone talking and laughing while they work makes it all seem more like play. Husband, wife and children go off together in their canoes collecting huge bundles of dry pandanus palms for roofing. They seem to work together much of the time except when the men go fishing and the women go to the gardens.

"Girls dive for clams, and outside on mats in the sun we saw hundreds of clams drying on long skewers looking like *shishke-babs*. They had been boiled first and put out to dry and will keep for two to three months. They were to be sent down to relatives in Honiara on the trading boat."

## THE TARO GARDENS

Brady: "Today mum and dad took us to the taro gardens. We had to wear jeans because of the damned mosquitoes and I just about died of the heat. It felt like having a 40-pound scuba tank strapped to your legs for half an hour. The taro gardens are divided into small blocks of land. Each one is lined with stones. All around the edge, next to the stones, *kakaki* is grown, another sort of taro with bigger leaves. In the middle grows the plain taro. That day we had lunch in the village, which was really great. We had green coconut — the inside was like ice cream, very refreshing after our long walk."

Jan writes:

"The women work in the taro gardens twice a week — on Tuesdays and Fridays. Wade and I go on Friday and enjoy it so much that we take the kids and Rebbekah back the next Tuesday. We walk along the curving lagoon beach for about a mile. On the way we pass groups of women coming back with huge bundles of taro leaves and turmeric on their backs.

"The track winds through the bush and all along the way we pass family taro patches. There are tall, brilliant green leafy plants on the higher, less swampy areas called *kakaki* (*Colocasia*); a coarse species of taro. The smaller taro (*Cyrtosperma*) grows in wet swampy areas like rice paddies and the women stand up to their knees in mud, bending over with their breasts tracing tracks on the surface as they plant out the tubers. Between the swamp plots, paths have been built up so you can walk without sinking in the mud. On the dry areas many plots are set aside for growing turmeric. All the plots are edged with coral stones. I think this must be done to keep out the grass.

"There is a spreading weed growing everywhere along the paths but inside the plots everything is free of weeds. They practise shifting cultivation in the family plots. Every six months the plants are lifted and at the same time tubers are replanted. Men assist with leaf mulching, strewing tree leaves around. Otherwise men avoid the taro gardens unless a wife has nobody to help her.

"Groups of women sit here and there resting under the shady trees chatting and laughing before they go back to the village with their heavy loads. Some are switching their backs with a sprig of the *lala* tree. Sweet scented like sage, it is also used for headaches; the juice squeezed from the leaves is swallowed or inhaled.

"As we approach one such group they gather up some turmeric leaves and make a discreet gesture that they want to make a

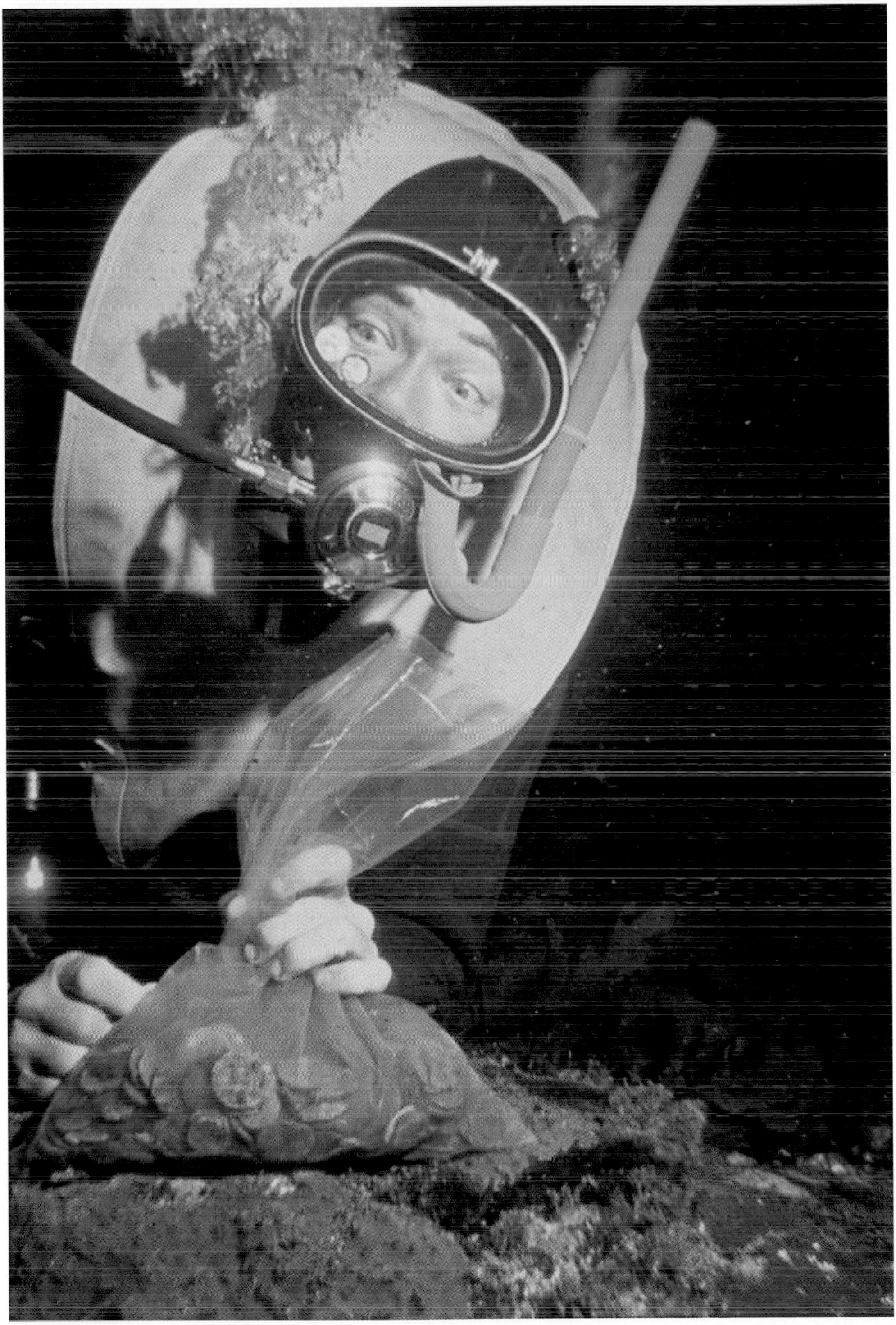

Wade with treasure; gold in mask for safe-keeping.

Gold half soveigns minted in Sydney same year *Elingamite* sank: 1902.

Treasure hunters; Wade in middle.

Just as his ancestors for centuries have fished the reef edge in front of Laulasi island, a village boy and his bow.

Stanley, the court jester of the villlage, grinds his share of shell money.

Georgi, the social chief of Laulasi, wearing ceremonial shell money bands.

Old Amoko leads the village men in singing ancient ballads which tell of the history and customs of the shark worshippers.

Paketi with his accurate model of ElTorito, is filmed by an admiring Walt.

Canoe landings where cargoes are exchanged. Firewood is being stockpiled for the Maoma feast.

Laulasi kids dance on the village square as the sun sets. On nights of the full moon young people play moongames here until sunrise.

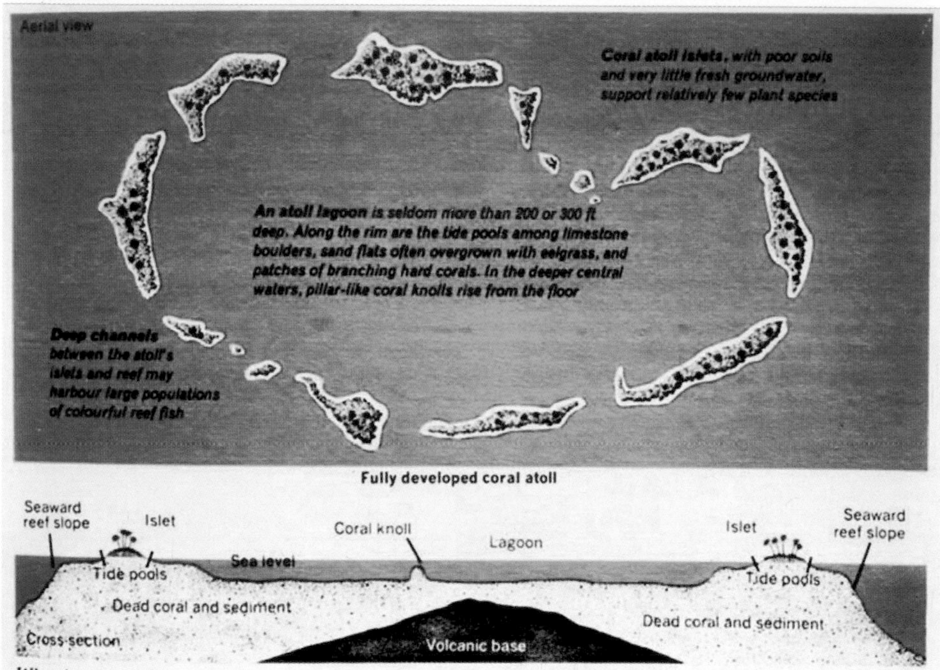


*When the volcanic island drops below the surface, the reef – now an atoll – continues to grow. Waves and wind bring debris to fill the lagoon and erode the coral. It stops growing only if the sea floor drops too quickly to keep the coral in shallow water*

An atoll is a circle of coral cays resting on the rim of a submerged volcano.

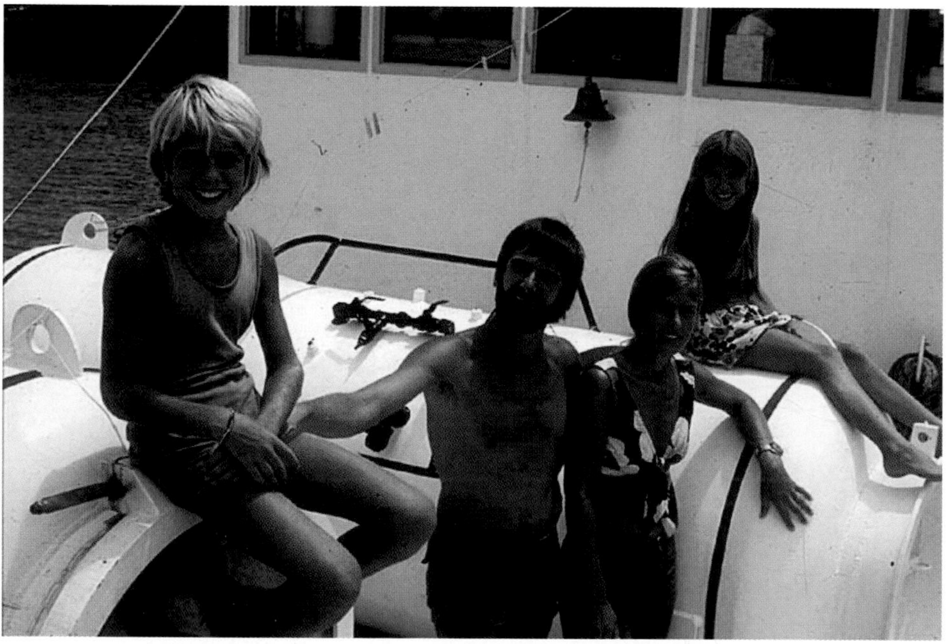

Doak family: L-R: Brady, Wade, Jan, Karla. on *El Torito* foredeck.

The diet of atoll dwellers is adequate although extremely limited in variety. The girl on my daughter's left is her own age — nine years.

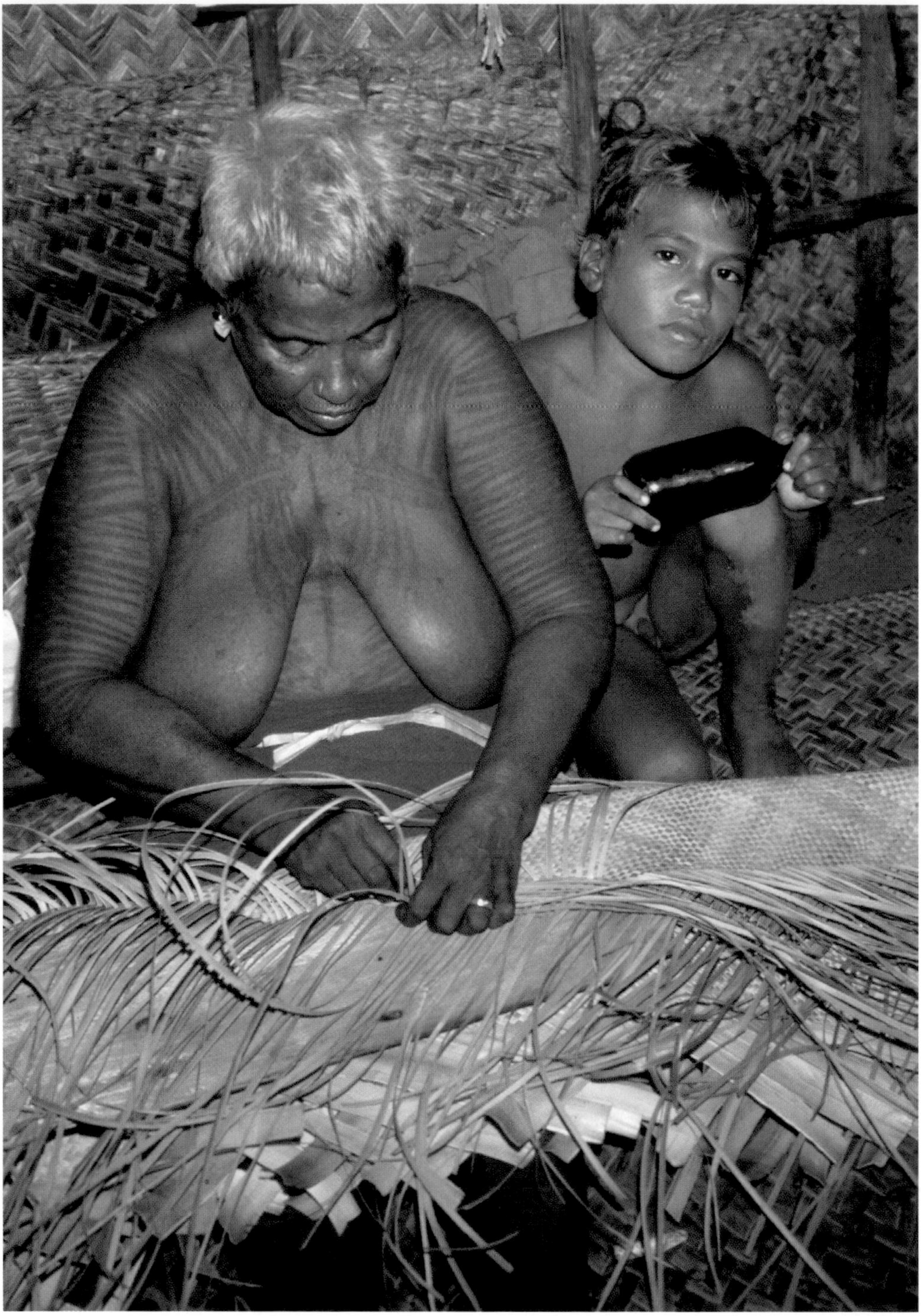

Florence is weaving a pandanus mat for a wedding gift. Having seen our films of women in other villages working, she had come and invited us to film her.

Ukelele girl, with your sisters and cousins, what fun to sing and strum, enjoying being together.

On two days each week the women go to work in the taro gardens harvesting and replanting in their family's taro patch.

To transport coconuts to the village children haul them along the lagoon shores in long chains. The coconut is the basic element in atoll survival. Growing in the near hostile environment of an atoll sand cay it provides for a greater range of human needs than any other plant: food and drink, shelter and clothing; implements and fishing gear, medicine and cosmetics. In a traditional Polynesian culture the coconut is like cattle to the Masai, the seal to the Eskimo or dice in Las Vegas.

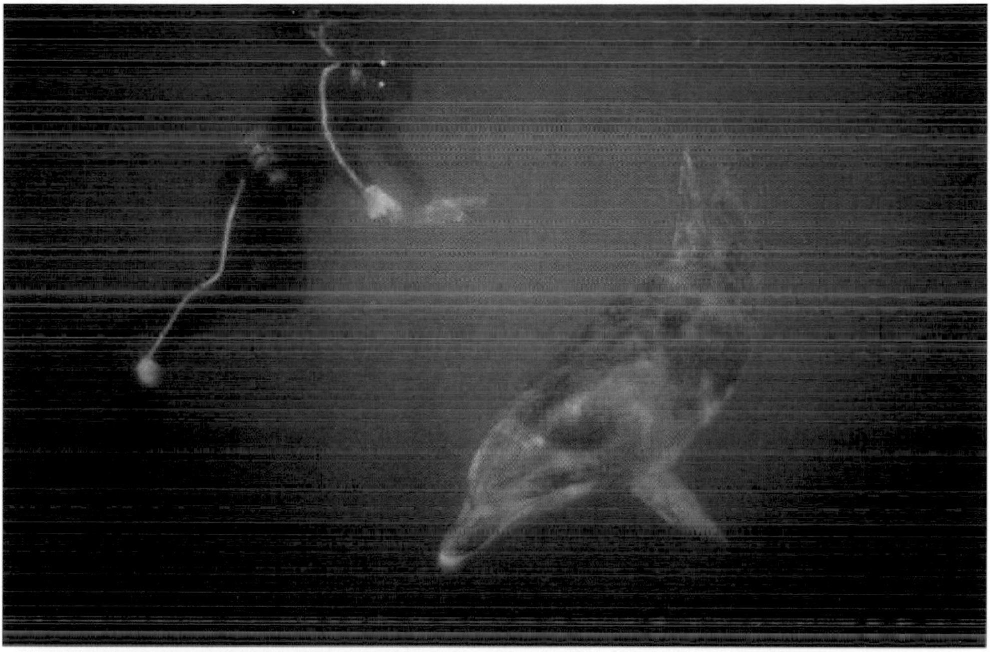

In the open sea near Napier, Horace played a game with seaweed and body language while Quentin Bennett took a sequence of underwater pictures. *Credits: Quentin Bennett*

Poor Knights Islands, 22k off Tutukaka Coast, Northland N.Z. / Wrasses and a goatfish

Rainforest scenes Northland, N.Z.

Polynesian catamaran *R.V. Interlock* in Rikoriko, world's biggest sea cave, Poor Knights Islands, N.Z.

Auckland green gecko, *Nautinus elegans*, on my neck.
*Credit: Sally Tagg.*

turmeric garland for us each. While we wait they rub the turmeric leaves on their legs and twist them into a cord. They have picked some fresh pandanus nuts and we are given some to eat. We are surprised that they taste so very nice — just like fresh sweet corn or green peas. They keep the gardens very tidy, not leaving any chewed nuts around. They carry them in a basket back out to the beach. We find out later that the rats love pandanus nuts and that is why the women don't leave nuts in the gardens. If rats are encouraged they will eat the taro too.

"Beside them, the women burn coconut husks to drive the mosquitoes away. They carry the burning husks with them as they walk through the bush as well. Their usual clothing is just a piece of calico around their waists but today, because of mosquitoes, most of them wear a piece around their shoulders too, or else an old shirt.

"It is beautiful here, so different from what I expected. I thought the taro gardens would be just a wide open patch of taro plants row after row. But instead they cover an area of about five acres winding in and out of lush bush. Seabirds are flying overhead. Lizards scuttle in the dead leaves and undergrowth. In the bush I recognise the huge pandanus trees and the hibiscus tree from which they make fibre for squeezing out milk from the grated coconut.

"The little kids run along the tracks playing. We meet three small boys with not a stitch on, slapping at mosquitoes. One has a beautiful white tropic bird in his arms. He has climbed a coconut palm and caught it while it sat on the nest. He is taking it home for dinner. One of the other boys has its egg in his mouth. He pops it out for us to look at. It is about the size of a ping-pong ball and a browny red mottled colour. The tropic bird has very long red tail feathers which the women use for decoration in their hair.

“On the way back along the beach the women stop to wash the mud off, standing combing their hair in the water then sitting on the beach by their loads making turmeric garlands and gathering frangipani flowers to put in their ears and hair. There certainly is no hustle and bustle. Ever since the night when we joined in their dancing the women have been much more warm and friendly towards us. They go out of their way to come and greet us. Before, they were very shy and would walk the other way or stand back at a distance rather than make contact with us.

“Back at the village the work of preparing the taro puddings begins. Groups sit outside the huts peeling taro. The whole process is done in groups and all the while they joke and laugh, making their work seem such fun.

“There are two methods of making taro puddings. When the taro has been peeled they boil it in a large pot on the fire. The cooked taro is drained and set out on *kakaki* leaves to cool. Then with a pestle, each taro is flattened and dipped in coconut milk or cream. It can be eaten at this stage and is very nice. To make it into puddings that can be eaten cold over a number of days, the cream coated taro is stacked in a pile on *kakaki* leaves, wrapped in a firm bundle and tied. They then scrape a large hole in the hot stones with a coconut shell; the taro puddings are placed on top, completely covered with stones and left to steam for many hours. When cooked it is left to cool, still wrapped in the leaves. Pieces can be sliced or broken off as required.

“The other method is used when they want to make a taro cake. The texture is much finer and it actually looks like a huge cake when it is done. For this they grate the raw taro with a shell or on special graters made from a piece of tin with many nail holes punched through. The grated taro is then mixed with coconut milk or cream and parcelled up in leaves and cooked on the cooking stones.

"I have a chance to sit with the women and watch the whole process. Mary can speak English and she is translating for me all the bawdy jokes that the other women are making. They are very open about sex, the older women especially, and talk and joke freely using plenty of action to describe what they mean. They asked Rebbekah if she is married. Florence, wife of Olau and mother of Mary, says that when you are old enough to have sex (going through all the motions), you are old enough to have a baby, which she described by squatting on the ground and grunting — and then you are old enough to be married. All the other women are screeching and laughing, slapping their thighs while Mary is translating.

"This night Walt shows the people of the village two films up on deck. They all come out in canoes and as many as possible crowd on the broad foredeck. They really enjoy them very much. We always get a great kick out of their reactions while they are watching the films. The next time we get ashore Florence comes and invites us to her hut. Olau is making a net and she is weaving a fine pandanus mat. They invite us to film them. Having seen our Laulasi film aboard *El Torito* they fully understand our interest in village life."

Wade: Clearly these gardens are the result of heavy labour to fashion regular basins in an interior depression that developed during atoll formation. In the cabin Walt and I discussed the atoll energy cycle in relation to the taro gardens. The amount of phosphates and nitrates removed from the gardens for food would be minute. For the most part the plant growth is a hydrocarbon cycle: hydrogen, oxygen and carbon dioxide, plus traces of nitrates and phosphates which would be replaced by the droppings of seabirds that rest in the trees there, and the leaf mulch gathered from the surrounding area. Atoll taro patches do not have the problems of those on the high islands with leaching and erosion. The centre of an atoll island is a nutrient stew. Even the coral substrate would release valuable nutrient salts, and from time to time a storm would inundate land areas with salt water and sea wrack.

## FISHING THE DEEP REEF

Strong winds are whistling across the atoll. It is the cyclone season. Two of the men from *India* clubhouse, Edwin and his brother, with two young boys decide to go out and fish the deep reef slopes on the lee side. Walter Hemoku tells us the men will be using specially rigged lines and traditional techniques belonging to their own family. He arranges for us to film them.

Skimming towards the pass their stone age canoe *Paradeis* overhauls *El Torito*. I have to run to our bow to keep level with it for a photo. Out on the open sea we catch up with them. The wind has dropped suddenly and they lower their sail. The men paddle north along the reef front on the ocean side of Luaniua. Then, stowing their paddles, they prepare their 100-fathom monofilament lines. Each has eight hooks arranged in pairs on wooden spreaders and baited with mullet. A hefty three-pound chunk of coral is the sinker. The last 30 feet of line is hibiscus bark fibre, a family heirloom. Incredibly durable, Edwin tells me later that it had been his father's.

I notice how useful the small boys are: they paddle the canoe nonstop, keeping it on station with light strokes while their uncles begin to fish. Two more adults would have overloaded the canoe. The boys are a valuable part of the economic unit, learning techniques and stamina while very young.

As we film them from *El Torito* black rain squalls sweep over us from the north, skeining out from the atoll and bristling the ocean with spear shafts. In the canoe the four unclad figures hunch their backs and continue to fish. Even on the equator a tropical deluge and driving wind can chill the body. Unused to clothing, their metabolism seems better able to withstand extremes than our own. Janice brews them a big pot of tea and we pull alongside to pass them four hot mugs full.

My diary reads:

"Mid morning. By now these fishermen have endured a dozen squalls. Lightning flashes throw the island palms in silhouette. Frigate birds overhead chase the white terns to steal their prey. Brady, Cliff and Rebbekah have gone off in the skiff to try to catch a silvertip shark — the only species Cliff lacks for his study. The men are catching strange deepwater species: red snapper, jobfish, cheilodactylids. Their fishing method is very productive. Almost nonstop they're hauling and lowering, the boys paddling to keep on station in the offshore wind. Fortunately an outrigger has very low windage or they would have a problem — needing an anchor or a motor. At this spot, only a quarter mile off shore, straight out from their village, the reef drops to 600 feet. The same distance again and it would be 1200 feet. The atoll slopes continue on down to 1000 fathoms. For these men to catch fish so easily only a stone's throw from their village is incredible. Men have lived here for centuries; reef fish populations are very susceptible to fishing pressure; yet right on their doorstep the Luaniuans can fill a canoe in a few hours. There must be some social system to avoid a concentration of canoes on this one method.

"Last night Frank told me he had spent the whole day trolling at sea and he got nothing. As with oil fishing, when somebody in one clubhouse catches a tuna, the men in the other clubs will go off and seek one. Maybe sport has a function in diversifying fishing pressure?

"Walt is getting some superb footage. Fishermen all over the United States will be green with envy at these Polynesians. From our vantage point on *El Torito* we were able to film right over their shoulders, zoom into the canoe and watch them through a screen of rain, tossing on the big swells. Their muscles ripple and ply, deftly hauling their lines, three or four large fish at a time, killing their catches with a swift bite on the back of the head."

By the time the men cease fishing the wind has lulled. Once they have carefully stowed all their gear, Walt invites them aboard for hot coffee while we tow their laden outrigger home through the atoll pass and into the lagoon.

Over hot drinks in the cabin we ask them the questions that have been in our minds all morning.

"But why don't you fish this way every day? Why not yesterday? Will you go back there tomorrow?"

In our time at Luaniua we'd never seen so much fish landed at one place. They just grin and shrug their powerful shoulders.

"We don't do it tomorrow. We got plenty today. Yesterday we fish for tuna. Tomorrow we can rest and drink toddy. Maybe, if the night is calm soon we go out for the oilfish."

From further discussion it becomes clear to us that all fishing trips are just games. You don't persist with anything once it becomes a bore. By treating food gathering as play these Polynesians have hit on a way of exploiting a diverse reef fish population that makes sense ecologically: never hammering any one resource, spreading their efforts wide; targeting individual species with an appropriate fishing method rather than the wastefulness of the non-selective net. Walt and I are staggered at the significance of this. But what if a diesel-powered fish cooler were established on the atoll, as has been suggested, linked to Honiara by a refrigerated vessel? The whole situation would alter: as on any other "developed" atoll, fish stocks would be depleted. A flow of Western goods would ensure a demand for foreign exchange and the long-term survival chances of this outlying Polynesian society would diminish to a level matching our own. The Luaniuans would discover the meaning of work and boredom, receiving money for their fish to buy the leisure they lost. And so it goes.

Back in the club house I question Henry Manuhea as to why so many different fishing methods are chosen when some are better than others. Was there any social organisation to conserve fish stocks? Why didn't everyone fish the deep reef as we had just filmed?

Henry says everyone is free to fish where and when he choses. Many people lack the long lines for *u'u* fishing. It takes much skill and experience. Even the method of baiting the hooks is an art. The pleasure aspect is important in determining choice. Tuna are very popular, preferred over the deep reef fishes as one good fish provides so much food and it is like red meat. The old men say that catching tuna is much harder now, because they are competing with the Japanese.

Henry explains that his people like to change their techniques and bring diversity into their lives. The weather bears an important part in this and all choices are strongly influenced by it: trolling is impossible during calms and onshore winds restrict exposed parts of the reef which, being circular, always offers some shelter.

Luaniuans freely adopt fishing methods from elsewhere. Diving with spears and hand slings is an innovation. Tuna lures are now plastic and rubber, from Honiara. Trolling under sail isn't traditional. They used to paddle along and troll a pearl shell lure. The men are convinced the outboard is no good for trolling — it scares the fish away. You may have a good school around you, an outboard arrives and they flee. It is good for oilfishing, on nights of flat calm, but not essential.

It comes to me later as I watch the outriggers skimming back into the lagoon from the pass, that family planning attempts have to reckon with existing social patterns. A village like this is not a cooperative commune: the extended family is the economic unit and there must be sons and daughters in order to fish and garden. I ask Henry about this problem. He says that about one-fifth of the village families are now involved in some sort of family planning: the pill, the loop and tubal ligation, but there is as yet no thought given to the social aspects of which he himself is aware.

Walt says dryly, "You just make contraception freely available and let selection take its course. The intelligent will use it and the rest perish."

I feel the converse may occur: the less intelligent could outbreed the others and drag the lot under.

## A NIGHT IN A POLYNESIAN VILLAGE

For a picture of an unusual day — and night — I turn again to Jan's diary:

"The afternoon has been wet and windy. A cyclone is in the vicinity but we don't know yet. We have been told there is going to be another wedding and we think that, even though the weather is lousy we had better make the effort to go since we have been to the other one.

"When we get ashore the wedding ceremony and feast are over but the women are all dressed in their custom dress and are beating the drums while the men dance. It is obvious that the men have been drinking a lot of coconut toddy and are really enjoying themselves putting everything they can into the dancing. The gong rings for the church service, which means the dancing has to stop. We wander round the village talking to groups of men here and there.

"We come across some of the men who were on the trip to Roncador with us, sitting in a circle playing ukeleles, singing and drinking toddy. They insist that we join them and even though women don't drink they offer Janice and me some palm toddy. We down a couple and almost straight away start to feel a warm, light feeling rising up from stomach to head.

"The wind is coming up very strong and we are worried about the skiff. We decide that we had better get back out to *El Torito* as it is growing dark. As we are leaving Edwin and Christopher come down to the beach and plead for Wade to stay and dance. We don't want to stay because we will have no way of getting out to the ship. The skiff has to go back now. We don't like to hurt their feelings so Wade and I say we will stay when they promise to take us out by canoe after the party, so Janice, Rebbekah and Karla take the skiff back. As we watch them depart with the wind increasing and rainclouds billowing up we have visions of sleeping under a coconut palm stranded on shore, especially as the men are already very much on the way with toddy.

"All I am wearing is a *pareo* and bikini top and I have silent misgivings. We must be crazy because even though it is very hot, when it is raining and the wind is blowing you get cold and the thought of having to spend a whole night on the island in the wet isn't very inviting.

"We walk back with the men and join in with their group. I get into a conversation with Alfred and Christopher, two of the men that came on the Roncador trip. They were very shy on the trip but with a few toddies they are now more relaxed and are trying out their English on me. Alfred asks me to dance. Patteson is amazed listening to Alfred whom he says has never spoken English before. He thinks he is doing very well.

“Patteson asks us to come to his hut. From a dark corner he fishes out a half gallon of wine. To our delight when we have a sip we find that it is a very good Australian dry red. We laugh. Ontong Java, one of the most remote of atolls, and we are drinking a good quality wine.

“We sit on the woven pandanus mats in the soft light thrown by a hurricane lamp and the flames from coconut shells burning on the fire and listen to Patteson talking quietly with his immaculate BBC English. Patteson’s wife Merrilee moves softly to and fro, setting plates out for the evening meal. Surprisingly there is no smoke from the burning coconut shells and the cooking stones glow hot under the pots, keeping them simmering. She takes a large pot off the fire and dishes up a huge plateful of fish; then takes a taro pudding wrapped in leaves and slices a portion for each.

“Merrilee’s father sits playing with young Patteson, aged eleven. He obviously loves his old grandfather. Little Lynda, aged three, lies in the hollow between her father’s crossed legs peeping out shyly from his arms. Irene, their older daughter, is sleeping with a girlfriend in another hut.

“We are pleasantly surprised when we take our first mouthful of fish. Using our fingers we carefully lift mouthfuls off the bones. The fish has first been boiled in salted water then coconut milk added. The flavour of fish stock and coconut milk together is delicious. I have not enjoyed taro pudding when I have eaten it before but this one, dipped in the liquid that the fish had been cooked in, is very good.

“After we have eaten we all wash hands and faces in a pot of water with a cake of soap; the dishes are stacked in a bucket and put aside until the morning. We sit talking into the night over hot cups of coffee and New Zealand Anchor full cream milk powder that Patteson mixed up for us. Patteson is a very intelligent man who has been to England and America to further his studies. Most of his education was done by correspondence. This year he will be teaching on Santa Isabel, one of the other Solomon Islands. He knows what it's like to live in cities and have all the modern conveniences but prefers the traditional way of life in Luaniua.

"Merrilee is a very sweet and warm person with a lovely Maori face. She can't speak very much English but sits beside us listening and understanding a lot of the conversation, her husband translates from time to time.

"Outside, the music and dancing continue. Every now and then a quick rainstorm passes over sending everyone for shelter. As soon as it stops, out they go again.

"Wade and I go down to the sea to the toilet. No one is allowed to pass urine outside the huts. Even little children at a very early age are trained to go down into the sea where special areas are set aside for men and women. When we come back we join in the dancing for a while.

"Patteson offers to take us back to the ship in a canoe but it meant launching it in the dark and the lagoon was still very rough. We ask him which is easier: for him to take us out in a canoe or for us to just crash in a corner of the hut for the night. He says it would be much easier if we slept the night but he hasn't liked to offer in case we don't want to sleep on the hard ground. We don't mind at all and are thrilled at having the opportunity to feel what it would be like sleeping in a hut on an atoll.

"Patteson's brother and a friend come in with some toddy to share with us. Merrilee lies down beside little Lynda. She is still being breast-fed. Later Merrilee shows me how to make rope out of the dried coconut husk fibres. They have a huge roll of rope in the corner which she keeps adding to whenever she has time to make some more. Merrilee twists husk fibres into strands for plaiting by rubbing them on her leg. She says that when they have a lot to do their legs get very sore and then they get one of the children to lie down and they do it on their bare bottoms until they get uncomfortable. Then they change to the next child. When the strands, which are about eight inches long, are made she starts the plaiting and joining, holding the end between her toes. I try it and manage to make rather a loose piece of rope compared with her very tight and neatly plaited sample.

"Merrilee sets out a mat for us which she takes down from the roof and gives us a pillow and a piece of calico to cover us in the night. Grandfather is already asleep with young Patteson cuddled up to him. There are two other children asleep in the hut too — Patteson's cousins. Little Lynda begins to cry in her sleep. Her father picks her up and cradles her in his arms, talking softly to her until she is quiet again.

"Wade and I lie down for a while but can't sleep. Around midnight we go out and wander round the village. Groups of people sit outside their huts drinking tea and coffee and eating cabin biscuits even at this very late hour. Little children are bending over the pot on the fire dipping out a cup of hot water, the light from the lamps making a halo around their hair. The low lighting effect is beautiful, casting shadows from the sugarcane, bananas and pawpaw trees between the huts. Everyone is laughing and talking; time meaning nothing to them. Single boys and girls are playing at chasing down on the beach in the *kalaniu* or courtship place, laughing and shrieking. We recline in the shadows silently watching and enjoying this very happy and tranquil scene.

"Back in the hut lying on the mats, I don't expect to sleep, not having camped on the ground for a long time. But I must be tired or perhaps it is that very warm feeling inside from the companionship of sleeping close to so many people in one hut and listening to the sound of the sea on the reef and the wind in the palms. I sleep well until I am awakened at four o'clock in the morning by the roosters crowing all round the village.

"I lie looking up at the roof and a rat runs along the rafters. The rats on these islands are quite pretty compared with house rats. I have one or two bites from mosquitoes at night but no worse than if I were at home.

"Merrilee gets up and starts to gather up the dishes from the evening's meal. I leap up too and we take the pots and pans down to the beach and rinse them. Then we sit on the beach and scrub the pots using handfuls of sand. When all the grime is scrubbed off we wade out to our necks rinsing the dishes and having our morning wash at the same time. The women always wear a *pareo* round their waists even while swimming and I am very thankful that I am wearing one too and cause no offence.

"We return to the hut and collect a huge container which we carry to the well between us to get water. As they sweep the village with coconut whisks the women are calling out to us, joking and asking Merrilee how I come to be with her so early in the morning helping with the chores. We wash the plates and cups with fresh water and soap and set them out to dry.

"Next we carry all the rubbish through the village to the seaward side of the island and dump it over the reef so that it will go out to sea into deep water. No rubbish is allowed to be thrown into the lagoon where it will wash up on the beach. This is also the women's toilet area and we all wade out to relieve ourselves. The women meet here and gossip every morning. I am really enjoying getting the feeling of what it is like to be a Luaniuan woman.

"When we get back the men are up so we fold the mats and roll the pillows and covers up in them and tie them in neat bundles hanging from the roof. With little reed brooms we sweep the hut and outside the door. Merrilee lights the fire and sets the pot of hot water on to heat. The men come back and we sit round on mats drinking coffee and eating biscuits, cold rice, taro cake and cold fish. A huge spider runs along the floor and over Merrilee's foot. She just glances at it and never bats an eyelid. It is just part of the scene along with the woodlice and occasional cockroach. The huts are kept very clean and not a speck of food is ever left around to invite ants and flies. Young Patteson sits making the sail for a perfect replica of an outrigger canoe which later I see him spending hours sailing in the lagoon.

"Merrilee takes me to the village store to get some sugar. I am surprised to find that the village has a cooperative store. The profits go to the village, not just to one person. A trading ship comes once every month to collect the copra and drop off supplies. The people get 12 cents a pound for their copra so can afford to buy things like lamps, towels, calico, coffee, tea, sugar and milk, not forgetting stick tobacco which most of them seem to smoke fairly heavily. The trading boat is due in a few days' time so Patteson is taking his family to their island (which belongs to Merrilee) to get their copra ready for loading. The shop is inside a corrugated shed and you wouldn't know it was there unless you were taken inside.

"Little Lynda has lost her shyness now that we have slept the night in her hut and is delightful, her little eyes shining as she chatters away.

"Patteson then takes us out to the *El Torito* in an outrigger. It glides effortlessly through the water. As we leave, I slip a little ring of mine on Merrilee's finger. We are so very grateful to have been able to stay the night and sample their way of life."

Wade: My own recollections are different, as this extract from my diary shows:

"Today I awake in the village beside Jan to the crowing of many roosters; a grey light at 4:30 a.m. and my head pounding like the rollers on the reef. Merrilee's father gets up and steps out between the two door flaps. The wind is gusting hard, but our hut, five rows from the lagoon beach, is well sheltered. My bladder is bursting and so is my head from all the toddy I drank with Patteson and his brother.

"I grope my way out of the hut, skirting the fire pit and its glowing embers and step out into the dark village. In the shadows the old man is sitting on a stool, a long cigarette glowing. I nod and make for the beach. At the end of the island, where the men go to void themselves I leave my clothes in the bushes and wade out to waist depth. A rain squall whips across the lagoon. I duck ashore to protect my clothes only to run into a startled but instantly friendly old man who is just leaving. My clothes, I find, have been carefully placed in the dry niche of a tree.

"During the night Patteson with his cultured British accent has told us quite a number of things about the village and himself. His has been an arranged marriage — all set up for him when he returned from Honiara training college. He had other ideas. He had already heard of boys who had been absent from the village for some time and returned to accept such marriages. Because they were out of touch with the young people of Luaniua, such marriages had often failed. He had insisted on a two-year moratorium. But then, within six months he'd found that Merilee was a very suitable wife and they were wed.

"As we yarn, his brother and a friend come in with a jar of one-day-old toddy — an ambrosial brew. At this early stage of fermentation I can still savour the bouquet of coconut flowers and appreciate that we are drinking pure, unadulterated nectar. Cloud cuckoo land: it has a sting despite its youth. Each round, you have to down a four-ounce slug and pass on the cup.

"In the cabin Walt and I discussed toddy production. He calculated that if beer and toddy are taken to be equal in strength it would take about 400 acres of coconuts to produce the money to buy beer equivalent to the annual toddy production of the 50 trees being tapped in the village.

"All the spikes of the coconut flower are folded towards the end and bound so that the nectar flows down the tips and is funnelled into a half coconut shell with a hole in it, fixed securely to the collecting bottle. Ezekiel told me that a flower can fill a quart bottle in a day and some trees may have up to five flowers, so there are half-gallon trees and gallon trees. Flowing untended this ambrosial fluid ferments naturally, without any additives. Within 24 hours it becomes a light white wine with a delicate bouquet and a hefty alcohol content. After six days it is dynamite and that's when the fishermen drink it.

"We were told that toddy was introduced from Sikaiana in 1950 and there, from the Gilberts. It is not made elsewhere in the Solomons.

"We had heard stories in Honiara that the Luaniuans were squandering their copra production making toddy. Puritanical nonsense, we decided, and it avoids the metholated spirits drinking problems we found elsewhere.

"Producer trees can still provide nuts: if the flowers are released at the right time nuts develop. The nectar serves to attract insects and then just falls to the ground. The toddy collector is like an outsized bee.

"Walt calculated that from ten acres of coconuts he could probably produce enough pure alcohol to fuel *El Torito*.

"'Wade, you know what we ought to do,' said Walt with that gleam in his eye. 'It would be easy to rig up plastic tubes and vats for a continuous fermentation plant.'

"The land of the gallon trees!"

## FILMING THE *OLIOLI*

Walt and I gasp and stop filming. Four bright yellow girls with bare breasts shyly join the circle of Polynesian women drumming a fast rhythm and chanting while the village men stomp and gyrate. Jan and Karla, Janice and Rebbekah — all the women from *El Torito* are wearing the traditional garb of Luaniuan women: their bodies completely coated in chrome yellow turmeric powder and glistening with coconut oil. Like their Polynesian sisters they are all stripped to the waist, wearing only a pareo of saffron-dyed calico and a belt of multi-coloured beads, garlands in their hair and necklaces of pandanus nut. The only way we can distinguish them is by their lack of tattoos.

Jan describes it in her diary:

"One afternoon we had gone ashore to film the *olioli* which the villagers were re-enacting especially for the movie cameras. Wade had been the only one ashore the night they had the real one.

"When we arrive everyone is getting ready and Mary the widow who can speak English and has been such a tremendous help, asks us girls to come and watch the women having the turmeric put on. She says that the women would like us to dress in custom gear too. We look at each other and think, 'Oh no, we can't.' But then we say, 'Well why not. It's not going to hurt us.' So we agree.

"They are delighted. We go into the hut and there on the mat is a large pile of golden turmeric powder which has been unwrapped from a cloth. We watch the other women, and then it is our turn. Mary says the custom is that only married women can apply the turmeric and decorate married women. The single girls have to be done by single women.

"Mary told us how she has lost her husband, who died in Honiara hospital. Widows are not to wear any form of decoration. If she marries again then she will be able to put on necklaces and custom dress again.

"We are undecided as to whether we should take off our bikini tops or not. Our breasts are so white compared with the rest of our suntanned bodies. As Mary rubs coconut oil into her palms and mixes it with turmeric powder we decide it will look silly with our tops on and the turmeric will cover our whiteness anyway. If we are going to have full traditional dress on we may as well do it properly. It is easy to be brave in the half-light of the hut. I wonder how we will feel in the full glare of sunlight outside.

"She starts on my back first and gradually works over every inch. I wonder if they are only going to do to our waists, but no: we are stripped and done completely from head to toe. It feels just as if someone is giving you a massage and Mary, completely natural, makes me feel at ease. Last of all she does my face. Two girls stand at the doorway chasing the children away who try to peek. Brady wants to ask Janice a question about loading the camera she has given him to use and he isn't allowed in either.

"There the four of us stand; we honestly feel clothed with this complete covering of body paint. They then give us a mustard coloured *pareo* each and one of their beautiful glass bead marriage belts to catch the *pareo* in at the waist. We feel very privileged to be able to wear these. We have scented turmeric garlands around our necks and necklaces made of pandanus nut. Next we have a crown of plaited coconut leaf and a garland of leaves of the *palmou* tree placed on our heads.

"The turmeric powder is from the roots of the turmeric plant. They dry the roots in the sun so that the soil rubs off easily. The roots are grated and pounded with a pestle in a large wooden bowl, then left to dry into powder. To make their mustard *pareo* cloths they take a piece of white cloth, wet it and rub the newly grated and pounded turmeric root into the cloth.

"Florence, the old grandmother, is wonderful. Since she has seen the films that Walt has shown the people onboard ship about the Laulasi people, she is really taking things seriously. When she unwraps her mustard *pareo* cloth, kept only for these occasions, she comes and waves it over each one of us before she puts it on. They keep the cloths wrapped up with fresh turmeric leaves so that they are always perfumed ready for use.

"We smell the heady perfume as it wafts past our noses. At last we are all ready. Out we go into the bright sunlight to join in the beating of the drums and dancing. A ground swell of excitement runs through the village and more and more people press in to see. Janice and I are to sit on one stool together and Karla and Rebbekah on another. Single girls are not to sit with married women.

"We are given a stick to beat time with the drums. It is a terrific feeling being right in with it all. The rest of the women crowd round, staring at us and laughing. The *El Torito* men make sure they take plenty of pictures. After a while with the coconut oil running into our eyes in the heat, it grows very uncomfortable. Janice is really having trouble because some has got under her contact lenses and Walt has to come to the rescue with a clean handkerchief because even our hands are smothered in oil and turmeric. Some of the men who can speak English come up and tell us we look pretty in custom dress. Florence is putting everything she has into leading the dancing group, singing and swaying with fantastic facial expressions. As the women dance we find out why some of them always drop out as the tempo increases. The faster they dance the faster their breasts flay and it hurts. They come back to their chairs laughing and holding their boobs! Some go on dancing with a thin piece of cloth tied round their breasts to hold them down.

"As we go back to the hut to undress we feel a warmth from the women who crowd round paying compliments which Mary is translating to us. It is really a wonderful experience. We feel totally involved. What trouble these people go to, putting this on specially so we can film it.

"We ask Mary and her family to come to tea on the boat the next night.

"When returning to the ship we get off on the stern platform because everything we touch turns yellow. Poor Cliff surfaces from his dive to see four bright yellow nudes in front of his mask. We get the boys to hand us a cake of soap each and we spend the next hour soaping ourselves down and leaping into the sea trying to get it all off. We feel like little girls again, laughing and sponging each other's backs. The mixture is difficult to remove. Once we have the worst off we go downstairs and finish with a hot shower.

"I guess the oil did our skins a lot of good but it certainly takes a long time to get it all off. The island women wash it off with soap in the sea but most of it just wears off. It's not so noticeable on their dark skins."

## LEAVING — THE HARDEST PART

Brady: "When I was lying in the cabin I remembered that in another week I would be lying in my own bed at home in New Zealand. Today is our last day in Ontong Java."

Wade: Ashore on our final day, a Sunday, a huge throng of kids and all the toddy men greet us warmly. Walt and I enjoy some toddy with Henry and Walter, Frank and Ezekiel, Edwin and Patteson, Alfred and Christopher and the fisherman of Luaniua. Before further succumbing I take photos of a family group preparing their copra for the trade ship visit, ramming the dry coconut into China rice bags with a wooden pounder.

Strolling through the village we come upon a group of women playing *kupu*, with black sea-heart *Barringtonia* seeds: ten metres apart two pairs of women kneel in front of grass mats. One pair has a pile of twelve of these large disc-shaped seeds (sea wrack from the high islands) which they are alternately tossing on to the others' mat. The team landing the fewest seeds on the mat retires and another pair replaces them. *Kupu* is played with great vigour and good-natured banter. Henry tells me that the men are experts and some can land all twelve seeds on the mat.

By this time the clubmen are getting steamed up and this time I determine to limit myself to only three tokes of toddy — sufficient to please our hosts and just retain the willpower to refuse more. As a visitor, some refusal is essential to survive but not to participate would put a very "dry" blanket on friendliness.

In the midst of a rip-roaring party the wind arises and the *Malaita* club withdraw to an adjacent hut with a raised floor. The women outside look on with good-natured indulgence and continued card-playing.

The sun returning, the revellers exit through the back door into the avenue beyond, where the party rolls all day — ukeleles, guitars, dancing, drumming. Big Christopher, with the Buddha stomach, signals me to dance with him. I bulge my gut out like his and advance towards him. Just as we are about to collide I retract until my backbone shows: a yoga posture. Buddha Chris tries with little apparent result. The village kids shriek.

While our team enjoy themselves with different groups around the village I spend the day with this happy bunch doused in powder and scent, garlanded with turmeric leaves and determined to resist the toddy. Then I notice that their drinking rate slows as dancing activity increases. The time comes to leave. "Aloha, aloha." "Sorry, sorry," and we shake hands, happy smiles and warmth. I feel very much akin to these fishermen. They could not be more kindly. Our final day at Luaniua has a charmed air with the whole village relaxed and games-playing.

To the ship for a farewell dinner, Rebbekah brings her village friends, the widow Mary and Hanratti, and their nine kids; what fun we have in the saloon, giving them all a big meal, with watermelon, ice blocks and a bag of glass marbles from Brady and Karla. We marvel too at their behaviour — they are not the least muted in this utterly alien world, just a delightful bunch of village kids. Alert and eager, they explore all through the ship and they each use the flush toilets. We give them plates and plates of watermelon and they are careful not to make any mess. Walt brings out the strobe light and we dance for them while Cliff plays music by the band Deep Purple. Jan transcribes Hanratti's tattoos — having gained the trust of the women she is building up a good collection of this art form.

Then a group of very pretty girls visit us, including the lovely sisters Elina (16) and Ellen (12), whom Janice and I have photographed bare-breasted. Tonight they wear their very best clothes. They try the typewriter and quickly pick up the keys. I manoeuvre the girls into the bathroom and shut the door. Just as they are getting ready to scream they catch sight of themselves in the full-length mirror on the back of the door and gasp with astonished peals of laughter.

Cross section: This afternoon Janice and Jan are in the darkroom printing photos for the villagers, Rebbekah and Brady are under the ship, Walt is reading *Playboy*, Karla is making a necklace, and Cliff is sleeping.

The children have written their last paragraphs on Ontong Java:

Karla: "Last night Rebbekah's friend Mary came out to tea on *El Torito* and she had nine children and a widow called Hanratti with her. Walt turned on the strobe light and freaked everybody out because everything went jerky and funny. Puggy the dog nearly shat herself because every time she went to go somewhere the ground flickered."

Brady: "It was really neat fun paddling back out in the rubber boat with Dad because every now and then we saw a powerful flash of lightning that cracked the sky as if it were glass. Dad told me there were different kinds of lightning. One of the strangest is called *St Elmo's Fire*, which appears as a big ball of flame, usually on a ship's mast, as it did in the sailing ship days, scaring the sailors out of their wits. That very night we got one on the radio aerial. It was only small but Walt said it would be 30,000 volts."

Wade: Following a second wild night of squalls and heavy rain and frequent anchor checks we don't expect a very pleasant trip to Honiara. At first light the decks come alive with feet: our passengers'. The list rises from an expected nine to seventeen, including three children. As president of the village council it is for Walter Hemoku to decide who has good reason to travel, as Walt wants to be helpful without causing trouble.

For the voyage, our passengers are laden with taro, cooked fish, coconuts and a big teapot full of toddy. Two outboards, new and nicely greased, are on their way to Honiara for servicing. Two secondary school girls (a rarity at Luaniua) returning to boarding school; a family going down to pick up the twin child of an urban daughter and bring it home. A boy setting out on a technical course in outboard maintenance; another with a suitcase stuffed with 6000 Australian dollar notes, his family's copra earnings, to buy a 30-foot fibreglass canoe, ideal for lagoon travel; Alfred and

Christopher off to work for the Japanese tuna fleet and Henry Manuhea, returning to his government post.

The day turns out to be quite pleasant — an easy following sea, intermittent sun and cloud and our company, all spread out over the little ship: under the skiff, behind the sub, on the wheelhouse roof, within on the settees and over the floor.

On the last leg of our six months' voyaging together we head south and I have time to think it over. During our brief stay at Luaniua we have been discovering that its inhabitants are among the happiest, healthiest communities on Earth, and in a crowded world increasingly beset with survival problems from pollution, poor sanitation, and over-exploitation of resources these people offer an incredible comparison: theirs may well be no end game. They live in balance with their environment; their healthy physical condition and sanitation are enviable by any Western standard, and there seems to be no problem for them in maintaining a well-balanced diet from land and sea, for in neither case is there over-exploitation.

One of the keys to atoll survival is the coconut palm. Its clusters of nuts provide such an abundance of water there can be little fear of drought. The nut meat is as versatile a food as any known to man: meat, coconut oil, coconut cream. From its husks strong rope and fishing lines can be woven; its shell burns with an intense and smokeless flame. The fronds are woven to make hut walls and food baskets; the trunk provides the stout framework. From the nectar of the flowers a sweet syrup can be distilled, a pleasant drink, or a mind-altering beverage for social gatherings. The kernel or "lolly" in the centre is a favourite with children. It also makes a poultice for dressing wounds.

To the coconut culture can be added the useful pandanus palm whose leaves thatch huts, form fabric, sails, mats; its yellow nuts are refreshing to chew or decorative on a necklace.

Taro grown intensively in flooded paddies provides one of the densest yields per acre of any starchy root crop or cereal. Together with these limited foods, the diverse resources of the coral reef provide an obviously adequate diet. On analysis Janice, our botanist, found it is basically sound. Her study shows that with the addition of a little pawpaw, banana, clam and chicken, all the daily needs of man — protein, calcium and essential vitamins — are being satisfied, but only just. The margin for survival is very narrow. Even though food is abundant the essential elements are limited in variety. Were atoll diet changed from taro and sweet potato to imported white rice, there could be serious inadequacies.

Tim Bayliss-Smith, of Cambridge University, has made a study of the human ecology of small island ecosystems. He compares the energy use of four pre-industrial societies at different stages along the road from total self-sufficiency to total involvement with the external world.

He points out that Ontong Java, copra producing since the 1890s, has been exposed to the cash economy much longer than his two New Guinean examples. "Imported foods are now an important supplement to the traditional staples of taro, fish and coconut, making up 24% of the total dietary calories. Four foods, rice, sugar, flour and biscuits, provided Ontong Java with 98% of its imported food energy, which absorbed about one-third of the total cash income. Of the fuels, kerosene was widely used for domestic lighting, replacing home-produced coconut oil in most houses, except in times of shortage. Fewer than one in 20 canoes are outboard powered, mainly for the transport of families between villages. Imported food and fuel contributed 5.1% of the total energy used by the Ontong Java population."

Since no islands are now without links to the outside world, he sees them as microcosms of the global trend towards a more and more exploitative relationship with natural resources and in agriculture, a less and less efficient manipulation of energy. Island populations were once among the few that were forced to view their finite resources more realistically and they developed forms of social organisation and land use that enabled an ecological balance to be maintained.

Scientists comparing the efficiency of food gathering in animals, including primitive man, have found there is a striking similarity running through them all, in the energy gained — energy expended ratios.

"By contrast," writes Bayliss-Smith, "industrial man is much less efficient in his use of energy. Much more energy is being poured into his food production process than is being gained from it. Only the low monetary cost of non-renewable fossil fuels makes intensive farming profitable. Yet the illusion persists that mankind has, as a result of astonishing scientific and technological achievements, solved the problem of production."

Wade: Most of the humans on this planet are assemblies of oil. Fossilised sunlight fertilises our crops and transports them to our tables; clads and houses us. Atoll dwellers have an age-old sustainable lifestyle mostly energised by sun, wind and water. Renowned ecologist H.T. Odum has it in a nutshell: "Industrial man no longer eats potatoes made from solar energy; now he eats potatoes partly made from oil." Our planet's resources have now been depleted; oil production has peaked. We face a brave new world.

This atoll is no utopian society, the achievement of a wiser, cleverer people. As commensals on the coral reef, the oldest and most durable ecosystem on Earth, atoll-dwelling man was moulded by his environment. As also with the Eskimos and the first Australians, its harsh realities did his thinking for him. Urban man could draw hope from this. If a high civilisation were to emulate the principles behind such living patterns, it might continue to evolve. Otherwise, as Gregory Bateson observes, "the creature that wins against its environment destroys itself — extinction by loss of flexibility."

When the crash comes for the developed world, these remote people may be among the survivors, the flag bearers for humanity; perhaps the transmitters of the precious message it could cost us our whole civilisation to learn: the absolute necessity for all life forms to live in harmony — the ecological imperative to maintain diversity and flexibility.

On her way through Boli passage, *El Torito* enters a harbour in the Florida Group. We are all standing on the bow except Brady, below reading a shipwreck story, *Survive the Savage Sea*. For many of the young atoll-dwellers this is their first sight of hills and forests. Suddenly with a traumatic crunch *El Torito* heaves up on to a coral bank and stops. Walt revs and revs, but his ship won't budge. To lighten the bow we launch the skiff and pump dry the forward water tank. Minutes before the tide begins to drop and leave us stranded, *El Torito*'s engines edge her sideways off the bank. Walt curses the ambiguous channel markers and dives to inspect her hull — the tough old girl is unscathed.

Soon after *El Torito*'s return to Honiara our long voyage together came to a close. As our family and Rebbekah left by air for New Zealand and Cliff flew back to college in the United States, Walt and Janice were busy preparing for the next major step in their plans: establishment of the research base at the Three Sisters Islands in the Solomons.

# PART FOUR

# ADVANCE NEWS

## A DEATH IN PARIS

On a sweet summer's day at the end of January 1976, I was standing on a cliff top overlooking the Pacific listening to music from a cassette player. There was a special resonance because this was music created by my Maori friends that I had recorded in this same exquisite place a few weeks earlier. Those musicians were with me, strolling about or recumbent, revisiting their sounds. Suddenly, while surveying the ocean horizon, I became aware of the rotundity of the Earth and then I remembered that my sister, a talented singer/songwriter, was out there, on the other side of the globe, painfully ill in the isolation ward of a Paris hospital.

There was a peculiar tearing sensation somewhere in my navel and a sudden surge of intense joy. I knew Susie had died. I felt no grief — just focused in the here and now. I even began taking photos of an insect on a leaf! When I got home a cable call had just conveyed the news to my family. I checked it out. The times corresponded exactly. I have since found that many people have had similar intimations of the injury or death of a loved one. It is especially common with identical twins.

Since for obvious reasons, such events are rare, the phenomenon has not yet entered the body of accepted knowledge. This was my most intense experience of another reality. Since then others have ensued.

## A SERIOUS ACCIDENT

Jan: "Wade and I were out on the catamaran during our dolphin research days. It was just after lunch, a beautiful sailing day when I got a strong urge to go home. This was so strange because I would not usually want to leave what we were doing on such a lovely day. I said to Wade, with a very firm tone that I wanted to go home. I didn't know why but I felt upset and knew that I *must* go back to port. Luckily Wade didn't object and we turned the sailing catamaran and headed for land.

"When we got home there was a message from our son Brady saying that my father had been blown off the roof while doing repairs and was in Christchurch hospital unconscious and injured.

I had reached home early enough to book plane tickets that day to Christchurch involving one from Whangarei to Auckland and another from Auckland to Christchurch. My father never really recovered from that fall."

## PETER RIPPON COMES TO OUR BEDROOM

Jan: "Our diver friend Pete had just died in a boating accident. His body was found — with an upturned boat and gear.

"In the middle of the night I sat bolt upright. I went to grab Wade and tell him Pete was here. I was just going to shake Wade when I realized it was all in my mind. How silly of me. He wouldn't be too pleased to be woken up with me telling him Pete is here when he was not. I'd had a very clear vision of Pete leaning over Wade at the side of the bed. I couldn't see his face but the top of his head and forehead. Pete had receding hair on each side of his temple and I knew it was Pete. It really shook me up and I lay there thinking about it for some time. I was burning to tell Wade but had to wait till the morning.

Next morning I related to Wade what had happened and that I didn't like to wake him at the time. To my amazement Wade said: 'That's funny, I've had a very strong dream about Pete in the night.'"

Wade: I had dreamt vividly that Pete, a very experienced diver and boatman, was trying to explain how he came to die at sea while on holiday in the farthest north. I recall something to do with an outboard fuel tank, which may have been empty. The significant aspect of this to me is that the subject of my dream corresponded with Jan's in these special circumstances.

## LOST CHILD

I was talking with our daughter Karla about our Melanesian experiences and subsequent discussion about their special capacities with the Solomon Islands anthropologist. She said she grew up with all that, having accompanied us at the age of nine to Laulasi on the second *El Torito* voyage and up to the atoll dwellers of Luaniua.

She has always had that feeling of connection to her loved ones; a sense of their location and how they were faring. One day when her family were living at Aotea Harbour on the edge of coastal wilderness her ten-year old son Mark went missing while exploring with a young friend. Karla says that very strangely she was not worried once she put her mind to the situation. Down on the beach, closing her eyes, she had a vision of a sunny place and lots of grasses and that he was okay. When the boys were found this remote sensing turned out to be correct, according to her son. She said she often finds things that are lost with this technique.

# PART FIVE

# OCEAN MIND: DOLPHIN RESEARCH IN NEW ZEALAND

## MY FIRST DOLPHIN ENCOUNTERS

I began diving in 1954. It was a compulsion. As a boy I made a diving helmet and walked on the seabed with air pumped down to me by two girls in relay. At high school I made my own scuba regulator and diving suit. My generation was the first to fly under the sea. By the age of thirty I had built up a large photo archive of marine fishes and invertebrates. Dolphins and whales were beyond my experience, as with most divers in those days. At best we only had hullo/goodbye encounters. But that was all to change.

In May 1971, I had been alone sixty feet down where white sand lies in drifts at the foot of Rikoriko cave wall at my beloved Poor Knights Islands, New Zealand. Suddenly everything went black. I glanced up in fear — the cave portal, usually a blaze of blue fire, had dimmed. It was seething with huge shapes — sharp fins, fast tails and jaws. Dolphins! One of them, in silhouette on the surface, smacked its tail and a pair of curving forms glided down in a spiral, circled me and rose to breathe. Each time the games leader smacked with his tail a pair spiralled down, curving on their sides to gaze intently as they passed me. Enchanted, for some time I forgot I had a camera: a large format Rolleiflex. Then with the last two frames left on the film I took my first dolphin picture: *Tursiops truncatus,* the bottlenose.

Subsequently I made voyages in the tropics aboard R.V. *El Torito*, about which I wrote two books. Then, in 1975, back in my old stamping grounds at the Poor Knights Islands, having just revisited the vast Rikoriko sea cave, largest in the world, I was driving our deep vee runabout homewards when dolphins moved to meet the fast-running boat. It seemed I knew exactly what I wanted to do if I ever met dolphins on the bow. *It seemed strangely prefigured; thought out by the back of the mind.* I would slow to a crawl, put the boat in a wide circle and leap into the centre. I wanted dolphin photos. Tony Ayling took the wheel and I plunged in. My strategy worked: dolphins were frolicking around the bow like circus ponies, with me as ringmaster. I fired off my dozen photos. Then I became aware that roles were changing.

The boat had stopped and I was now at the centre of a cyclone of dolphins. I called to Tony and the others to join me, but "one at a time; and let's all do the dolphin-kick." I can't recall why I should have said that, but it was probably an important factor in what ensued.

As an exercise in relativity it is interesting to imagine those dolphins' viewpoint. A diver bursts through the heaving mirror and points a third eye at them. He passes the camera up and starts to mimic the dolphin way of swimming. One after the other two more men join him, diving down in their wetsuits. Then — a subtle variation — a bikini-clad girl. Suddenly, a large nude male appears. Had this been planned we could not have designed a more effective introduction to humans. Poor Les Gray! He was supposed to look after the boat but our enthusiasm was too much for him. And the wind had died down. Almost! Barry Russell and I saw the boat start to waft away — faster and faster. We only just caught it, averting an embarrassingly long swim home in the dark.

During our dolphin games each diver in his sealed-off world became aware that the dolphins were demonstrating new tricks. I was weaving among them with a fluid dolphin drive, my fins undulating together like a broad tail in a movement that began at my head and rippled along my body. A dolphin drew alongside me. By counter-opposing its flippers, like the ailerons of a plane making a spin, it barrel-rolled right in front of my mask.

Maintaining the dolphin-kick I imitated this corkscrew manoeuvre, counter-opposing my hands held close to my chest. The response was slow as my pseudo-flippers were tiny and my speed a fraction of theirs, but I found myself rolling wing over wing. Then something startling happened. The moment my spin was complete a formation of six dolphins, abreast of me and on the same side as before, repeated that trick, in unison, reinforcing my newly acquired mimicry pattern. And so it went on, the sea wild with energy, a maelstrom of dolphins, their shrill echo ranging whistles dinning in our ears.

We gambolled with them for about an hour until utterly exhausted. Then one by one we hauled ourselves in over the stern. Around us we could now see salvoes of dolphins leaping in symmetrical pairs and singly for a mile in every direction. We must have met a whole tribe of bottlenose dolphins on their passage along the coast.

As we towelled ourselves warm I said how marvellous it was that such huge, sharp- toothed animals, each as heavy and as fast as my boat, had not even buffeted us by their swirling movements. "Only once," said Dr. Tony Ayling who had been the last on board. Just as he was approaching the stern one dolphin had rushed to within a metre of him, stopped short, vertical in the water, with flippers flung wide as if imploring us to continue. It then tugged his swimfin. We felt we had let them down. I gave the hull a resounding thump. From a short way off a tail smacked on the surface in answer. I thumped again. Eight times we exchanged signals, and that was it.

The words of Dr. Walter Starck aboard *El Torito* still haunted my thoughts: "Dolphins may lead us to unknown areas of the mind. That huge brain has got to be there for some function other than cute tricks to please tourists."

Those two episodes were to change our lives. With our Project Interlock Jan and I set out on a quest to discover the capacities of mind in the sea. I have now written four books about encounters with dolphins and whales.

## BOB'S FIRST ALIEN

From the day the dolphins whistled to him aboard our boat, Bob Feigel had been trying to put on paper the experience which first made him eager to know dolphins better and led to his coming to sea with us that Anniversary Day.

I once took a photo crossing Auckland harbour bridge on a wet night. Just resting my camera on the car window sill I made a time exposure of the city lights, neon signs, street lamps, buildings aglow, headlights and the wet roading with its reflections. My photo is a fantasia of light trajectories — a picture that records a third dimension: time. I showed it to Bob Feigel. That's just about what he saw the first time he experienced dolphins. Just before our film project he gave me an account. Bob is a professional writer from Malibu, California, but this was something almost impossible to put into words. I titled it: *Bob Encounters His First Alien*.

Bob: "On 12 November 1976 I was out on charter boat *Lady Jess* from Tutukaka heading back from a day of fishing around the Poor

Knights along with some friends. There were probably twelve or so people on board and most of them were either aft or on the bridge with the skipper. I was hanging out one of the cabin doors on the port side thinking of nothing in particular when the inside of my head seemed to come alive with high-pitched sounds and something my mind's eye saw as multi-coloured dots zigzagging all over the place. If you've ever seen one of those early digital ping-pong games. It was like that, but in colour and multiplied by thousands, and the visual experience was connected with the auditory one. It wasn't a very pleasant feeling because of its intensity but it only lasted a few seconds when *BLAM!* — out of the water right in front of me jumped a dolphin.

"It was huge and I've never been that close to any creature of the sea before, but of all things I remember feeling, fear wasn't among them ... only a very intense awareness.

"Its jump was a tight arc and when it reached the level of my face it seemed to hang in the air and look me straight in the eyes and then dive back in the water. It came up a short distance away one more time, and everyone on the boat *ohhed* and *ahhed* and then it disappeared. All in all I estimate the time involved to have been no more than sixty seconds.

"The bouncing, multi-coloured dots were just as real as everything else. It seemed as if my perception had widened. The reality I had been experiencing a moment before was put into the background with this new overlay happening simultaneously — like a double exposure.

"There was a hint of another dimension. The multi-coloured dots seemed to zip and zap all over the place, points of light moving infinitely away or close around without becoming larger or smaller, as if there were no up or down, or in or out, but a total 360-degree awareness.

"There were more subtle movements too, slight changes in the colours and patterns of the 'atmosphere' within which I seemed to be seeing the points of light. This atmosphere was crystal clear yet at the same time produced a sense of colour; a dimensional thing like layers of subtle, changing colours. The discomfort was not caused by the intensity of the sound. It seemed I was not hearing in the usual sense but listening to sound registering in my head without coming through my ears. The sound was so beautiful, like some absolutely perfect electronic music. The discomfort came from trying to listen to it without hearing.

"Both the sound experience and the visual seemed connected, just as the music and light at a rock concert can be connected, yet at the same time they were distinct and separate. Despite the intensity of the experience and discomfort, after it was over I felt as I would if someone I loved very much but hadn't seen for some time had come into my life for a short visit. I felt relaxed ... I felt comfortable ... and I felt full of love for everyone."

## WE ARE NOT ALONE: ANNIVERSARY DAY ENCOUNTER

31 January 1977: The midsummer ocean was so calm. Five miles off shore the only sound was the distant rumble of Anniversary weekend traffic. Our runabout drifted over a translucent plain. The tape of the whale songs had played right through.

Bob Feigel let out another shrill whistle. The common dolphins *Delphinus delphis* we'd been following were moving off now. They were working about half a mile to the south. We found ourselves listening to their breathing and splashing sounds. Then it happened. Our ears thrilled to a raspy, hollow whistle — it came from amidst the dolphins. One had answered Bob. I saw a large dolphin surge off to the west. It sounded and emerged, whistled boldly and dived. We were hanging there, Jan, myself and the two girls. And Bob was standing at the grab rail, whistling across the water and listening to the responses, hardly believing each time that it was not one of us — that a sea creature was making such sounds. Our experiments had taken an unexpected turn.

From the outset it had been the most perfect day — not a breath of wind, the sky a cobalt blue to match the sea and the water so very clear. Boats were everywhere.

Halfway to the Poor Knights with Bob Feigel, our daughter Karla and her friend Lisa aboard we had met the dolphins at twenty-five minutes past ten. This time there were no birds working. One or two gannets and shearwaters were sitting around on the ocean and occasionally taking off for a few circuits.

Jan donned her gear. We cruised along with the dolphins and they seemed very interested in the boat. We had humpback whale songs playing on the tape and the girls were ringing the cowbell, our acoustic signature.

Just before Jan got in, the small group of dolphins we were cruising with joined up with a larger school. Bob climbed up onto the bow and was leaning over close to the water. It was time to leap in: the dolphins were all around us.

As Jan hit the water and dived down dolphins came from all directions to have a look at her, sweeping in to within ten feet. She dolphin-kicked energetically until she had to ascend for a breath. There were dolphins on the surface only ten feet away. She dived again and they came in, circled once and withdrew. She could hear their sonar whistles all round when she was below. Once they had satisfied their curiosity they left. From examining body marks and dorsal fins it seemed this was a different group from any we had met before.

The second time Jan got in with them was much the same as the first. They had a look at her twice before rejoining the rest of the group. It seemed that only some of the group would ride on the boat and check us out while the majority kept apart, possibly with the school of fish they were working. On every occasion that we have followed common dolphins, this same thing has been apparent.

A large launch cruised past quite close. Two dolphins tore in to have a quick look at Jan. The dolphins did not go over to this boat to frolic on the bow wave as might be expected. Yet our boat was stationary with the motor off.

We caught up with them. I got in this time and shot some 16mm movie footage before they left. Filming is a problem. It destroys interlock playfulness. I can't frolic about spontaneously and shoot movie at the same time. But I badly needed some action shots — it would be my third roll for the film proposal. Each time I dropped in they would do one burst round me and leave. I wanted to film Jan in their midst wearing her dolphin dorsal fin but there was no way. As I was returning to the boat after my second attempt I got a real jolt. From the depths air bubbles were rising in sparkling screens. "There can't be a diver down there! Methane gas? No, it's not coming up steadily enough.

At depths beyond visible range the dolphins had released large gulps of air which expanded as they rose and as pressure diminished, swirling silver bells exactly like the exhaust of a scuba diver. But out here it was over 300 feet deep. Was this an attempt at communication, a visual game, or just indigestion? Future observations may reveal its significance. At that time no dolphins were in sight — they'd all left the scene, I assumed. So maybe the bubbles had been released at some considerable depth.

I took some movie of Jan dolphin-kicking with her dolphin fin and some of the boat approaching me in the water with the kids hanging over the bow. Then I made four more attempts to approach the dolphins with Jan and camera but they sounded and came up further away each time. We wondered if the boat motor drove the schoolfish they were herding deeper as we approached. It was twenty minutes to twelve. We had been moving with them for one hour and fifty minutes so far and we weren't getting anywhere. By this time we were sure this was a new group of dolphins. We decided to try a different approach, starting again from scratch to establish trust.

Bob, having been shown only a few minutes previously how to handle the boat, suddenly felt at ease with the controls. I was very happy at being able to concentrate on the dolphins and not the boat. In fact we were all feeling quite ecstatic. Karla and Lisa were leaning over the bow gliding gently in the midst of a dolphin parade. The taped dolphin sounds finished and Pink Floyd started. At twice its normal speed "Echoes" has a crazy carnival rhythm. Somehow it sounds just right in that setting and the dolphins all around us showed clearly they were listening to the tape: when the tempo increased a surge went through them and they began to frolic.

I never thought when David Harvey and I first tried that tape one winter's day on the coast, six months back, that we would ever manage to play the entire experiment to a group of dolphins and feel certain they heard the sequence of acoustic logic it expresses. From the outset David and I had hoped that if dolphins ever heard these experiments they might realize that the communication barrier between man and dolphin is the great gulf between the sound frequencies which each species uses. We hoped there might be some significant response if ever they grasped the analogue message on our tape. So I was particularly interested in this quickening of pace with the Pink Floyd piece. They definitely responded to its jingly, dancing music — a festive mood was induced in dolphin and man. I felt as if we were in a Mardi Gras procession.

Bob was driving sedately, letting the dolphins lead us. When the humpback song came through the tape he began whistling the same whistle over and over again, mimicking the whale sounds. The dolphins were all round the boat, riding the bow, rolling over and looking up at the girls. Every now and again one would leap out of the water. It was so clear you could see every mark and scratch on their backs. We started to note in our minds things that we would be able to recognize at another time.

There was one with the top of its dorsal bent right over: Bentfin; another with a nick out of the top of his dorsal: Nicky; another with a nick out of the lower part; one with two grill patches on its left side in front and behind the dorsal; one with a diagonal scratch on the left side in front of its dorsal.

I saw one roll over on top of another as it went to get in front of the boat. I've never seen them actually touch like that before.

A rush of understanding: of course, every time we meet a new group of dolphins we have to start from the beginning and let them get used to us first. They seem to accept us as long as we are responsive. We must let the dolphins lead us and not the other way round. A new ethic: they are teaching us the rules.

[Note: Even after the E.S.P. hypothesis developed we still felt a mutually acceptable interspecies meeting ethic should be followed at all encounters. It would be rude to withhold courtesies involving mutual trust on the assumption of an E.S.P. link. As we had learnt in Pacific island villages an overt display of body language ensures understanding and respect.]

We were only doing four knots, Bob whistling all the time. The dolphins were getting much more friendly, milling about under the boat, in front and behind in the wake. They seemed to be swimming in pairs or fours.

We were now halfway between the Sugarloaf and the shore. There were a few gannets and shearwaters in the vicinity. They weren't feeding, just following the dolphins. Then the dolphins seemed to form a line which broke into three groups. We were with the middle group, some were to the west and some to the east.

Broadside to the keel the dolphins came streaking under the boat rolling on their sides as they passed close to the girls' dangling feet. Then the three groups came together in one mass. All this time we had the tape playing the songs of the humpback. It ran out and Bob turned the motor off. We could easily hear their sonar squeaks. It was so calm and still with a continual low rumble coming from all the weekend traffic on the land. It was now ten minutes to twelve. Bob continued to whistle like a whale. Then all of a sudden we looked at each other. What was that unearthly sound? We were all stock still, hardly breathing. Once more Bob whistled. We heard it again. It was a dolphin making an aerial sound with its blowhole, as if it was trying to master the whistle and couldn't quite make it. Blowing raspberries! Bob kept whistling and we noticed that the answering call seemed to be coming from one particular dolphin.

Dolphins in captivity have been trained to whistle with their blowholes in air but for a dolphin to attempt this in the wild was just too exciting for words. By now the dolphins were at quite some distance but we continued to drift silently listening while Bob kept up his whistling. Then we noticed they were getting closer. While Bob whistled they came nosing through the clear water right back to us. Defecating as they went (some sort of signal; perhaps an olfactory greeting such as goats give when they urinate as one approaches) hurtling under and around the boat. It seemed Bob's whistle had drawn them to us again. One group stayed close to the boat and others spread out around.

Bob and the girls were leaning over the bow. Bob whistling. Every now and again we would hear the return whistle. The mimicry was getting better and better until in the end it was quite perfect and we would look at Bob to see if it were he or the dolphins who had made the sound. Three times we stopped the motor and the tape and drifted while Bob whistled so we could hear the answering whistles.

We were looking at the group of dolphins ahead when Jan suddenly stopped jotting down notes. She felt as though she had been interrupted. She turned and her gaze joined ours. At that moment out of the water shot a large dolphin. A trio were travelling north very fast to join those ahead that we were concentrating on. As they approached the others we heard two more whistles. Both Bob and I felt this strange premonition too — that something was going to happen. We were all looking in the same direction just as that dolphin broke the water, whistled and plunged back in.

It was now 1:25 p.m. We started up again. While we circled Bob was leaning over the bow with his arm outstretched over the dolphin backs riding on the bow, whistling to them gently. I saw one answer Bob ten feet from the boat. Bob touched one, lightly rubbing his fingers along its side. He said after, that he was amazed at the softness of its skin. The dolphin gave a start, splashing the water with its tail. It came back up again, rolling on its side to look at Bob, then it did a sideways wriggle.

We kept cruising with them in this manner until 1:50 p.m., heading towards the Pinnacles now. Each time we caught up with the dolphins we had whale sounds playing and would ring the cowbell. We wanted them to recognise and get to know us by introducing ourselves the same way every time. Then we would turn everything off and let Bob whistle.

We decided to try getting in with them again. I manoeuvred the boat until we were in front of them. Jan leapt in three times while I kept the boat circling. Much the same thing happened as in the morning. They went away after she had dived down twice but both times as she dived they came and circled and had a good look within ten to fifteen feet range. The second time one swept in close to about six feet and then went away. She got out at 2:15 p.m. and I decided I would get in on the end of a tow rope. We had various arm signals worked out: go faster, slower and stop.

I was towed behind the dolphins for half an hour but they were moving just a little too fast for me to catch up. More speed and I would lose mask and arms. It was unlikely they were aware of my presence behind the boat because of engine noise and the white water from the wake.

The tow proved more interesting than I'd hoped for; here was a way to move fast like a dolphin. At slow speeds I found I could still do the dolphin kick even though being towed. It relieved the strain on my arms. I could readily veer out from behind the bow wave by thrusting one arm obliquely ahead.

Eager to get amongst the dolphins I signalled Jan to speed up by stages until the water pressure was all that I could stand. *Chain salps* and jellyfish whisked by. Movie footage shot like this would be incredible. I was hurtling through innerspace — a giant marlin bait! Uneasy thought, but the dolphins ahead were a source of some comfort. Little did I know there was a mako shark in the vicinity. Aqua-sledding has its small risk factor but could be worthwhile. It would be possible to build an elaborate tow sled for this purpose with built-in scuba tank, tape recorder and movie rig.

They were moving faster by this time in a southeast direction so we decided we couldn't afford the fuel to follow them any more, even though we wanted to. We took off to the Poor Knights and as we detoured to pass near the Sugarloaf, noticed a fin in the water. Preparing to leap in we slowed down and circled. It turned out to be a magnificent mako shark. The water being so clear we were able to see him very well. We watched for a while and then he swam off into the light. He looked tremendous as the sun lit up his huge blue-grey form. We could even see the gills opening and closing on his side. I had almost joined him! Mako sharks are deepwater animals and we were lucky to have seen it so close.

We continued over to Nursery Cove where the girls and Jan snorkeled and enjoyed the fishes. The demoiselles were thick in against the cliffs and they lay on the surface watching these little fishes spawning. There were newly-hatched demoiselles everywhere no bigger than a thumb nail. And males guarding nests against all-comers — other than dancing females of their own species whom they courted and whose eggs they accepted. That night we all slept with dolphins before our eyes.

## THINKING THINGS OVER

On thinking it all over, it seems possible that common dolphins, *Delphinus delphis*, may be nomadic herdsmen, pasturing schools of baitfish along interfaces and thermoclines. There is so much of their behaviour that could only be understood if we studied the schools with side-scanning sonar and observed how they are being protected and husbanded.

Another factor in trying to interpret their manoeuvres is that in many instances only about half the dolphins would be surfacing at one time. Very often it seems there would be one group swimming near the surface while others spend longer periods submerged. The surface swimmers may be more available for play as some can be spared from fish-tending. They may even be detailed to distract the boat by playing on its bow. The surface swimmers are often younger ones and mothers with babies.

When we approach a dolphin group with a fish school under surveillance, they often sound. This may be because we frighten the schoolfish which they must then pursue and round up. We must avoid this in future. Another ethic.

Dolphins rounding up prey: One method seems to be to form a long line, which may then divide into three groups. I can visualise them driving the fish at five knots and then suddenly sending down three groups beneath the school to completely surround it. The preyfish form a dense "meat ball." Those dolphins on the surface rush together to close the gaps and feeding may occur.

## VOCAL MIMICRY, KEY TO FIRST STAGE OF COMMUNICATION

Vocal mimicry is the first stage in communication between mother and child. The dolphins have now shown they can adapt to our low-frequency airborne sound signals with perfection. Physiologically it is not easy, a highly consummate feat by an acoustic gymnast. But once the actual production of such sounds was mastered they rapidly perfected their modelling. Like a man first learning to make a sound on a trumpet and then playing a recognisable tune.

In captivity it took scientists weeks of reward/punishment training to elicit airborne sounds from bottlenose dolphins. But these were lonely, touch-starved creatures with little choice other than to comply with the research pattern imposed on them. In the wild the dolphins have the trump hand — they can withdraw at will. In this situation man can only proffer himself to be taught by the dolphins.

Our message tape is a logical acoustic statement. It may act as a rosetta stone, or a bridge between two acoustic cultures whole wavebands apart. I don't think the dolphins regard us as particularly interesting yet. We offer little diversity of behaviour. Our canned music can't communicate because the element of response is missing. "OK — you're making cetacean sounds but that's no more intelligent than the wind whistling over wave crests if you don't respond to us."

First the tape establishes the concept of changing speeds through the four-stage recording of dolphin sounds, slower and slower until their whistle calls become much more complex to the human ear than the shrill whistles we hear normally. Next, a piece of western music which incorporates imitation whale sounds is presented at increasing speed until it becomes to us, musical nonsense. Then the humpback whale songs start and Feigel begins to copy the whales. "That's it," the dolphins may think, "they make meaningful sounds in air, at low frequencies. Let's try them out."* (Maybe they tried for some time but we didn't notice until the motor stopped.) They pucker their blowholes experimentally, sometimes a bit too tight and the air is released in explosive clicks. Too loose, and a hoarse, rasping sound. Then they get it right and manage to whistle in air instead of the high-pitched calls they generate inside their heads underwater. We respond with more whistles but it's hard to show them a patterned performance as yet because they're not on the surface long enough to hear a series of calls. I had the uncanny feeling they must have known when Feigel whistled, because immediately after, one leaps out and responds, but this is just a hunch.

[*Note: Much of this prefigures the section of my story ahead, when the solo dolphin Rampal at Whitianga hears our sound output and responds in air and water in a major way.]

At first we'd tried hard to engage them in the water. Each time we dropped a diver in they made a turn about him and left. Perhaps the preyfish school had been frightened and had to be overtaken. But once we motored along quietly at the same speed as the dolphins we got our first lesson. Perceptively Bob had begun to notice certain signals which seemed to indicate which way the group would veer. It was this that enabled him to anticipate their turns and so keep right up with them. As long as we did this, dolphins that were surface-swimming came close around the boat and cavorted on the bow wave. They responded to changes of pace in our tape and inspected us closely through a mirror calm surface as they swam in at right angles to the boat.

At these times a wave of happiness seemed to cocoon the whole boat, all its occupants and those below: all moving through the same field of sound and light, the whale songs and the summer's day. I'd kept wondering whether I should get in but didn't want to spoil what was developing between Feigel and the dolphins. I'm glad I had the sense to refrain or otherwise we may not have learned anything new that day.

The dolphins showed us their hunting patterns, they inspected us closely alongside the bow and displayed a range of antics indicative of joy and exuberance. Even while the motor was going we heard some very loud sonar whistles which penetrated the hull. These may have been earlier efforts to communicate before attempting the airborne sounds. We are Brobdingnagians unable to see finer realities that underlie the coarse-grain world view our culture admits.

The dolphins have whistled to us on a fine summer's day. The eerie sounds still echo in my thoughts — the most uncanny and haunting I've ever heard — something alien, droll and utterly perfect — a comforting response from a mind in the sea — an assurance that *we are not alone*, that bridges can be built and both sides can cross them.

I recalled seeing a movie about pre-contact hill tribesmen in New Guinea. When gifts were left on the track, they emerged from the jungle, unaware of a telephoto lens, gathered up the parcels and hurled them down the path. Mutual respect and game sharing, self-effacement and flexibility are all essential for transcultural exchanges. We may be on the brink of something exciting if we develop a flexible, creative approach.

When we meet a group, if they respond to the boat manoeuvres by following around in a circle, they are amenable to further interlock in the water. But if they only play on the bow when we head along their course, they cannot be induced to stay and play. *If they are busy hunting we should stay clear.*

We've now tested this repeatedly, and it seems they have other duties to perform. In such situations only the surface-swimming dolphins are amenable to vocal interlock. It could be that, like the early explorer and missionaries, we are mainly encountering the young ones and mothers, rather than the acoustically more sophisticated elders, who probably manage the schoolfish. This may hinder the development of interlock, so we should be patient. In all cases observed it was the larger, older dolphins who learned to whistle in air.

## IN CONCLUSION

After months of experimenting with dolphins in the wild, we have just met a group who heard our message tape. And they have acknowledged it. The tape is an acoustic statement about the vast communications gap which may exist between air-dwellers and sea-dwellers.

In response they learnt to make low-frequency airborne sounds within our hearing range. Then they used the new wavelength to mimic us perfectly. The ball is now in our court. Can we show them we are acoustic games players too? Can we offer them a diversity of interesting sounds? How complex could their responses become?

Had we known then what was to unfold exactly one year later with this same group of dolphins, we would not have been ready to believe it. Perhaps we had to grow in understanding.

# PART SIX

# BOB'S DREAM
# MEETING WAIPU PITA
# OUR FILM: *THE FIRST MOVE*

I figured by making a documentary film it would enable me to document something of our work and communicate our procedures to others who might try them. I was eager to share our discoveries and see how dolphins would respond to others who approached them creatively. A wild dream to stimulate a global interest in dolphin games.

But I wasn't to know just where the filming would lead us. Now it is over, I see it provided the energy to document a strange episode of human/dolphin communication exactly as it unfolded.

During filming, with a television team camped on our forest land at Ngunguru, by an immense stroke of luck we managed to shanghai Bob Feigel to join us on the catamaran by fast boat. Bob didn't hestitate. He knew we wanted to record his strange dolphin experience on film. I'll never know how Bob could sit on our sunny foredeck and give an interview with such vivacity and warmth twelve miles out on the ocean.

When the film was in the can he turned quietly to me to say he had had a dream. He saw me up on the bowsprit of the catamaran* (a foot-wide plank that runs fore and aft midway between the hulls, from the foremost crossbeam to the next) surrounded by seven dolphins. In the dream he saw the interlock *rondels* fitted on our bows, although Bob knew nothing of them. One large dolphin communicated telepathically, directing towards me a Maori word: *tepuhi* or *tepuke*. Now Bob is an American and knows no Maori. As it proved, this is a rare expression anyway. "Find out what it means," Bob urged.

[*To further our work Jan and I had sold our Matapouri house and bought a Polynesian style Wharram catamaran, fitting it out extensively for dolphin research and naming it R.V. *Interlock*. We'd also purchased a bare piece of rainforest land at Ngunguru as our base.]

For the next two days we sailed and sailed but not a sign of a dolphin — just superb weather and a deserted ocean — no gannets, no schoolfish, no action. The film shows us in Rikoriko Cave again, endeavouring to "think dolphin," calling the dolphins in the vast echoing rock chamber.

Then the heavens opened up on us and for the next six days we could not go to sea because of bad weather and strong onshore winds.

## MEETING A MAORI ELDER

Television director Jason Olivier and I took the opportunity to drive up the coast to meet Waipu Pita, an elder of the Ngatiwai tribe, and see if we could arrange a filmed interview with him. As we pulled up at his door Waipu was just getting off a horse. The stocky, silver-haired Maori apologised for the tear in his shorts.

"Just breaking in this racehorse," he explained politely, nodding at the sleek creature tethered to the fence. Jason and I were mentally reeling. We knew Waipu was 76 years old, but age had not diminished his powers.

We met his young wife and their pretty five-year-old daughter. In their lounge we discussed dolphins with Waipu and later arranged to film our questions and his replies. Waipu told us that to him the dolphin was like a human in the sea. If a canoe or boat were in trouble, dolphins would appear and the distressed Ngatiwai would follow them to safety.

"When they start to jump and dive you know you are clear. Our people once used dolphins as an echo-sounder."

He told us how dolphins would reveal new fishing grounds to them. He confirmed my own observations: big snapper follow the bottlenose dolphins. (Fish eat dolphin wastes.) "The Maori once regarded the dolphin as some kind of a god or influence to direct them to things they wanted to know. To me it is a human being in the sea," he repeated with conviction.

"I swim with them, I play with them. Where I live in Whangaruru Harbour very near the water, we hear a splash and then a pip and we know they are in the harbour. Early in the morning we get up and go out and all the family swim with them. You can ride on them. But no funny tricks. I've seen my uncle Hohepa Pita play a flute to them. The dolphins may be spread out over the sea. When the flute is played they bunch together and frolic around the music."

Jason asked, "Could you tell us about calling the dolphin?"

"We only call dolphins when we need help in a rough sea, or in difficulty or if there is something we would like to know about relatives at a distance over the ocean. If a relative is sick when the dolphin appears it will give a sign whether or not that person will recover or has already recovered. We can tell from the way it leaps."

Jason: "Do you call dolphins as individuals or is it a general call?"

"You can't call a dolphin as an individual. The dolphin always swims in a group. Therefore you call them in a group. When you try to separate dolphins it's a sad moment for them. The Maori people nowadays mostly live in European society and to them it's just a story or a dream. It would not work for them any more — like a young animal, a horse, you train to suit you and then neglect. When you go to it again it will refuse to do what you taught it before. That's why calling the dolphins doesn't work for most people now. Some Maoris still have the gift — even a European may.

"Dolphins can always tell whether you're genuine in your feelings. I don't know whether you've noticed or not. If you are genuine in your desire they will do exactly what you want."

Waipu explained to us that you don't call the dolphins directly but through a special bird that flies with them — *Tukaiaia*, the sea hawk. (In the global esoteric culture, such a bird would be seen as an *auxiliary*.)

Waipu sang us an incantation to the sea hawk. He showed us a sacred walking stick with a snake entwining the shaft and the seabird's head for a handle.

"That bird is the emblem of the Ngatiwai people."

Then I put the question I had been longing to pose: "Waipu, we have a friend called Bob Feigel who seems to have the gift. He's had some interesting dolphin experiences. The other day he told me he had a dream and in that dream he could see me on the bowsprit of our catamaran with the dolphins around. He said there was a word in the dream that seemed very important — something like *tepuhi* or *tepuke*. Does that mean anything to you?"

The elder smiled gently. "That's the flowing out of the breath from the dolphin's blowhole," he told us. "It's not a dream when it's like that," he added. "It's real."

Finally, Waipu explained, it conveyed a subtle point: the third syllable of the word *tepuhi* was neither an *h* nor a *k*, but a Maori aspirate something in between. Onomatopoeically, *puhi* mimics the rapid exhalation and inhalation of a dolphin. Try it.

[Note: Maori attitudes and relationships with dolphins compare interestingly with those of the ancient Greeks. A Maori elder from Hawke Bay told me later her people believed that if one reached a high level in this life, one became a dolphin or a whale. In the oral tradition the first two migratory double canoes to reach New Zealand were guided here by whales. Most families formerly had a dolphin that was their family member in the sea, a protective ancestor or "aumakua." I compared this with the shark beliefs of the Laulasi people. Hawaiians have similar beliefs.]

## ANOTHER ANNIVERSARY DAY

The camera crew had been with us for two weeks. Every aspect of our work on sea and land had been filmed. But no dolphins. Fair weather eluded us from the start. Jason Olivier, the director, got an extension of time from head office. The very next day *had* to be our dolphin day or the whole film would flop.

There were thirteen on board that Anniversary Day. As we sailed over the big swells those of us who had previous experience with the dolphins (our family, Hal Chapman, Eric Kircher, Bob Feigel, Barry Fenn, Karen Buckley) communicated a quiet confidence that they would appear. By contrast the film crew were getting pretty twitchy. Even the cool jazz from our bow transmitters couldn't dissipate all the tension on board. But the dolphin gamesters remained serene.

"They're here!" Jan yelled. She was holding the tiller and saw them gliding through the water from behind us. The motor was silent, our ship dancing downwind. Those dolphins were acting in a strange way. Not rushing in exuberantly and cavorting on the bows as usual. Just lying in the water quite still, and then moving gently into the ship's path and sweeping around in between her hulls. The games began.

The film crew dashed off in the inflatable to shoot our bow activities from dead ahead. This upset the usual pattern of interlock procedures, and from this point I realized that in documenting them it would be very difficult not to interfere. Yet somehow that day the dolphins seemed to be running the whole film show themselves. While Jan wriggled into the dolphin suit* the film crew were surrounded by dolphins. I've never seen them behaving in such an intimate manner, really hamming it up: cruising straight towards the camera on the surface, several fins converging on the lens like a *Jaws* fantasy, making delicate arching leaps right alongside the inflatable — it was all happening at such an intensity they would have needed three cameras. It was as if the dolphins really knew our purpose.

[*To extend our increasingly complex body language exchanges with dolphins, we had developed a special monopode wetsuit and a full set of dolphin appendages. The first time Jan had tried it one dolphin adopted her and would not leave her for several hours.]

When Jan slid in wearing the dolphin suit the slow pace changed to a frenzy of excited manoeuvres as dolphins whirled around her, imitating her actions, filling the sea with sounds and graceful forms. Waggling their heads and rolling on their sides they swept by her over and over only to turn sharply and come speeding right back, veering aside at the last second. As usual one particular dolphin seemed to adopt her, coming closer and staying longer.

"I've never felt such joyousness and excitement generated from the dolphins," she told us later. "I could hardly breathe."

In the water with her I felt an electric heat — my suit became too hot and I would have liked to swim free of it. I saw a dolphin with a bent fin — like one I'd seen before — but when? Another with the tip of its fin missing and one with a scratch on its left side.

At one stage our inflatable auxiliary stopped suddenly. The cameraman kept going, just managing to toss his $25,000 *Arriflex* back aboard before he flopped on the dolphins. Normally with such a shock the dolphins would vanish. On this occasion they stayed in close but never again allowed the cameraman while on the water to get on the same side of the boat as themselves. If John changed sides, they switched to the other. It seems clear that trust is a delicate affair; man is still a dangerous, unpredictable creature from their point of view, and you can only go so far.

As I dolphin-swam among the curving forms I closed by eyes, just hearing and feeling the ocean. My mind screen registered something like canoes with latticed patterns of green. All of a sudden it came to me: that word in Bob's dream. I removed my mouthpiece and yelled it into the ocean, "Teeepoooheee!"

At that moment a dolphin released a huge plume of air from its blowhole just like the exhaust from a scuba diver. My hood may have prevented my hearing any sound it may have made so I swam down and gulped at the swirling screen of bubbles — an improvised response gesture such as the food exchange rituals we shared when meeting people from different cultures in South Pacific islands.

That very instant all the dolphins gathered into a tight formation, a phalanx with a leader at the centre. Beneath Jan and me they swirled around in a clockwise turn, spiralled powerfully towards the surface and vanished out.

As my mask cleared the water, I saw them all poised in midair — some three dozen dolphins in perfect line abreast. Off they sped, the whole row surging north towards Whangaruru in a series of superb leaps. When I climbed aboard *Interlock* every person on board had seen that gesture. (The film captures it perfectly.) And everyone knew it was a final gesture; we would not see the dolphins again that day.

I recalled the words of Waipu Pita: in the old culture when the dolphin leaps in a special way, that is a sign.

*Tepuhi*, I have learnt, is an especially easy word to pronounce underwater. It has an energy all of its own.

Two nights later, as the film crew were preparing to leave, Bernie the sound man played to us the tape he made that day, when surrounded by dolphins. We heard their blowholes and the music of the catamaran approaching, voices, whale sounds, Bob Feigel whistling. And then we heard airborne whistles close to the microphone.

"Just a minute," said Jan. "Did those whistles come from the dolphins' blowholes? " John the cameraman said, without any surprise, "Yes." He thought this was quite a normal thing for dolphins to do.

And then, when the film crew left, I had time to follow up my hunch that we'd met Bentfin and his group before. There it was: Anniversary Day 1977, the whistling dolphins.

Why didn't we do them the courtesy of remembering them, Bentfin and his group, responding intelligently in a manner consistent with our previous contact: the message tape; complete silence; then

Bob's whistle calls? We might then have recorded their responses and taken another step into the unknown.

Our belief models are still too inflexible to allow the dolphins memories better than our own. Will we be given another chance?

[Note: Jason titled the film *The First Move*. He had picked up a phrase I used in an interview: "We're the manipulators. We have to make the first move."]

## *TEPUHI*!

When the film was televised — 3 July 1978 — we started to receive some exciting feedback. But the letter we got from Sam McHarg prompted us to sail fifty miles north to meet him. What Sam has to say is extraordinary but we found him to be a no-nonsense headmaster, a Rotarian and a man for whom the sea has been a lifetime passion. Here is what Sam wrote:

"For over thirty-five years I have spent most of my spare time sailing boats. During that time I have had many happy experiences with dolphins, two scary experiences with orca (Tasman Bay) and one very interesting meeting with a half-grown humpback whale (Tasman Bay 1948).

"For some years I have thought that by whistling at dolphins I could sort of make contact. Many of my friends tap their heads, and look upon me as one might a person who talks to trees.

"November 1978 I was helping to deliver a yacht from Auckland to Kerikeri. It was fine and dead calm. We were about one half-mile west of Hen Island (all of thirty miles south of the Poor Knights), doing four knots under motor. Common dolphins were feeding nearby and broke off to play around our bow. As usual I lay on the bow with my hands above the water doing my whistling act much to the amusement of the gang in the cockpit. After having a very good look at me, one dolphin came right in under my hand

and I stroked it. I did this to several. I then called '*tepuhi*' and the dolphins all jumped and crowded in for a stroke! Silence from the cockpit and wide eyes.

"'How did you do that?' I was asked.

"I told them I had given a Maori greeting to the dolphins.

"'Rubbish!' they cried as they called 'Hi there,' 'Knickers,' 'Muldoon,' etc., to the dolphins with no reaction.

"I then called loudly '*tepuhi*' again and the whole sea erupted as the dolphins all jumped (for joy?). The crew still wouldn't believe it and kept up their own greeting shouts. No reaction from the dolphins who were swimming on their sides to get a look at us. Three times I shouted '*tepuhi*' and each time the sea erupted. A photo of the crew's faces would have shown open mouths and wide eyes. The dolphins then left us to carry on feeding.

"Good luck with Project Interlock. I think you are really onto something. In the meantime I will keep talking to a creature that I believe has tried to communicate with me."

In the months to come we were to receive a series of letters from Sam — we had found a fellow enthusiast whose dolphin experiences parallel and extend our own.

## WITI MCMATH: A MAORI TOHUNGA COMES TO SEA

Until the completion of the film *The First Move* in February 1978, in all our dolphin expeditions we had not once interlocked with the big bottlenose dolphins, *Tursiops truncatus*. Strange, considering it was these dolphins that set our whole project in motion, the day we danced with a huge gathering of them back in 1975 (as described earlier). And there was that unrelated event in 1971 when they met me alone in Rikoriko Cave, before I became interested in dolphins.

My diary records that the bottlenose meeting which was to change the whole pattern of our dolphin encounters occurred two days after we took our Maori friend, Witi McMath, to sea. To me in retrospect, it is important to mention this link because of the contribution his knowledge made to the evolution of our thinking about dolphins; so many seminal ideas that are easy to forget, but which later bore fruit, came from this source.

It was Witi who had directed us to Waipu Pita, the Maori elder, and from Witi I learnt the historical context of our research: the coastline on which we operate has a pre-European history of very intimate human/dolphin relationships which, with western influence, have gradually wound down during this century. To the Maori people the Pelorus Jack, Opo and Horace episodes, in which solitary dolphins bonded with humans* were a carry-over of traditional relationships into modern times.

[*Note: My book *Friends in the Sea* describes these episodes and many others in detail.]

From Witi I learnt that the Ngatiwai, the people of the sea, formerly lived also on the offshore islands including the Poor Knights, Great Barrier and their stronghold, Hauturu/Little Barrier. He told me that if their people on Aotea/ Great Barrier Island were in need, a dolphin would arrive in Matapouri Bay and give the message.

At the time I found Witi's story difficult to credit although I knew this was just a cultural problem for me — like a bushman encountering television.

As things unfolded with the bottlenose dolphins, I came to understand we were once again raising the veil of ignorance that has separated humans and dolphins in this part of the globe for only a relatively short time — and that it would take organic growth of our own belief patterns before the bond could re-establish. It would take that Maori reverence for all living things of the forest and the ocean and a deep seated response to the Earth as our nurturing mother, and that activator, the sky: Papa and Rangi, Yin and Yang. Only when we felt truly connected to it all, could we have intimations of the old bond that linked cetaceans and people.

"What is water, Te Rina?" I asked a powerful Maori woman environmentalist whom I stayed with in Napier.

"Water is our mother's milk, Wade. It flows from her breast to the sea. *Waiora*, water of life. And if we ever poison our mother's milk, we most surely will die."

So often I have found in Maori tradition these simple, powerful statements of ecological principle. Whereas these statements once sustained a whole way of life, modern society now pays mere lip service to the science of ecology, spinning environmental impact reports in lieu of prayer wheels, before going on — uncaring.

"Look what they are doing to our mother," said Te Rina, as she drove me to Napier airport across Ahuriri estuary. A dragline was ripping up the streambed to load trucks with gravel. "They are tearing open her belly and killing all her babies. There will be no fish in the sea." Then she told me that, to her, the visit of solo dolphin, Horace, to Napier was an ecological warning.

The late Witi McMath was my Matapouri neighbour. One day when I visited his home he was planting potatoes out the back. But he was only too happy to stop. Gardening was not his scene, he explained with a grin. He was a warrior. In Maori society you could be a gardener, a fisherman or a warrior he explained. None of these roles bore any more distinction than another. He had served in the army in Vietnam and even acted as personal bodyguard for the prime minister of Singapore. Planting spuds? Bah!

We got to know each other and began a series of yarns along with my friend Simon Milton at night. Only after midnight could you really communicate, Witi insisted. And on those occasions his words were unforgettable. He told us that he was one of the last to be inducted fully as a *tohunga* or priest. To do this the candidates, a select group of young men, would accompany a venerated tohunga into the forest. There they had to build him a fire. And maintain it all through the night. On the third night, after twelve o'clock, things started to happen. At this stage they were thoroughly sleep deprived and so in an altered state. The fire keeping duty ensured they were wakeful. Suddenly, Witi told us, they saw a procession of figures: all their ancestors, paraded past them in the flesh! Their teacher pronounced all the names from their progenitors Rangi and Papa (sky father and earth mother), up to recent times: their precious *whakapapa*: ancestral lineage that connects Maori to all life forms back to the first nothing: Te Kore — our big bang! With such a genealogy lesson nothing could be forgotten.

## WITI COMES TO SEA

Diary, 14 February 1978: "Today Witi came to sea with us and I saw the Poor Knights and our whole project through Maori eyes."

"My first time to leave Tutukaka by sea," Witi told me as I steered through the entrance. He loved the Polynesian catamaran, so close to the water, so intimate. He stooped and washed his fore-arms and face with the sea. "Makes me feel like a kid again," he grinned. But from our Solomon Island experiences I knew it was a *tohunga*'s ritual cleansing.

Out around the Sugarloaf and Pinnacles we motored over the summer calm, to approach the Poor Knights beneath the massive rocky bridge of Archway Island, all for Witi's enjoyment. Anchoring the catamaran in South Harbour I whisked him off in the inflatable, around into Shaft Cave. The immensity staggered him, gazing up at the vast rectangular chimney that pierces the very centre of the island, with its rim of trees far above and shafts of sunlight playing like searchlight beams on the dark waters of the cave. Then Witi began to chant. Powerful Maori words that echoed and sparkled with ancient wizardry, sending my mind into a timeless space when carved canoes probed these caves.

A short distance further on we entered The Tunnel, paddling silently while Witi gasped: black diamonds slipping by in the blue-black depths, about forty long-tailed stingrays seemingly plankton — feeding in the tunnel currents. But stingrays *do not* feed on plankton. They browse the seabed. Again Witi chanted; to my delight and awe, he set the echoes ringing to notes that hadn't stirred there for almost two centuries. It was as if the echoing voices were Witi's ancestors who once lived here. Suddenly all the stingrays surged up to the surface, fluttering to and fro just beneath us as if in response to this chant. In fifty years diving out there I have never seen the like.

Through Blue Mao Arch we zoomed to the sheltered western corner of Labrid Channel, where forest trees almost reach the ocean edge. We skirted the shores of Aorangi until a concealed portal opened in the cliffs. Again we paddled the inflatable in silently. As we entered the interior harbour Witi was in ecstasy. At the first chance he slipped into the water and landed on a kelpy rock, half awash. For a moment his powerful figure seemed to commune privately with that enchanted place. Then I guided the inflatable into a low cavern that opens off the internal harbour, delicately manoeuvring until we were in the farthest recess.

I had only recently discovered this space — most magical of all the Poor Knights' temples. At the end, the cave roof suddenly soars skywards and the rock walls sweep up in parallel towards a lofty forest ridge. At the base of a funnel we clung to the rocks trying to steady the inflatable on the surges. Witi felt that such a place would have been a tapu ground where island-dwelling *tohunga* (priests) once came to commune with natural forces: an intimate meeting-ground of sky and sea, earth and air. A place to leave the body.

We went back to the catamaran, hove to nearby, for my cameras. As we returned to the island I had a certain foreboding. Just then, from the slope above the portal a puff of dust grew into a small landslide, rocks fell into the water at the very entrance. In sixteen years out there I had never witnessed a rock fall. Should we enter with cameras? Witi paused in thought. Then he said it would be okay. But that untoward event raised our awareness to another level. As we paddled in, dust from the slide petalled the surface. I recalled my readings of Carlos Castenada about Mexican shaman Don Juan, wherein he heeded unusual manifestations in nature as significant.

Witi steadied the boat as I trained my camera within the temple. A green space: even the rocks glow verdantly. With each ruck and wrinkle the tide edge is slightly translucent a greenstone jade world. Above us the fronds of ferns hang like greenstone feathers all the way up the funicular slope to where grotesque, wind contorted *pohutukawa* stand on the high ridge, their trunks and branches silhouetted and leaves sparkling in the sunlight. The ocean gurgling around us and the songs of forest birds overhead.

On our homeward voyage, Witi imparted a wealth of Maori tradition which I have never been able to find in any of the books. This area of sacred knowledge was not often vouchsafed to the missionary scribes who wished to eradicate it.

I asked Witi if it would be possible to commune with dolphins in a space like the one we had just visited. Witi said you would have to be obsessed with the subject. Then you start noticing signs like the stingrays and the landslide. Things happening on another level of reality. You then carry right on through. He said he had only seen two places like that cave before in his life. A stairway to heaven. In places like that a priest or tohunga would practise his divining rites, leaving his body on the far journey.

We sailed home talking of *tohu*: lucid dreams, eating snacks and sipping tea while the ocean changed colour from gold to silver and silver-grey, reaching our mooring just on dark. Somehow that day I felt very close to the dolphins, yet none had appeared. But two days later....

## THE DAY OF THE SEA HAWK — TUKAIAIA

16 February 1978: "That looks just like Tukaiaia*, the bird Waipu Pita and Witi told me flies with the dolphins," I was telling Robin Solomon, a Maori friend, as a dark bird flew up towards our stern and banked sharply. As I finished my sentence, Graham Mosen looked back as I spoke: just then he saw a dolphin breach in our wake.

[*Also called Korotangi, the bird of stone. This is a highly mysterious stone carving in the National Museum, Wellington, cognate with the Indonesian Hindu bird carving Garuda, placed in the bows of sailing craft. It is a non-Maori art form, discovered beneath a tree on the remote Aotea Harbour shore where a famous migratory Maori canoe of that name is believed to have landed.]

"There they are," shouted Robin. And so it began, our first interlock with the big dolphins — *Tursiops truncatus*. Three of them, cruising south along the coast, right at the harbour entrance. We changed course to follow, but they were difficult to establish a bond with.

Everybody was so excited, whistling and calling to them, that we kept it up for miles past the sensible "give up" point. I was curious to know what would happen if we kept on going. We could just keep their fins in view about two hundred yards ahead, breaching in close sequence — a tall, thin white-tipped fin with a tear at the base of the trailing edge like a protruding thumb. Then a short, stumpy ragged one and a perfect black scimitar usually appearing in that order, white tip being the boldest of the trio. Occasionally they would breach off our starboard bow or drop back to within 100 feet of us, but no closer. All the while, the black bird was swooping about, now above us, now out to the east, the west, overhead, astern and always leading our eyes back to the dolphins so we could use the bird as an indicator whenever we lost contact. Funny — ever since I met Waipu Pita his story about the bird had worried me. Everything else the elder told us had proven true. But we had never seen a black petrel with *Delphinus*.

Then it happened — when we were past all hoping, the dolphins came to us and took up position in between the bows, two at first, huge muscular forms that suddenly made the bows of the cat seem fragile and small. The finely sculptured tail pumping up and down and the long, lithe trunk. They turned, nosed towards us, fixed us with their eyes and nodded their heads.

When I asked one to turn on its side, two responded in unison. The one with the perfect dorsal had a nick in the left lobe of its tail: Nicktail. The human response was ecstatic: a constant high-voltage euphoria enveloped the seven of us that smoky northeast morning. The music tape ran out. Jan restarted it. When the tape came on the dolphins slowed visibly in front of the bows.

Twice they came in and took up positions on our bows. We wanted them to go on forever, but then, they may have had other concerns. Robin saw Nicktail "flicker flacker" its tail, then dive down steeply.

"That's it," Robin said, "they're off!"

We did not see them for some time; then they surfaced well ahead. I jumped into my suit to try meeting them in the water. I leapt into the inflatable and Graham and Tony zoomed me ahead of the cat. Directly in the path of the dolphins I tumbled in wearing the dolphin dorsal fin. A dolphin passed beneath me. I tried it again. The dolphin passed and then suddenly dived straight down at least 100 feet before disappearing into the blue. That was it. Interlock over. No sorrow. It felt so complete.

We were about eight miles down the coast, off Pataua. We set sail for the Knights. With us all the way flew Tukaiaia. People joked, "Look, there's your bird — leading us to the dolphins." Would he, I wondered, accompany us to the pelagic dolphins further off shore?

"Maybe it's the dolphins on our sail," thought Jan.

It was about three o'clock when I slipped below for a nap. "Here they are," someone called.

I snapped out of it at once to find the ship alive with excitement. We'd met them — *Delphinus* — both dolphin species on the same day! About forty dolphins close to the Poor Knights, an active hunting group pursued by about a dozen sooty shearwaters — but not a single gannet. Fast-moving rushes, complex groupings, leaps, tail thwunks, that funny twisting movement in small groups of about three. Jan slipped into her suit and so did all the others — never so many keen games players at the ready.

The dolphins rode our bows while the ship spun around and took a reverse course, downwind. People in the bow hammocks, trailing over the sides, hanging on to the stern ramp; for five minutes humans and dolphins exchanged glances but it couldn't last: the day was late, a strong southeast wind had arisen and it was soon too rough for interlock games.

Graham said he felt confused and uneasy at the sea conditions. Just to prove a point we still tried to establish contact. Tantalisingly the dolphins kept half a mile ahead — we followed. It dawned on several of us, independently, that they were leading us towards Tutukaka — for a time invisible in the haze swaddling the coast, but eventually visible. We got home just as the fierce thunderstorm struck.

[Note: Some time later I met a neighbour with a dolphin story. Bill Shanks was crewing on the fishing-boat *Busy Bee* when it was servicing a huge experimental trap net up at Whale Bay. One morning they found a big bottlenose dolphin in the net. To release it necessitated hauling the dolphin on board, but it did not resist in the least. They steamed three miles out, soothing it and pouring water over its skin. When set free it leapt clear of the water and vanished.

Next day as the *Busy Bee* left Tutukaka Harbour two dolphins met them off the entrance with a series of superb leaps. One of them they recognised as the dolphin they had liberated the day before: a nick made by a rope in the rear base of the dorsal fin.

I showed Bill our first bottlenose pictures. That was how we came to name that big dolphin Busy Bee.

A diver friend reported seeing at Aotea/Great Barrier Island, six hours sail to the south, a trio of dolphins exactly fitting our descriptions. They dived with them for half an hour. The two big ones were copulating.

A short while later — on 22 January — we sighted these same dolphins on our stretch of coast, fifty miles to the north. So much for Witi's story of the messengers coming fifty miles from Great Barrier Island to Matapouri Bay.

Subsequently the vessel *Busy Bee* was wrecked. The bell was given to R.V. *Interlock*. It hangs from our forward beam. This is the bell we ring whenever we meet dolphins. A link."

## RAP-ON-THE-KNUCKLES-DAY — E.S.P. OR NOT?

29 April 1979: Just three of us aboard — Jan, myself, and veteran diver Mac McCaffery — we were heading south along the coast toward the Hen and Chicks Islands when I thought I saw a dolphin leap, but wasn't sure. In a matter of minutes bottlenose dolphins were making the most spectacular leaps off our bows.

It was during a hard gust and the catamaran was screaming along. The rough water and strong winds didn't seem to worry the dolphins in the least. They were magnificent, completely free and at ease in the rough conditions.

Jan yelled to them, "We can't get in the water and play with you out here. It's far too rough. We'll see you in on the coast in the shelter of the land."

Heading straight towards the coast, I decided to play Jan's game and assume that they *did* understand us. Having to handle the boat in rough seas we didn't recognise any of the dolphins at this stage. We saw them heading north, then they disappeared. We felt a bit silly, actually sailing away from where we last saw dolphins. However, we carried on towards the coast. Mac began to get into his wetsuit and I did likewise. As we entered the lee, out of rough water, we suddenly saw the dolphins pop up just ahead. This was wonderful. We rang the bell and they came towards us. They swam on the bow for quite some time. I was on the port bow and Mac the starboard. Jan was at the tiller and could see our delight. Mac leapt into the bow net hammock and shortly after yelled that they had gone.

Jan replied, "No they haven't. They are back here with me."

The stern platform is so low in the water that the dolphins seemed almost on the same level. They were cruising along on their sides looking up at her. She felt a sudden surge of pleasure to have them near again. Two were swimming along beneath the inflatable, upside down. Then Splitfin and Stumpfin surfaced beside her. There were two other smaller dolphins side by side surfacing together. Their fins were identical, with no markings. She glanced behind and saw a dolphin surface. She yelled excitedly to me, "I think it's Busy Bee." I looked back and at that moment the dolphin surfaced again. Sure enough, it was Busy Bee. They played around the boat as we went along. Busy Bee has never come close to anyone in the water in all the time we have seen him but always seems to stay around and expose himself long enough for positive recognition...

The conditions were still not good enough for us to leave the boat so Jan said, "We'll see you up at Goat Island." There we knew it would be flat calm in the sheltered little cove. The dolphins vanished and we continued on our way.

Then we noticed a few dolphins close in the shallows on a golden sandy beach. I took a photo when one surfaced. Mac looked down at reefs through clear water and said, "This looks a good place for a dive."

I felt it was a bit absurd keeping up this "talking" game with the dolphins. We couldn't very well refuse Mac a dive but at the same time we had said we would meet the dolphins at Goat Island. We decided we might be going too far. What if the dolphins didn't turn up at Goat Island? We would look as if we were quite mad. I decided to drop anchor so Mac could have his dive. The dolphins we saw in the shallows had disappeared. Once we had anchored the wind began to gust. The boat swung too close to the reef for safe diving. Jan felt really unsettled about not keeping her word and continuing to Goat Island. We decided not to stop. Eating lunch we moved along the coast slowly with only the foresail so we could ignore the squalls. We had wasted an hour by the time we got to Goat Island. It was very calm where we anchored. I took Mac inshore in the inflatable and dropped him off for a dive, then, still clad in my wetsuit, climbed to the top of Goat Island, an old pa site or lookout. There I had a panoramic view for many miles. Not a dolphin.

Jan lay on the boat thinking of dolphins but they did not come.

Just as we got home Dave Brind walked up our driveway. He said, "You should have been at Goat Island earlier today. About an hour before your boat arrived in the bay the dolphins came in and were playing and jumping all round in the shallows!" Dave had been on the beach watching them.

That was a great "rap on the knuckles" for us. If we had not stopped; if we had just kept going without worrying about lunch and taking our time, as we had intended, we would have been there with the dolphins. We had let them down!

It was a lesson for us: either we accept E.S.P. or "visualization" and stick to it, or dismiss it entirely — with communication you can't sit on the fence. We had shifted to another model of reality. Thinking it over, I realized that we really expected the dolphins to stay with us, if they understood Jan's words. But from their point of view that would be absurd — it would only mean they had followed us. With their speed what better response than to head off and await our arrival?

Several of these were dolphins we had met before. Would we ever get another chance?

# PART SEVEN

## SOUND EXCHANGES WITH A WILD COMMON DOLPHIN

Over a period of four years a highly unusual dolphin situation unfolded in a fast flowing tidal river 113 sea miles south of our Ngunguru home. At Whitianga a female common dolphin with her offspring and a second adult appeared, to the locals, to be living in the river. Only when Jan and I sailed down with our catamaran and lived on the river did we discover the dolphin trio were only using the estuary by day. Each night they would slip away to sea to return at first light. It is not at all usual for this open sea species to frequent a river. Nor is it the pattern for common dolphins to form a male/female pair with an offspring — as we were to discover. But even more exceptional were our complex sound exchanges with one adult, whom we called Rampal after the famous French flautist. And at times, there seemed to be a degree of mind transmission.

### FIRST EXPEDITION TO WHITIANGA: MAY 1986

That first morning I played some musical scales on the synthesiser that were amplified and directed out into the river through a powerful underwater speaker. In a moment an adult dolphin was alongside the grey metal housing, gently nudging it with its beak, lifting it slightly on its head and rubbing it with its belly. A metre below the surface, the dolphin hovered beside the speaker for long periods, rising for a breath, curving in an arc and returning to the sound source. Through the adjacent hydrophone I could hear its high pitch signature whistles in a regular pattern and the staccato clicks of its sonar. At times I could see it release a large bubble-gulp from its blowhole — a familiar gesture to us, and usually made in a communicative context. To my delight I was now able to see it and listen at the same time; I could at last determine that this was not simply a by-product of sound production but more likely a visual signal. The hydrophone was not picking up any phonations when the dolphin released a gulp of bubbles, but when thin beads of bubbles emerged from its blowhole I did hear sounds and recorded them for later analysis.

For some considerable time the dolphin maintained a pattern of diving out of sight, circling around and rising just beneath the stern platform to release a bubble-gulp. I wondered if this could be a method of adjusting buoyancy as it faced into the current, no more than an arm's length below. But in due course all my doubts as to the dolphin's signal-intention were to vanish.

## NEXT DAY

I had an inspiration. Among the jumble of gear on board I found a length of plastic water pipe about a metre long. I suggested to Jan that she might sit on the stern platform, just awash, her legs dangling in the water. The tube would carry her voice down into the river and she could mimic the dolphin's bubble-gulp gesture prior to each sound transmission. Then I switched the recording machine to the public address mode and plugged in an extension speaker, placed on the stern near Jan's head. Now she could hear all the noises of the busy river and the dolphin's constant, high-pitch signature whistles and sonar click chains each time it approached. Jan said she would try and make the sort of noises a dolphin could readily mimic using its blowhole.

In her own words: "Well, then it started to happen! If I blew a large bubble the dolphin would come up under me and release one too. Then I made a sound along with the bubble and the dolphin did that too. For the very first time in two days its bubble-gulps were now accompanied by sound. I then made different noises and talked through the tube. I was so excited! The dolphin responded with amazing sounds such as we have never heard before in all our recording sessions at sea. What made it perfect was the feedback system Wade had rigged so I could hear the dolphin's responses. We could actually have a two-way 'conversation as with a telephone.'"

The dolphin's behaviour indicated that it was as excited as Jan at getting a human response each time it completed a sound sequence. It wriggled and shook with seeming pleasure and made each ascent for breath briefer and closer to the boat. Sometimes it would approach us on the surface, making raspberry sounds with its blowhole exposed, maintaining visual contact before diving alongside our acoustic array once more. We varied the pattern, either making the initial sound, once the dolphin was in position, or waiting for it to initiate and then responding ourselves. We strove to avoid the usual human-dominant situation because with a free dolphin, we feel it is essential to adopt a flexible, open-ended approach that is the essence of communication. In actual fact, it was more the other way around, with the dolphin able to manipulate us: rewarding responses it liked and ignoring those it didn't appreciate.

As time went by the dolphin was outdoing Jan. It had mastered blowhole sound output (not a normal dolphin channel) to such an extent that Jan was easily surpassed. It showed how many nuances and varied patterns it could create, blending the air release noises with click chains and modifying the latter so that, at the bottom of the scale, they sounded like somebody running a fingernail along the teeth of a hair comb at varying speeds to produce changes in pitch. As the clicks accelerated they often merged in a rising tone, much like a phonation but with a distinctive quality.

## SECOND TRIP: DECEMBER 1986

Later in the day of our return, Jan and I were alone with Rampal. I had been itching to try something which would take a lot of concentration and demanded a situation free from distraction. I wanted to play the dolphin a special recording I had made after analysing hours of tape recordings from the May trip. I had collected all the best "takes" and put them through a special digital synthesiser, shifting them up and down the keyboard scale. Now I hoped to play this back through the underwater speaker, one phrase at a time, pausing to record any responses. To signal our readiness Jan tapped on an aluminium tube. The dolphin came over and immediately started vocalising beneath Jan and alongside the acoustic gear. Then it emitted a long, low reverberating sound such as we had never heard before, and rose gently to the surface where it made a sequence of blowhole sounds in air, as if demonstrating what had just been done underwater.

At this point I took the opportunity of trying the playback tape in which each of the dolphin's most interesting phonations pass down the scale, slower and lower; then up the scale higher and faster, before returning to normal speed and pitch.

For the next hour Jan and I entered an amazing space — the dolphin almost made the water boil, such was the intensity of its responses. At times it would surface beside us and raise its beak as if desperately trying to communicate, as we in turn strove so desperately to understand.

At one stage I told Jan, 'Now I'd like to get a few photos." To our surprise, the dolphin seemed to grasp the situation because it lay there on the surface longer than at any time before while I took four shots in a row and then another sequence.

Eventually we were utterly exhausted. Concentrating on the complex task of manipulating the gear and staying tuned to Rampal's space had my head pounding. Then the dolphin did an incredible thing. It swam over to us on the surface. Slowly it curved its body like a banana, head and tail right out of the water, dorsal skin all wrinkled. Even the lobes of the tail were curved upward. It opened its blow-hole wide, releasing air freely — and sank below. There it turned 180 degrees underwater and sped across the river to its favourite mooring buoy. The clearest body language you could imagine to express, "I am exhausted. That is it." We were amazed at the empathy it showed towards our own feelings. We felt satisfied yet humble. Out in the river Rampal lay resting on the surface alongside the moored vessel *Easy Rider* with its companions: the mother and baby.

## THIRD TRIP: FEBRUARY 1987

For us the greatest surprise of all was the way in which we learnt the gender of the sound maker. By the third day of our third expedition we were burning to discover this. A scientist who published a report on the river dolphins for the marina developers, after a brief visit, stated that the second adult was "almost certainly a female." This was totally at odds with our own intuition, based on a pattern of small clues.

That afternoon, up on our catamaran bows I had just explained to the local Calder family how to sex a dolphin if they should glimpse its underside. I was drawing the patterns of genital openings for them, when suddenly, as a launch roared past, Rampal streaked after it and began to treat the stem as if it were a female: upside down, his body curved around it, pectorals embracing the sides. We all stood there, rigid with astonishment at this unusual display while Rampal repeated the performance *five times*. Mentally we were all asking: what gender are you?

Next morning as I sat in the starboard cockpit sipping my coffee, Rampal came in from the open sea straight up to me, made eye contact and dived beneath the vessel and the mother dolphin who was on the surface beside our port hull. Just beneath her body but slightly to one side Rampal lay upside down on the surface and extended his penis twice, very deliberately, from the slit in his belly, like a periscope. (The dolphin penis has muscular control.)

This did not appear to be a sexual act and the mother showed not the least response. We had seen no courtship behaviour in any of our past or subsequent observations. From then on, we could have no doubt as to his gender!

Then Rampal approached us for the first of a series of communicative exchanges such as on our previous trips. But this time so many things were different. No longer did we signal to Rampal with the ringing of a bell or some acoustic output. From the outset he made it clear he would come of his own accord when he was ready and from then on, no signal from us would entice him over. He selected the time for the acoustic exchanges excellently — at periods when the current flow had slackened — and now he took the initiative in all the exchanges. No longer did he explore the underwater speaker or bother with irrelevant games. He seemed to have grasped where our capacities lay. With the calm conditions that he chose, no longer did we have to cope with our acoustic array vibrating noisily in the strong current, nor did he extend the sessions to the point where we were exhausted. Our richest exchanges were just under an hour in duration, sometimes twice in a day, and always in perfect conditions.

Because the river was now discoloured from rain sweeping down from the foothills, we were ignorant of his presence beneath our stern platform until he made it known. Our acoustic array, broadcasting per the P.A. system, made us aware of his clicks and whistles in the vicinity but his actual position was a mystery until a huge gusher erupted beneath us. Jan noticed that the initial bubble-burst was always the greatest. "Like an atomic bomb cloud," she remarked. Rampal then established a regular pattern of exchanges which made it easier for us to respond appropriately and to analyse our tape recordings later. Each bubble-burst would be acknowledged by Jan with a matching unvoiced burst from her tube. This was equivalent to a telephone ringing, setting up an exchange of communication. Then, as regular as clockwork, Rampal would make a new sequence of blowhole sounds. As time went by these became increasingly complex and prolonged. To let him know that we had heard him, I would make an attempt to copy his sounds or make some variations of them, weaving together previous patterns he had taught us into a new synthesis. This appeared to stimulate the dolphin to more intensive efforts and the session became rather like a two-way telephone conversation except that neither party could communicate much more than joy and creative spontaneity as with two jazz players improvising.

Following our final 1987 visit the common dolphin trio began to spend increasing time at sea. In early April 1988 they left and did not return until 20 July. Thereafter their periods at sea grew longer until in June 1989 they were last sighted in the estuary.

For a female *Delphinus* dolphin to spend nine years in a river estuary is without precedent anywhere in the world, as were our complex acoustic exchanges with the male, Rampal. They were filmed for television, photographed and sound recorded.

# PART EIGHT

## USA: UNTOWARD EXPERIENCES

### THE BRIDGE: MICHAEL WIESE, DOLPHIN FILMMAKER

Word of our research must have travelled farther than we thought, as the letter, dated 9 May 1979, came from San Francisco:

"I recently heard about your experience of swimming with wild dolphins and wanted to ask you about this. I am a filmmaker and have just completed a fifty-eight-minute film *Dolphin*, about our experiences swimming with, being with, and playing music underwater for a school of wild dolphins in the Bahamas. The film will be released in June in San Francisco and later in Los Angeles. Our intention in making the film is to raise human awareness about this magnificent creature and the benefits which could come to humanity through a relationship with another intelligence.

"Our film begins with basic background on the dolphin (evolution, history, brain size, intelligence, marine parks, tuna fishing, the Iki dolphin massacre in Japan) and quickly moves into our own research for dolphin contact in Hawaii, the Florida Keys and the Bahamas.

"My feeling is that we only scratched the surface. We feel that we were very fortunate in setting out to meet dolphins in the wild, that they were attracted to us and did play and swim with us and relate to us in their own environment providing us with absolutely magnificent film footage. Music was our primary means of reaching them although my sense is that our 'intention' — wanting so badly to join them — had much to do with our encounter: as if we were sending out 'psychic messages' as well. While the film does not get into this area directly, it is something I would like to explore, perhaps in another film.

"It's still too early for me to tell what I will do next as far as filmmaking goes, but I would very much like to hear from you in as much detail as possible about your experience, sensations and reasons for swimming with the dolphins. What kind they were, the conditions, locations, and any other information you'd be willing to share.

I want you to know that my desire is to make a contribution through my filmmaking to human and dolphin relationships ... to share the magnificence of the dolphin in a way that supports their life here. I've enclosed some information about myself, the *Dolphin* film, and my other work, so that you can get a sense of me.

"Thank you for your cooperation. I look forward to hearing from you. Warm regards, Michael Wiese."

From this letter and enclosures a correspondence developed to the point where we desperately wanted to meet Michael Wiese and his co-worker, Morgan Smith, to see their film and share experiences — this was like one of those evolutionary convergences and the parallels could provide some invaluable pointers towards interlock procedure.

Then one day while in a waking dream state I had an inspiration: for many months we'd had two return air tickets to the United States. I'd won them with a science fiction short story about dolphins as time travellers. We felt the tickets had to be used to further the dolphin study in some way and could see no purpose in visiting the United States at that stage in our work. That would come later.

Michael and Morgan accepted our offer and arrived in Ngunguru in early December 1979. My editor Neil Robinson and his wife, Flora, picked them up at Auckland airport, gave them breakfast and brought them 140 miles to our door for lunch. We shared an intensive eight days together, viewed their film twice, showed them ours and took them to sea. In the course of all this I was able to put together the story of their Bahaman dolphin experience.

As Jan wrote in her diary, Michael and Morgan were some of the nicest people we had ever met: "...very gentle and truly dolphin people, all the way from the other side of the world yet approaching dolphins in the wild in the same manner as we have been doing and achieving the same results."

We were very sorry they could not stay longer in New Zealand. On the mangrove-lined road to the airport Morgan asked us to stop the car. They had something they wanted to do in private. We were told to shut our eyes and both felt something being placed around our necks. We each had a tiny gold dolphin on a golden chain.

"Don't feel you have to keep them," said Morgan. "Give them away if you want, or throw them to a dolphin."

The seed for their *Dolphin* film was planted in 1967 when Michael Wiese was walking along a beach south of San Francisco and encountered a dolphin stranded in the shallows. He assisted it back into deep water and as it swam away he was overcome with the intense resolve to make a great film some day about dolphins in their natural habitat, as a plea for their protection. He was impressed with the sounds that dolphin made and the general presence of the creature. "I sensed something very special that was not going on with other animals. I'd swear it was trying to communicate with me."

Ten years later he met Hardy Jones, who shared his determination, and they raised a $200,000 budget to make a feature-length film. Buckminster Fuller narrates a segment of the film reviewing the history of dolphins over the past thirty million years and their amazing brain capacities. The film takes a look at their plight today, drowning in the giant nets of the American tuna fleet and being slaughtered *en masse* by Japanese on the island of Iki. It reviews the approaches being used to understand dolphins in captivity with a sequence showing dolphins being taught sign language at Flipper Sea School in the Florida Keys. And then they started to hunt around for stock footage of free-ranging dolphins.

"We very quickly found out that nobody had filmed humans and dolphins together in the wild." At that point their documentary became a quest.

On the Hawaiian island of Maui they met a whale-filming expert, Jim Hudnall, who agreed to help, but an attempt to film the Hawaiian "spinner" dolphins yielded little human/dolphin interaction. Next they tried Southern Florida, assuming it would be easier down there — but found they could not get near them. In Florida many bottlenose dolphins were being captured and tagged for research.

Around 17 June 1978, having been given a tip by the famous treasure-hunter Bob Marx, they set sail on the seventy-foot schooner *William H. Aubury* for a remote location forty miles from Florida called the Lilly Bank. There they encountered a group of some fifty Atlantic spotted dolphins *Stenella plagiodon*. They played with them for three days for periods of forty-five minutes to three hours, each day ending when they were too tired to swim any longer.

At the outset the dolphins rode the bows of the schooner while eleven men and two women crowded around the bowsprit. Then Hardy Jones and cameraman Jack McKenney, clinging to the chain plates, dangled their bodies in the bow wave amidst the dolphins, establishing mutual trust.

Although the film shows a different sequence, it was a flute that initiated the interlock. When the boat anchored, two hydrophones were suspended beneath her keel over the shallow ocean floor. Through them Mary Earle played "Appalachian Spring" on the flute. To their delight the dolphins returned to the boat and members of the party began to enter the clear water.

One of the most successful at relating to the dolphins was Dr. John Siebel, an experienced snorkel diver, who could hold his breath a long time. He imitated the motions of the dolphins and would often hum to them.

The interlock developed into an elaborate and graceful interspecies ballet when sound engineer Steve Gagne drifted down, cradling in his arms a pneumatic underwater piano. Using the exhaust of his scuba Steve had devised a keyboard instrument which produces high-pitched crooning notes.

Morgan Smith was dolphin-kicking when a dolphin swam above her, gently touching her on the back. Humans and dolphins cavorted in perfect conditions: water that was extremely clear with more than 100 feet visibility, eighty-three degrees warm and only twenty to thirty feet deep — a featureless, white sand bottom. Only the two cameramen Jack McKenney and Jim Hudnall and Steve wore scuba but the dolphins showed no fear of them.

On the second day contact began at five in the afternoon. "Three of us were on the bow," Michael told me. "Beautiful weather and light. We said, 'It's so perfect — now if only we had dolphins!' Seconds later the ocean was filled with leaping dolphins, heading to our ship to ride the bow wave.

"When I was with the dolphins I felt as though I was communicating with them telepathically about the film. Certain dolphins seemed to pick me out of the bunch of humans and I felt that if we had been able to remain on location longer individual relationships might have developed.

"On the third and final day the dolphins were summoned by Steve's underwater piano. At first about six to eight dolphins came in, almost like a scouting party, and then others arrived. About twenty minutes later they left, apparently to feed. We could see birds feeding a mile or so away in the direction they headed. That evening the dolphins hung around the ship and watched us. They played games with one of our rowboats, twisting and pulling on the tow rope, tangling the boats up.

"The most powerful communication to us from the dolphins was this. We had spotted some very large and nasty-looking barracuda one day while swimming with the dolphins. They obviously knew of our fear because occasionally they would chase the barracuda away. The next day, in one of the motorboats towed behind the schooner, we found a very stiff, dried out and very dead three- to four-foot barracuda with curved tooth marks in its back. The dolphins seemed to have tossed it up like a gift during the night as if saying, 'Hurumphff . . . barracuda! Nothing to be afraid of here!'"

Following the success of this filming expedition Hardy Jones made three return trips. In June 1980, after an eight-day search, his team re-established contact and filmed a sequel to *Dolphin*.

In a brief note, Hardy said: "We identified sixteen individual members of the pod. The dolphins began to mimic our musical output and would touch my flipper when I took it off. We are beginning to discern the social order/hierarchy of the pod."

[Note: Jan and I subsequently made two expeditions to meet these Atlantic spotted dolphins undoubtedly the most friendly dolphin tribe in the world. I described them in *Encounters With Whales and Dolphins*.]

## A JOURNEY TO AMERICA

Opening the mail on 18 March 1980 I found the offer of an expense-free journey to Washington D.C. A letter from Dr. Ray Gambell, secretary of the International Whaling Commission, invited me to attend their special meeting at the Smithsonian Institution on the intelligence of cetaceans and the ethics of killing them. After the four-day conference I found myself being passed along a benign chain of contacts that took me to Los Angeles, San Francisco, and eventually to four Hawaiian islands. With the influence of Michael Wiese I was meeting people with a psychic interest in dolphins and showing them our film *The First Move*.

From my diary:

2 May 1980: "This is the first peaceful moment since I left our Ngunguru forest home eight days ago. This morning I am stretched out on the sofa in Michael and Morgan Wiese's lounge here at Sausalito, San Francisco. I arrived at mid-day yesterday after flying in from Washington D.C. ... Above me on the wall is a huge blow-up from their film *Dolphin*..."

"On my last night in San Francisco, parapsychologist Dr. Jeffrey Mishlove arranged a second showing of our film, this time to a group of his friends, all people interested in parapsychology and curious to know what has been going on in this field between humans and dolphins, through dreams, visualizations and physical transactions. I had with me a file of such reports, a fast expanding aspect of our project and something we were quite unprepared for when we set out to observe dolphins in the wild.

"Among Jeff's guests was an architect involved with N.A.S.A., a top particle physicist, two authors of books on dreams, a Jungian scholar, and several advanced students and lecturers in parapsychology at Berkeley. I was amazed at the interest our film aroused in these people and the acceptance this subject has gained in the U.S. I asked the particle physicist why dolphins and psychic matters interested him. He explained that he was working with a major particle accelerator and that, in researching quantum physics scientists were encountering areas of reality that defy ordinary understanding. For this reason they were more receptive of alternative realities."

From my diary I offer extracts about events in San Francisco, Los Angeles, and Hawaii that relate to my theme:

## OUT OF BODY AND HOME TO JAN

"Richard and Cherie Gierak have been exploring the possibilities of E.S.P. communication with dolphins through group hypnosis. Richard offered to show me how such an episode was possible. We went to his chiropractor rooms in a quiet Concord suburban mall on a Sunday. I sat in a chair while he told me to relax and visualize my favourite beach at home. He asked what I could see. I replied: seagulls. He told me to go to one end of the beach. 'What is there?' he asked. 'Rocks and tide pools.' He asked me to go to a tide pool. I immediately imagined a clear pool among rocks at the south end of Ngunguru beach. He asked me to look down into the pool and suggested there was a tube at the bottom down which

I could descend in the form of the single cell from which my birth eventuated. He said that in this state I could go anywhere in the Universe I wished.

"In an instant I was back home in Ngunguru. I was looking over Jan's right shoulder as she typed. On the page I noted she was typing up a letter describing the first encounter to come to our Project Interlock archive of a person meeting a rare little Hectors dolphin.* I noted she was at a very small desk in our bedroom, a place where she would never normally do typing and that she was wearing a batik decorated shirt with a handsome male Sandagers wrasse on it, made especially for her by a friend. This is one of her favourite fishes.

[*Note: At that stage in our research we had collected many anecdotes involving encounters with all three of the other dolphin species in New Zealand. But when I flew to America we had none on file for this rare species.]

"Following this experience, that night I noted the basic details and date in my American travel diary. To me it was quite low-key and not particularly remarkable. I gave it no further thought.

"Many months later, as I was writing a passage for my book *Dolphin, Dolphin* about cetacean-oriented people I had met in America, I came to notes made while in California. On a whim I read them to Jan. She gasped. The details fitted her experience exactly. She keeps a regular diary and was able to correlate the dates. She explained that she was typing in this unusual spot because she had visitors. She was wearing the batik shirt to please the person who gave it to her who was among the guests. As the shirt did not fit well, she did not usually wear it.

"I often wonder about this out of body experience and the implications of such a journey."

## DR. JOHN LILLY'S ISOLATION TANK

12 May 1980: "While visiting the famous dolphin researcher at his home in Decker Canyon, Los Angeles, John gave me three of his books that I'd not read. One of them, *The Deep Self*, is on the subject of isolation tanks. Flicking through its pages I asked if the isolation tank was still going.

"'Yes, want to try it?' asked his wife Toni.

"I showered, donned a bathrobe and just on sundown picked my way up the hill to a nondescript shed. A hothouse warmth flowed over me as I entered a gently lit space, full of gadgetry and dominated by a large fibreglass tank with a curving, counter-weighted entry hatch. Boarding the inner spaceship nude I found ten inches of lukewarm Epsom salts and stretched out. Just as in the Dead Sea the saline water supported my body perfectly and I relaxed into a nice drift of thought. My journey and all those I'd met sifted slowly through my mind.

"At times I rested my hands on my head or abdomen rather than let them float extended. This relieved a discomfort that developed in my arm joints, distracting the mind. The sound of a jet plane, the plop of condensing water or a sudden sting of cool, were major events. In the steamy warmth there was no awareness of any odour or light, while touch and sound were almost absent.

"There was no question of sleep but my consciousness must have undergone quite a change when an emerald lake appeared on my mind screen with, at its centre, a dense black void. And then I caught a glimpse of the stars as through a steamy window. This gave me such a shock I jerked out of it, back to the blackness of the tank.

"I enjoyed eidetic displays of people's faces, undistorted and not emotionally charged. Lying in the isolation tank was a pleasant, low-key relaxation, a space I would like to explore further while listening to cetacean recordings. After what seemed like an hour I decided I should make a move. Reaching the darkened house I was staggered to find more than *three hours* had elapsed. What I thought was a low-key experience had drastically altered my sense of time. Everyone but John's son-in law had gone to bed!

"When I got back to Malibu where I was staying I read *The Deep Self* and found it contains the experiences of about eighty people who have tried the inner-space voyage. Most interesting was that of a Mexican shaman who said it provided the sort of out-of-body experience to which he was accustomed within his own culture. He then gives details of how he would communicate with dolphins while in such a state."

## OAHU, HAWAII

20 May 1980: "The psychic scientist, Dr. Ron S. Nolan, picked me up at Honolulu airport in his convertible, handed me an iced beer and whirled me across Oahu to the weather coast. This island is one continuous suburb. Last night over a seafood dinner Ron told me how the psychic change came into his life. Now aged thirty-three, Ron heads the highly successful environmental and fisheries consulting firm, Orca Ltd., has a doctorate in marine biology and is a long-experienced diver and underwater photographer.

"While working for three years alone on the west coast of the island of Hawaii, the Big Island, near the Polynesian temple at Kealakekua, he had become aware of the spirituality of the place. Then he met Adele Tinning, a psychic in San Diego, and began to develop this faculty.

"He told me of his primal cetacean experiences: seeing a mother humpback teaching her calf to leap, and then the day he had a feeling of precognition that he was going to communicate with a whale. With scuba he was swimming along the foot of a typical

Hawaiian lava-flow cliff. He began to feel as if something was inside him, scrutinising him. Expectations grew but nothing came. Ron swam up to the boat and climbed in, expressing his disappointment to a puzzled companion.

"Just then the water beside their Boston Whaler heaved in a glassy mound. Out of the centre a huge form thrust some twenty-five feet into the air and flopped over on its side in a crash.

"He told me of a mission to get photos of a captive *Pseudorca* at Sea Life Park. Inadvertently Ron fired his strobe very close to the creature. The cetacean seized his camera gently by the strobe unit and placed it in the centre of the pool. That was it — no more photos.

"Ron was keen to assist me along a journey through several Hawaiian islands along a chain of contacts set up for me by friends in Los Angeles: Michael Wiese, Steven Schwarz and the Mobius Group. I had a strange intuition that for once in my life it would be best if I just trusted in the process and let myself get transmitted. I had not planned for this when I left New Zealand for the conference in Washington D.C. I had no idea as to what I was in for- and virtually no money! Just a delicious feeling of anticipation."

## WITH JIM HUDNALL

22 May 1980, Kihei, Maui: "So this calm Maalaea Bay with its nearby islands, Lanai to the right, Kahoolawe to the left, and just the western tip of Molokai visible beyond Papawai Point, is the world's hottest spot for human/humpback relationships. It was out here that the finest footage of humpback mothers and their calves was shot by whale researcher Jim Hudnall.

"During a taped interview with Jim Hudnall today I asked him a question which I'm finding of increasing interest with people dedicated to cetaceans: the primal experience is often something of an elevating nature.

"'How did you get drawn towards cetacean research, Jim?'

"'Well, I first became really intrigued by cetaceans in 1963 while a geologist at Scripps Institute of Oceanography. I was working in a little cottage on a cliff overlooking the sea at La Jolla. During a coffee break one morning I was sitting out there on the cliff edge with my secretary watching some dolphins body surfing about half a mile up the coast. They'd been riding the waves for about fifteen minutes when we saw a grey whale heading along the coast very close in. It swam through the Scripps Pier and became entrapped by a reef diagonal to the shore below us.

'The dolphins left off surfing and headed down the coast. They lined up on the shore-side of the whale near its head and either pushed it or were very close. If touching at all, it would only have been a gentle nudging. They oriented the whale towards the opening of the 'trap' and accompanied it out. When the whale began curving shorewards a little north of the reef they got on the inshore side again, near the head region and seemed to guide it out to sea. Last seen, the whale was on course for the northward migration. I looked at my assistant.

"'Did you see what I saw?" And she said "yes" and we both decided it would never be believed, so we mentioned it to nobody.'

[Note: My archive now has several well documented accounts of dolphins assisting whales.]

"Jim went on to explain how he had then done his draft stint with the Navy, in sonar work, as an anti-submarine warfare officer during which he learnt to distinguish various whale sounds and understand acoustics. Later he got involved with guiding tourists out to see whales up on Vancouver Island and became increasingly interested in cetacean behaviour. This led him to Hawaii and his outstanding humpback study."

## FULL CIRCLE DAY

21 May 1980: "Those sleek spinner dolphins at Lanai seem like a dream to me now that Jim Hudnall has brought us back to Maui after two days with them. When I set out on this journey from New Zealand to Washington I hadn't the least inkling it would lead to interlock with another dolphin species. I had steeled myself for a world of words and cities.

"On Sunday Jim's inflatable whisked us over the eight-mile stretch of indigo blue ocean between Maui and Lanai. Three of us: Ingrid Orbom, the girl who makes such vital ceramic dolphin busts but had never met a live dolphin, Jim and myself.

"During the crossing I kept a hopeful eye open for humpbacks but most have left these waters by now. As the steep cliffs of the volcano island drew near Jim followed a hunch and took us straight to the dolphins: the black fins of eighty spinners, *Stenella longirostris*, cruising slowly in a bay where they pass the daylight hours. At dusk the spinner dolphins move offshore to feed on squid 1,000 feet below as they, in turn, prey on the rising night-time plankton swarms (once called "the deep scattering layer") until by midnight there is a squid feast near the surface.

"Leaving the inflatable adrift on a sea anchor, we dived straight down and the dolphins came around us. I felt as if I were already back home, in a dream involving a strange species with extra long beaks and salmon pink bellies, yet so similar in their body language and responses to our presence. How I longed for our catamaran and all the communication gear that enables us to interlock more intensely, but at least these dolphins accepted us in their midst, circling tightly within arm's length and maintaining eye contact. Jim saw one trailing a piece of plastic or tatty seaweed from a flipper. I remembered how *Simo* back in New Zealand did this. Same behaviour; different species!

"We wore no wetsuits and I found the Hawaiian waters not quite tropical enough to avoid chilling. After three warm-up spells in the boat Jim and I decided to hang back and let Ingrid meet the dolphins alone. As the pod advanced over the surface *en masse* towards the boat, Ingrid swam into their path. They circled her very slowly, including the Zodiac in their course and then circled her again. Full circle day: the dolphins showed themselves to the girl who had been sculpturing their forms with such devotion. Ingrid said when alone with them her residual fears emerged and were overcome."

Later I would learn much more about these Lanai spinners.

## JIM LOOMIS: *HOMO DELPHINUS*

27 May 1980, Maui: "Both Jim Hudnall and Ingrid insisted I should not leave Maui without meeting Jim Loomis, director of the Cetacean Relations Society. This morning I found him in his office, on the edge of town, where he sells solar heaters. Without a moment's hesitation Jim shut his desk and I spent a very pleasant day getting to know him.

"Jim Loomis is *Homo delphinus:* a former maths teacher in California, owner of four ocean-front wilderness properties on various Hawaiian islands probably worth millions of dollars, a tall dreamer/philosopher with the physique of a Greek athlete (6'3", 180 lbs). At 45, Jim is in his prime: a perpetual sea boy with virtually no possessions who rows from one island home to another with a sixteen-foot dory.

"Since founding the Cetacean Relations Society in 1973 Jim has established six centres which offer a variety of facilities for the human/cetacean interface: from the Dance Centre on Maui to the

Cetacean Observation Station on Molokai, boat and dock facilities at Lahaina and Lanai and the Sensory Enhancement Centre over at Malibu.

"Jim whisked me out to his Hoolawa valley property, the Wingdoor Cave-pool. He led me along a string of pools and waterfalls to a vast pool-side cavern and down there we lunched and swam together. I learnt that Jim is a man totally inspired with a vision of the dolphin/human interface that makes my own dreams seem timorous. For Jim, dolphins are divinities and our greatest teachers if we wish to join the cosmic dance.

"Warming ourselves on the volcanic rocks beside the pool Jim told me his plans: 'I'd like to see all my twenty acres in fruits, gardens and flower and no paths, and full of active, healthy people engaged in the common goal of living with dolphins and like dolphins when ashore. A community of divers, dancers, actors, singers, musicians, artists, scientists, gardeners; futurists whose aim is to celebrate cetacean consciousness.'

"As we talked young people began to come down to the pool from small cabins dotted through the bush and dive from the crest of the waterfall. Jim believes that as extramarestrials we should adopt a dolphin viewpoint to see ourselves more objectively.

"'The contemplation of cetacean consciousness leads to a new perspective. Away from the anthropocentric position and towards biocentrism, essential for continued survival upon this planet. Modern man seeks more and more technology to solve his distresses. From the viewpoint of a highly encephalised, large-brain mammal that's evolved with no need of technology, the tool has become a crutch for human survival. They *became* their technology rather than use it as we do.'

"In the pool by the cave Jim is training with a group of swimmers to achieve synchronous dolphin-swimming in readiness for an interspecies ballet. He already knows that dolphins respond when humans approximate their breathing and diving patterns.

"'Man is *Homo ludens,* the playing mammal. At his best when at play. Dolphins are the masters of play. When we approach them as our friends and teachers, the drama of interspecies ballet will begin.'

"Members of Jim's 'School of Humans' must have 100-second breath hold ability and feel at ease sixty feet below, moving like dolphins and following their breathing schedule. He believes such delphinic formation swimming is too dangerous to attempt unless the swimmers develop a new perception, a total watching and awareness of one another underwater such as dolphins possess, instantly ready to offer 'mutual assistance.'

"'This generalised buddy system is imperative,' Jim insists. He showed me the little shrine above the pool in which his son died. 'Its lack cost Gannon his life.'

"To develop the necessary group consciousness Jim plans to use a circular isolation tank that will take six trainees in a spoked wheel, head-to-head within a twelve-inch diameter. 'Water is a better conductor than air for sensitizing yourself to group perception.'

"Then Jim Loomis told me about his favourite bottlenose dolphin, *Guruthgill*. Dating back to December 1976, meetings with Guruthgill have made Jim think deeply about the implications of E.S.P. communication or visualization transfer. He gave me a detailed account of one such meeting wherein the bow-riding dolphin responded to a sequence of four spontaneous questions with explicit answers right on cue. Many dolphin-lovers have had these experiences and wondered about them.

"Jim has written: 'There are at least four modes of viewing reality. They are complete within themselves, but contradictory taken together. All satisfy different parts of our being. Those parts that aren't fed, starve. No explanation is complete. All the lists of axioms of the perception structures include as their bottom lines — "All the above statements are true, all other realities are false." That is what is false. A total human wouldn't be bound by any of these perception structures, but would feed the parts of her/his being that was needing the sustenance these structures were making available. All structures are incomplete models of reality. What's more, the notion of there being a reality which holds still while we study it, is false. Reality is created-discovered much more than it is perceived-reacted to. So what is the reality that you would like to experience? Tune in. The reason that people get so sure they are looking at *the* reality rather than *a* reality is that the world does perform "as if" the reality were so. And it contradicts other realities at face value, which they lack the flexibility to experience. Seems so simple. Is. There is a great revolution in human thought close at hand. I think Kant began this one. It holds more potential than anything that I have considered for years.'"

## HAWAII, THE "BIG ISLAND"

2 June 1980: "From Maui eighteen minutes in the sky and here I am on the island of Hawaii — the 'Big Island,' as it is called. From Kailua airport a small truck rattled me along the foot of a soaring volcano cone over a cinder black lava flow, an inert moonscape crazy with hibiscus flowers, to the sea front dolphin research house where I now write. Sitting here at dusk, in a chair on the sea wall, watching a six-man outrigger canoe cross the bay I am astonished to find this is the very spot the psychic scientist Dr. Ron Nolan, back on Oahu, had wanted me to visit: Kealakekua on the Kona Coast bay where Captain Cook was killed in 1779. The beetling cliffs curve around to Ka'awaloa Point, a low promontory where a white monument stands at the sea's edge.

"Nor had I realized there would be a full-scale dolphin research project here. With eight students from the University of California at Santa Cruz, the diurnal behaviour of spinner dolphins is being studied. There is an estimated population of 200 to 300 spinner dolphins along this western coast and anywhere from four to eighty spend the day in Kealakekua Bay. From a transit site 245 feet up the cliff researchers have been following them using a surveyor's transit telescope and plotting their general movements on a map to provide an accurate picture for comparison with the bay's submarine topography.

"A more intimate view is gained using the Boston Whaler *Makaala* which has been fitted with a sunken well and plexiglass windows. Student Christine Johnson lies in this and has been observing the social behaviour of dolphins on the bows. Then, further along the coast, at Kona, Jody Solow swims out with dolphins, attempting to gain acceptance much as the chimpanzees of Gombe Stream accepted Jane Goodall.

"Research so far shows that the spinner dolphins' day falls into several phases of activity. They usually enter the bay quietly just after sunrise. A period of active socializing ensues with vigorous leaping and spinning, somersaulting and tail slaps. During this time the dolphins rub and roll over each other, push each other in the middle with their beaks, chase each other just beneath the surface, and copulate. Then follows a quiet period when they draw close to each other in groups, diving and surfacing together. In the afternoon they socialize again with even more spectacular leaps than in the morning. Finally comes the "zigzag swimming" period when they speed towards the mouth of the bay with abrupt changes of direction and slowly cruise back in. This may be repeated several times before they finally leave.

"Each day there is a change in the individuals that return. The researchers have been recording the dolphins' underwater sounds and find that they become very noisy during the socializing periods — 'It's like a news bulletin jabber in a foreign language.'

"Researchers have noticed the way distinctively marked individuals often take the initiative in approaches and suggest these may be dominant animals. I'd wondered if they can sense that our attention is directed to more easily recognized individuals. Christine tells me Jody studied the Lanai spinner dolphins two years back before coming here and had remarked on an individual that habitually carried a plastic bag around — probably the one we had met.

"The girl researchers are very glum. There have been no dolphins in the bay for several days. They are refusing to ride on the bows of *Maka'ala*. Some male researchers recently captured a spotted dolphin and attached radio gear. A clear example of the clashes that arise between benign research methods and the more traditional approaches for which, it appears, it is much easier to obtain funding from industry. The men plan to track the dolphin using satellites."

## KEALAKEKUA BAY — CLIFFTOP REVERIE

3 June 1980: "At dawn tomorrow my homeward flight begins to New Zealand from Hawaii, the volcano island, this bay where a seaman from the west took his last breath, this anchorage strewn with ship bones where the tourist boat comes daily to see the Captain Cook monument out on the point; where the dolphins come on their coastal visits to pass the hours till squid night.

"And now I sit here on these massive tumbled rocks, an ocean surging over sea-worn boulders, my body fresh from scuba diving in the clear bay and all the brooding spirit of this volcano island arises around me — our mother, 'Papa' to the Maori, 'Gaia' to the old Greeks, who mightily moved this month at Mt. St. Helen on the Pacific rim, her life force welling from the planet heat, a primal birth process. Our mother, Papa, palpable. Touchstone. Earth me here.

"As I wrote these words I entered a reverie or altered state that invoked all the people I'd met in the past thirty-five days wandering through America. I think it started when I noticed a couple along the shoreline gazing out to sea just as I was and felt a common bond. I wrote on my pad:

*One ocean rims this world*
*And on its shores*
*Who hear its surging breath*
*From self to one*
*Unfurled.*

"A string of names follows, arranged in playful patterns. Somehow this verbal game induced a state of trance, an abstracted state in which I was fully conscious but my writing finally petered out.

The next words on my pad are: 'a canoe passes. I wave at two men. Dolphins appear in their wake.'

"There ensued the most elevated interlock with dolphins I have ever experienced. Something I find very hard to articulate other than the basic facts. For at least an hour, possibly two, six spinner dolphins gambolled below me. There was a mother with a baby and four others. They came in quietly behind the canoe from the direction of Ka'awaloa Point and the Captain Cook monument and moved over to an area directly opposite me and adjacent to a pair of moored yachts. In all their activity they kept these yachts between them and the houses at the head of the bay. The initial move was that typical spinner dolphin gesture, milling close together with their long beaks and heads waving around above water. This they did on the seaward side of the trimaran hull. Then began a session in which they leapt and tumbled in synchrony with my thoughts and questions. Something which is really too much for me to believe afterward and yet so distinctly remembered like freeze-frames in a movie.

"At times I would glance over to the dolphin research centre, and *Maka'ala* moored out front, wondering whether the research students would notice the dolphins had returned. Then I wondered whether the dolphin movements were being masked from that angle by the boat hulls. In mid-afternoon they left the bay quietly along with any doubts I still harboured about mind links.

"As I returned along the shore I suddenly noticed the massive stonewalls of the Polynesian temple *Hekiau Helau* in the corner of the bay. With my thoughts on the sea I'd walked right past it this morning. At the cliff base I even noticed human bones protruding. Very near was the monument to Captain Cook, marking where he had fallen. Had he violated a burial ground?

"Back at the research centre house nobody had seen the dolphins today! I have a hunch those dolphins I observed had deliberately avoided being visible from that angle. Was it the satellite tagging programme?

"Then, still fresh from a long flight, Jody Solow arrived — every inch a sea girl. The dolphins could not want for a more devoted and sensitive student. This is the first time I've met anybody else trying to gain the trust and acceptance of free-ranging dolphins. She swims out with them each morning in the nude, making delphinic noises, observing individual markings and trying to understand their social patterns.

"Back in New Zealand some months later I had a lucid dream in which I translated *Kealakekua* from Hawaiian into Maori and then I guessed at its significance: with a consonant shift between the languages *k* becomes *t*, *l* becomes *r* — so it is *Te Ara Te Atua*: Pathway to the Ancestors! And, just as with the Maori, these ocean nomad Polynesians of the northern hemisphere believed that dolphins were ancestors. Hence the temple in the bay so named, where spinner dolphins spend daylight hours. Later I was to learn that in a boulder field on Lanai there are ancient petroglyphs or rock drawings that depict the shamanistic out-of-body experience: the dolphin/man. And these also exist at Easter Island and in South Canterbury, New Zealand. At the three corners of the Polynesian triangle, the dolphin cult was celebrated, just as in Melanesia, the parallel shark cult was represented by the shark/man carvings I had photographed. In Fiji at Namuana village on Koro Island they call turtles. In Gambia Africa, crocodiles are revered.

"With this dream I think I came to understand why I had been led along a pathway through four islands of Hawaii to gain an insight into the ancient beliefs of Oceania."

# PART NINE

# MIND AT LARGE: FOREST AND SEA EXPERIENCES

"We need another and a wiser and perhaps a more mystical concept of animals. Remote from universal nature, and living by complicated artifice, man in civilization surveys the creature through the glass of his knowledge and sees thereby a feather magnified and the whole image in distortion. We patronize them for their incompleteness, for their tragic fate of having taken form so far below ourselves. And therein do we err. For the animal shall not be measured by man. In a world older and more complete than ours they move finished and complete, gifted with extensions of the senses we have lost or never attained, living by voices we shall never hear. They are not brethren, they are not underlings; they are other nations, caught with ourselves in the net of life and time, fellow-prisoners of the splendour and travail of the earth."

— Henry Beston, *The Outermost House*, 1928.

## THE GIANT NATIVE DRAGONFLY

Helicopter designers could have sped up progress had they first examined dragonflies. I had just been reading a book on how designs in nature parallel human technology and was fascinated about dragonfly structure, when I met a giant dragonfly down in our valley one fine summer's morning. I was not going to tell this story, fearing my credulity would be stretched.

The bush giant dragonfly *Uropetala carovei,* Maori *kapokapowai* or "water snatcher," is the largest of New Zealand's eleven dragonfly species, with a body length of up to 86mm and 140mm across its gossamer wings. With its bold yellow markings it hovers in forest clearings and along the edge of the bush in summer, hunting insects. It is a voracious predator observed to catch up to twenty flies in an hour.

When one swooped noisily around my head the desire to scrutinize it closely was immense. In a flash of inspiration I extended my hand. For a miracle to happen I had to make it possible! On my fingertips it alighted broadside on. I overcame the reflexive urge to flinch. And I drank in the details of its body, from the male appendages on its tail to the set of down-facing jaws on the head. But I yearned for a frontal view to inspect its large compound eyes. It took off and circled. Again I extended my hand. This time it settled facing me! I drank in those huge convex view ports like blister domes on an aircraft.

My only regret was not having a camera to document this rare encounter. When I got back to our barn one had recently entered and died there. I got my pictures. For years I have kept the experience in the back of my mind.

## SHOOTING A GOAT INVADER

To my horror I discovered a goat had invaded our land at the stage when I was strenuously trying to revegetate open areas. In a clearing far from our dwelling I came across the tree muncher. It would have crossed the highway from the forest reserve adjacent. What could I do?

Early next morning I went into the forest near our barn with a .22 rifle. I have never been a hunter but the gun was essential for putting down trapped possums.* I felt a huge compulsion to try and do something. It was better than naught! But the moment I entered our forest I realized it was hopeless to try and find a goat in all that wilderness, when every footstep would rustle the leaves and alarm it. Besides, it could be anywhere in our 44 acres.

[Note: These are introduced Australian marsupials. New Zealand has a major problem with exotic mammals that destroy its lush vegetation and prey on its unique birdlife. For responsible landowners pest control becomes a way of life. As I write we are delighted to find endangered kiwis have now returned to our rainforest.]

I decided to do something absurd. I sat down and selected a patch of sunlight in the distance. I aimed at it with the telescopic sight. With a sense of dedication to the forest — *I imagined it standing there*. At least, if a goat stood there I would have a chance. I could hardly believe my ears. Trit-trot over the leaves came goat hooves. It stopped precisely where I was aiming, in that patch of sunlight. My bullet penetrated its skull and it never moved again. I dragged it out to the driveway, buried it and planted a plum tree on its grave.

Some years later a neighbour let fourteen goats go. They set up camp in our forest. At first light Jan and I set out. A farmer's daughter, she knew where they were camped. She drove them past my ambush behind a tree. After four sessions we got the last goat. They all became fruit trees. I do not know where the accuracy came from that endowed me to kill those forest destroyers with such an inadequate gun.

## GECKO ENCOUNTERS

Then there are the lovely emerald green geckos of New Zealand. They mystify me with their appearances at unusual moments in my life. It is so very fortunate that on one occasion a professional photographer was visiting us, collecting pictures of odd New Zealanders for a book which she has since published. [*On Top Down Under* by Sally Tagg and Witi Ihimarea, 1998] It was an honour to be among pages with people like Sir Edmund Hillary etc. But the picture she took of me was unbelievable in origin: we were relaxing on our hilltop, gazing out at the sea, surrounded by a fringe of tree crests. Her quest for photos was over for the day. Suddenly she gasped. She grabbed her camera. She snapped a shot of me with a green gecko perched on my shoulder. Were it not for her picture in the book I would not dare to relate this story about the shyest of creatures.

The first green gecko I ever saw was an episode just as strange. Jan was there beside me in the bush. I turned aside and pointing a short distance up into some sunlit foliage I said to her: "There's a gecko" — *a moment before I had seen it*!

I will stretch credibility with another. I had lost my wristwatch while working on our long bush-lined driveway. Next day I walked down feeling how hopeless it would be to find it. Suddenly my eyes were drawn to an emerald green creature perched on some sticks at the base of a blackwood tree. A green gecko! On the ground! And right beside it, *lay my watch*.

Then came the time we were taking my aged mother for a short walk in a park in the heart of Whangarei City. It would be the last walk she would accomplish in her life. As we ushered her old legs along the well trodden way towards the Hatea River edge I gasped: there at her feet was a green gecko!

With one exception all New Zealand's twenty species of geckos and thirty of skinks produce live young — unlike most of those elsewhere in the world. Our geckos usually produce a single pair of live young, which makes them particularly susceptible to exotic predators such as rats, stoats, cats and possums. No wonder they are so rare.

From an interpretation gained in the Solomon Islands, I now think of the gecko as a totem animal for me; a powerful and motivating bond with nature that spurs my conservation efforts. But it was not until I encountered South Sea cultures I was able to come to terms with such things

## THANKS, TANGAROA!

For one very intensive year Jan and I dived hard, month after month, to make a pair of undersea documentaries about the lives of fishes and the complex fish community of the Poor Knights Islands for *TVNZ Natural History*. We called our films *Masters of Inner Space* and *City Under the Sea*.

During this time we had many lucky breaks such as finding the only electric ray I have ever encountered out there and getting fabulous film of it shocking me and rotating like a music record!

We came to look on our work as a celebration of ocean life. Half in jest but with an underlying sincerity, we would put our luck down to the Maori sea god *Tangaroa* whose offspring we were praising. But it was no joke the day Jan found the rarest of our moray eels, the mottled moray — virtually to order! There are four species of moray at the Poor Knights Islands. The grey and yellow species are quite abundant. Mosaic morays are frequently found at certain locations in deeper water or around shady archways and tunnels.

We had reached the stage where we had those three species "in the can." It would be quite a quest to get the fourth: the seldom seen mottled moray. Jan acted as our scout. She would go off and find things for us so that we could more easily follow up with the big, bulky Betacam video camera linked to the catamaran R.V. *Interlock* by several hundred metres of black cable plugged into a recorder in the cabin. The day came when it seemed appropriate to make a major effort to get that mottled moray. As Jan prepared to dive I said half jokingly: "Go and find us a mottled moray." "Right," she said resolutely and swam over to Trevors Rocks in Maroro Bay. Her fins vanished. Seconds later she surfaced. "It's straight down here," she yelled in triumph. "Thanks Tangaroa!" we chorused and in no time the elaborately patterned eel was on the television monitor aboard ship and recorded on videotape.

## OMAHUTA RETURN: MIND AT LARGE

The Omahuta Kauri Forest Sanctuary in New Zealand's far north is the most powerful forest I have ever entered. A green palace where the centuries are chronicled in opulent plant growth. Virginal forest. As if the place were a sworn secret, we saw not a soul in the thirteen kilometres of lovely winding, forest entry road. It is truly a retreat of the highest order.

Seven months had elapsed since Jan and I first explored the sanctuary. From that day in autumn, when orange red *Metrosideros fulgens* rata vines spread over the canopy along the portal road we now came to a spring time festival: white *M. albiflora* ratas were in bloom, spikey red rewarewa and white hinau in clusters of tiny, tooth-edged bells. As previously the route to the sanctuary enraptured us and much delayed our arrival: a very tall rimu, its craggy trunk entirely enshrouded in the tiny leaves of the *M. perforata* rata that flowers white at Christmas; the delicate pink leaves of a wineberry sheltering beneath the towering canopy and massive boughs of a kauri. Its imposing might defied capture by our cameras.

Near the Sanctuary we stopped once again by the road sign pointing to the giant kauri stump. This time we were prepared. We measured its circumference, its diameter and the distance to its fallen crown. We took photos — myself protruding from a hole in the centre; Reggie at the rear edge. The perimeter of the stump is a little eroded so measurements could not be precise. But we got a circumference of 18.8 metres: *greater than any living kauri*; a diameter of 6.70 metres (four of my body lengths!) and a trunk height of approximately 17 metres. From nearby came a gentle spicey aroma emanating from a giant lily called kauri grass: *Astelia trinervia*, with its dense clusters of emerald spears two metres high surrounding a spray of tiny flowerlets like stars.

It was late afternoon by the time we pulled up in the Sanctuary's small car park. A sweet place, on a high plateau, calm and sunny — the best of times. With our friend Reggie as an extra set of eyes we chose the northern fork in the path to check out the avenue of rare tawari trees. They were not quite in bloom. Just a week or so too early to see them burst into flower. Tawari are said to be the most spectacular of our native tree flowers. Their symmetrical clusters of buds resemble the most elegant and finely wrought minarets, nestled among long, narrow, tooth-edged leaves. The foliage of the narrow leaved trees glowed with a golden orange effulgence.

There is much that is unusual elsewhere in our native bush but here, rarities are side by side. There can't be any place one feels more privileged to visit: not the Louvre, not the Taj Mahal, and all of it so much older than our finest buildings and in pristine condition. It was so hard to keep my eyes on the well-formed, well-drained pathways. My neck became sore from staring into heaven. It was so difficult to move from one exhibit to the next. At times it was an effort to hold back tears of joy — especially when a grey warbler chorister resounded through glades of vertical garden.

Among those titanic, branchless kauri tree columns the spaces are completely infilled with a rich texture of so many different leaf shapes and sizes and tones; like orchestral music with a powerful melody from the ancient giants, interwoven with the harmonies of so many other sweet instruments. Gaia is excelling herself in diversity and creativity in this forest.

Along the path the full realisation came to us: *this relict grove of giant kauri trees is truly an old growth forest.* For millions of years nature has cycled this community of plants, great and small. We felt a special energy in the place; its virginity induced a euphoric sense of tranquility and happiness. Our companion told us the forest created such an altered state he would not be able to drive a car!

I realised that such a thriving community was linked as a whole and interconnectedness had developed through time. Each plant was dependant on all the others to maintain the habitat. The overhead canopy created special conditions of shade, moisture, shelter and nutrients that suited the under-storey of ferns and mosses, vines and shrubs and beneath that layer, myriad root fibres were feeding; exchanging nutrients with fungal threads. At the foot of a kauri, in damp moss and fallen leaves, I discovered a rare patch of tiny native irises *Libertia pulchella* with dainty, fanlike leaves and blooms of pristine white petals in a perfect triangle.

Why did the men with giant saws spare these trees? They were as readily accessible as the cutover forest adjacent. Was it the collective power of eight mighty kauri columns?

I am aware there is a culture all over this planet that regards virgin forests as natural temples. It is believed power emanates from them. Perhaps we intuit the intensity of plant cell activity in progress there — akin to that background roar of downtown New York I once thrilled to, but sweetly regulated and harmonious. Whatever it may be, the emotional state the ancient forest induced in us was profound and enduring. I have only to reflect on it and life takes on new meaning and inspiration.

Those virgin, old-growth groves still accessible on this planet are all the more precious because of their rarity. They have the potential to elevate our minds and redefine what it is to be human — to be *a part* of the natural world and not *apart* from it. The health and wholeness of the forest enhances our sanity and boosts our energy. Entering a successful community of living things dominated by millennium-old trees so persistent and triumphant, we feel deliriously good and invigorated. Just as Jan and I have found beneath the sea, at our beloved Poor Knights Islands. In such worlds, time is not a linear progression as we see history but a continuous series of cycles. Lines of old poetry kept coming to my mind: "On this bank and shoal of time" — "Heaven's breath smells wooingly here" — "Earth hath nothing to show more fair" — "A sight so touching in its majesty" — "A thing of beauty is a joy forever."

Finally, over coffee and long delayed food, in folding chairs and the last rays of warm sun, we were there at dusk, high on a ridge plateau in the midst of a green kingdom, our hearts brimming with emotion from revisiting those massive trees, each one bearing an eminent Maori name: *Tokoiwa, Ngapuhi, Hokianga, Kopi* (now fallen and hollow, like a crashed spaceship), *Tokerau, Rakaunui, Ngatuahine and Taniwha*; eight colossi, each at the end of its own courtly aisle. It is a wrench to depart. One wishes to sleep there through the night, to dream, wander in groves of trees begemmed by glow worms and awake to it all, fresh and renewed.

## RIKORIKO CAVE: UNDERSEA TEMPLE

Like a giant chianti flask lying on its side half full of ocean this is the greatest sea cave in the world. No location at the powerful Poor Knights Islands affects me more spiritually than Rikoriko, cave of echoes and dancing light. Topside its vastness fills visitors with awe — even terror. Two girls on kayaks once told me they had called to the echoes in there and then skedaddled as fast as they could paddle. They felt so tiny and vulnerable out at sea, surrounded by rock. I like to linger within until all boat racket dies away. Only then does the cave's eerie presence register fully. The susurration of wave energy from the slightest surge excites this resonant sound shell with white noise.

At the neck of the bottle the entry foyer is high enough to clear our catamaran's mast tip fifty feet above the surface. Within the main chamber the dome roof rises another thirty feet. From the ceiling delicate ladder ferns are pendant, seeking bounce light from the water. I consider the volcanic birth throes of Rikoriko and the titanic forces that created this massive space: explosive gases, molten lava, and the millennial erosion of ancient sea levels. Like wainscoting, a mauve tide line encircles the walls. At low water this gives way to skirtings of yellow and red sponge. Out by the eastern portal the water glows with a lovely turquoise radiance from light bouncing off the bright wall below.

A dive following the western wall from portal to innermost recess is really a journey into the abyss through a continuum of change. Diminishing light levels and food transport in Rikoriko Cave compress the living conditions of great ocean depths within the scope of one shallow traverse.

I set out with Jan who carries a powerful movie light. I watch her swim in around the entrance corner, passing a patch of tangerine sponge, a vertical fringe of kelp plants and a small cloud of dainty butterfly perch.

As Jan fins along the wall of the entry hall eight metres down the slope begins to jut out into a complex of ledges and crags extending down to house size rocks that rise from the bottom. At this stage the wall journey is spectacularly rich with delicate encrusting life much more intense than those on a coral reef. But until Jan illuminates the decor I see only sombre slopes of muted colour. I can barely distinguish a pale mauve from a muddy yellow. As the circle of her light progresses an artist's palette of brilliant hues glows momentarily and recedes to dimness as she passes. To dive these splendours without a torch is like exploring a shopping mall in darkness. Even after years of visitation I still find it hard to believe such wonders can exist, only revealed by an imported light source.

As Jan swims towards the twilight a retinue of wrasses follows. She passes over a huge flat rock elaborately carpeted with sponges of varying hues: orange, mauve, purple, red; each patch battling with its neighbour for dominance using subtle chemical warfare.

Halfway into the cave a major change occurs: like an igloo entry, the hallway joins the sphere of the main chamber. This junction is a zone of turbulence. Swells see-saw along the wall and jostle on the corner. Near it Jan lights up a big patch of brilliant yellow sea daisies or zoanthids with delicate circlets of 24 tentacles. These are really stalked corals that dispense with a calcareous house and settle on other creatures: an encrusting sponge or a sea fan. Photographers delight in finding such large patches of them so close to the surface.

Rounding the corner to the right we enter another world. Light levels have now fallen dramatically. We're on the edge of the abyss. As we travel the curving cliff we notice the effect of reducing food transport: less and less diversity, until a bland region of tan or white sponges predominates: bulging, knobbly, nodular structures. It was in this dimmest part of the giant dome we discovered the fluorescent green solitary corals *Paracyathus* that hitherto had only been known from depths of 5,000 to 6,000 feet. In deep recesses and crannies crimson clusters of cup corals are the main life form. As we skirt the rear wall something clicks in my brain. I feel as though we've reached a realm far from the sun; a dark, still world. We are experiencing the ocean abyss without venturing deeper than 50 feet.

Rounding the cave's innermost recess our journey back to the light along the eastern wall begins. The eastern wall is quite different, especially towards the entrance hallway. With a reverse slope that shelves 100 feet to white coralline sand, it supports a luxuriant forest of sea fans, all oriented at right angles to the prevailing water movement. Interspersed are massive vase and castle sponges; tube sponges like organ pipes; gnarled hydroid trees, pink lace corals; orange soft corals, and stunning carpets of jewel anemones, each colony a different colour combination: fluorescent pink with brown tips; deep maroon with pale citron centres.

The darkest crevices swarm with big eyes, agile feeders of the night plankton. Close by clouds of demoiselles flit around the sunlit entrance, snapping up day plankton that swarm close to the vertical kelp forest.

A virtue of the Rikoriko wall journey is that when our long excursion terminates we're close to the dive boat anchored mid-cave. There is no current to contend with; little need for decompression, no long surface swim. And we gain the experience of a whole series of deep dives.

These same virtues make Rikoriko Cave the most rewarding of night dives. I have found it best to give the fishes a few hours to settle into sound sleep patterns before diving. By day I never see the fluorescent pink maomao in Rikoriko. They are all outside on the western point, plankton feeding. But at dusk they return to their secure dormitory. Under our torch lights their bodies glow with fluorescent pink radiance, often mottled with blotches for night camouflage. At the foot of rock slopes and on ledges, in pairs or solitary, lidless eyes wide open they enter a state of rest wherein they show no response even when I approach closely, flooding them with light.

As I traverse patches of white sand and cobbles I meet a lizardfish, propped at an angle against a rock. It bears my name: *Synodus doaki*. With a big mouth it lies around doing nothing all day... a lurking predator. Over the bottom a toadstool grouper spurts in search of prey. Its white spots have now become blue. When I hold my light behind a sleeping butterfly perch its body is suffused with an orange glow. Then to my delight I encounter a half banded perch with its newly acquired supper. Like a Salvador Dali moustache the legs and filaments of a decorator crab protrude from its mouth. Eighteen times it gulps to engulf the awkward meal, finally spitting out a twist of legs and spines and cruising off.

Encouraged by the range of lifestyle changes found at night I decided to try diving at sunset. I slide down the portal wall and set up vigil standing on the white sand beside a tall rock. The sea grows dimmer. Suddenly I am witnessing a new sight: a ghostly school of pink maomao is passing by, heading into the cave. I switch off my lights and watch a cavalcade of dayshift plankton feeders coming to bed in the cave. Then, out from beneath the rocks emerge the night shift: all the big eyes are leaving their daytime dormitories, heading out into open water where they feed by starlight. Standing there at dusk alone at the giant cave portal as the two shifts pass each other, I had a profound oceanic feeling. I felt I was a part of the living rhythm of the sea.

I recalled that magic moment when I first met dolphins in this cave portal. One day I am gazing out into the sunlit world beyond. Suddenly, my vision is disrupted by a screen of huge shark-like bodies hurtling to and fro, blocking the light. Fear turns to wonder. For the first time in twenty years' diving I am meeting dolphins. Alone, at the entrance to Rikoriko! I hover there, astounded beyond belief as pairs come down to scrutinise this strange forked creature. Eventually I snap to my senses enough to click off the very last shot in my camera; a pair of bottlenose scrutinise me and our eyes meet at close range: my first dolphin picture was framed by Rikoriko Cave.

# PART TEN

## A NEW LOOK AT LIFE: PATTERNS THAT CONNECT

For me, a diver from the age of fourteen, and utterly obsessed with the sea, there had come a time when I emerged and, with my wife Jan, began to discover linkages between land and ocean that are profound, invisible and never to be broken. With an expanded consciousness and the empathy with nature this provides, recognition of these patterns and adaptation to the underlying blueprint may well be the key to our survival.

To quote British scientist James Lovelock: "The physics, chemistry and biology of the oceans are once again being recognised as interdependent parts of a huge global process." Humans of the new millennium face an enormous challenge: can we develop sustainable agricultural technology? Can we tune into the world's huge internet database and apply all the fresh knowledge flooding in from our extended sensory systems: submarines, weather balloons, satellites and deep drilling rigs; space telescopes, electron scanning microscopes, cat scanners and particle accelerators?

Can we then reshape our society's direction fast enough to cope with the greatest problems humans have ever faced, survival against immense odds, problems that, as we sit here, are day to day realities for so many in the third world?

For fifty years this headland Tutukaka Coast and the adjacent Poor Knights Islands have been among my deepest interests. Gradually I have come to understand the undersea world as a vast energy system supported by plankton and sunlight.

On the undersea cliff every firm surface provides foothold for an immense diversity of plants and animals. A wall of mouths filters the passing parade of microscopic plankton. Mobile animals range out over the rock faces by day and by night, grazing upon the cliff dwellers or preying on each other. Through time such an abundance of life forms has become mutually dependent for living space and food: an ecosystem.

When my mind rose from the sea to explore the forest I found a parallel web of life. The same diversity of shape and colour I loved so much down below was all around me on the headlands. Then I discovered a new scientific view of life on Earth is emerging. Planetary biologists are now projecting the concept of a global environment: *a living Earth*.

Whether I explore above or below, the cliff is seen as one body of life, each organism having its particular function and as intimately related to all the other life forms around it as my eye is to my heart and to my toe. Just as the cells in my body struggle for nutrition, nature is a continuous self-devouring cycle, each life form entirely dependent on the others for its existence. A body of life wherein the components are not simply competitive and aggressive, as in the old world picture, but fundamentally co-operative in keeping the system functioning properly and maintaining stability in the face of changing environmental conditions.

## MIND AT LARGE

I was discovering what philosopher Gregory Bateson has called an ecology of mind: "In so far as we are mental processes to that same extent we must expect the natural world to show similar characteristics of mentality" he wrote. [*Steps to an Ecology of Mind*, 1972]

Or, as I put it, whatever may be intelligent in our own minds, there will be an expression of that intelligence in the organisation of the world around us. I found that by comparing patterns from two very different worlds, ocean and rainforest, I could arrive at a basic blueprint, the pattern common to both. This is what Bateson called "the pattern that connects."

To me this all seemed to point directly to the modern crisis in humanity's relationship with other life forms from dolphins and whales to the fungal threads that feed the tree roots in the forest. I saw the great thrust towards a new conceptual model given us by people like Gregory Bateson and Buckminster Fuller, or Jim Lovelock (the "Gaia hypothesis") and John Lilly.

I saw the crisis expressed succinctly in Bateson's words: "The organism that destroys its environment destroys itself." And I realized why, in coming to terms with the convergent evolution of terrestrial and oceanic intelligence, normal science is hamstrung. This will continue while potentially intelligent creatures are assessed according to rules whereby it is presumed the researcher and the experiment can be isolated from affecting each other except in controlled and understood ways; rules which expect that the experiment, if valid, can be repeated by any other researcher and that the conditions under which it was carried out can be duplicated. From the very frontiers of hard science, the world of the particle physicist, such assumptions are no longer acceptable. We are, right now, in the throes of a scientific revolution with crucial implications for life in this part of the Universe.

The Gaia hypothesis postulates that the Earth can be regarded as a single living system including the biosphere, atmosphere, oceans and soil.

According to one of its leading proponents, Jim Lovelock [*Gaia — A New Look at Life on Earth*, 1979]: "The air we breathe can be thought of as being like the fur of a cat and the shell of a snail, not living but made by living cells so as to protect them against an unfavorable environment."

That the oxygen in our atmosphere is of biological origin has long been accepted, but Lovelock claims the same is so for atmospheric nitrogen, ammonia, methane, nitrous oxide and a whole range of gases, which are the products of the metabolism of various micro-organisms. Thus the atmosphere is a highly sensitive regulating mechanism maintained by Earth's life forms, making the whole planet, in effect, *one life*.

In that concept I see the fusion of science and esoteric tradition. That is the way of our future.

## EPILOGUE: ONE LITTLE ROOM AN EVERYWHERE

Twice in my life I've had the fortune to find treasure. Back in 1966 the *Elingamite* wreck up in the far north yielded such a hoard of silver and gold Kelly Tarlton and I were able to devote our lives to the ocean. We set up our families in a big house in Matapouri Bay and started exploring the adjacent coast and the Poor Knights Islands underwater. Many decades later I can see how those dusky old treasure coins and the book I wrote on their salvage became the key to getting my diving wife Jan and myself to the Tutukaka Coast and our next major treasure find. After writing a score of books about our sea adventures and making natural history documentaries for television, Jan and I decided to explore thoroughly, above and below, the diverse coastal stretch we had been diving for so long. Working on programmes for network television can be frustrating because only a broad overview can be given. We wanted to get right down to detail and photograph and video it all underwater: the fishes and marine life, and then document all the diversity of life on land and in the mangrove estuaries.

Only then could we prove our deep conviction — that every person who sets out to explore the Tutukaka Coast will discover himself or herself truly to be a millionaire! Because of our region's thoughtful system of public reserves at so many strategic places, we all live on an enormous piece of coastal real estate and have access to a fabulous treasure: the finest bits of maritime scenery this planet can provide. [In a global 2010 survey conducted by *National Geographic Traveller* magazine, it was rated as the second best coastal destination in the world, and best in New Zealand.] I realise these are pretty bold claims to be making, but the proof is in the pudding. We have made a huge effort to document it all with words, photos and video over a period of half a century.

As our books testify, Jan and I have explored coral reefs, atolls and sand cays from the Bahamas to the South Pacific, Hawaii, Melanesia, Polynesia, and the Great Barrier Reef.

Nowhere is there a solitary pinnacle of delight. But there are plateaux of superbness and this adventure coast of ours is certainly one of them. During our work we keep discovering new wonders. It just gets better and better. At the outset we thought we knew this coast pretty well but now we are totally smitten with it; the infatuation of a first love affair.

With still and video cameras we have now explored topside coastal panoramas from the Tutukaka lighthouse summit, Wellingtons Reserve trig station and the curving sand- gleam beaches at Matapouri, Woolley's Bay and Whangaumu; we've penetrated the tunnel at the back of Marsden Cove to reach the Mermaid Pool and entered the big hollow tree at Whale Bay and sipped sepia whisky at the Soda Spring and measured the giant kauri behind Tutukaka: *Tane Moana* is 11.16m in circumference. Meanwhile our son Brady has gathered video sequences for us such as divers descending on the funnel of *Waikato*, a sunken warship, sliding through hatches, finning along passages, the wheelhouse, a pair of big gun barrels, a propeller at thirty metres on the sea floor. From Matapouri bridge we glided up a crystal clear, high tide boulevard flanked by mangrove trees, fishes and shrimps darting among their branches, flounder skimming the sand. Or explored the frantic nightlife of a Ngunguru estuary reef where a tropical convict grouper lurked. With our long lenses we joined the frenzy and rhythm and festive joy of a major *waka* canoe race day at Kowharewa Bay; skimmed wave crests with board riders at Sandy Bay, or stacked out on keeler yachts racing down to Goat Island in a stiff offshore breeze. Kids zigzagged their frisky *Optimist* dinghies across Whangaumu Bay at Sunday sailing school. And everywhere there were jaunty, bright coloured kayaks. We learnt that nowadays kayak prows are probing every secluded nook and rock passage along this enchanted coast, up estuaries, across broad bays, around deep water promontories and each adventurer finds his or her own private universe.

At dusk out in the low-tide Ngunguru estuary the wading birds of Pimanu sandspit are silhouetted on rippling black velvet as beaks probe and spear prey: all is silent now but for the liquid plop of a rapier beak or the shrill warning cries of a bossy oystercatcher. Upstream the sun, bound for Australia, sends out spokes of light over the steep dome of Cape Horn and the Old Cemetery.

At dawn a silver carpet extends from Cabbage Tree Bay 25 kilometres across to the boldly silhouetted Poor Knights. There is no wind. The tide is low. Twin arms of the bay seem to reach for the offshore islands. The whole, forested haven with its elaborate, bush shrouded Maori pa site, is holding its breath. Perhaps, because of its long association with Stone Age humans who left so little impression on the landscape, this seems to me the most spiritual place on the coast and its wilderness values are supreme. I imagine that special full moon night when brown eyes surrounded by tattooed faces look out along a river of silver to where Marama is rising in the gap between two islands, each not quite a perfect reflection of the other.

After a lifetime exploring the marvels of marine life, the cameras of two veteran divers have recorded, month by month, the moving feast of coastal forests, their trees, flowers and berries. On rugged, exposed promontories, especially at Whale Bay and Tutukaka Lighthouse Reserve, Jan and I have poked our lenses at fragile and delicate sun orchids, magenta, cornflower blue or pure white. We marvel at the unexpected beauty of such tiny, insignificant blooms. That is an important aspect of the New Zealand rainforest, probably because of the nature of the pollinators: there are so many inconspicuous flowerings, especially rewarding to the keen eyed discoverer. Hidden jewels. Not so the gorgeous gold of the kowhai, the virginal white of the clematis and the eye candy crimson of pohutukawa. Our exploration has tried to inventory all the coastal vegetation, establishing each plant and then zooming in closer than the unaided eye can see. Then, to provide further insight into nature's diverse riches in this district complementary to that in the adjacent sea, we set about documenting the birds, butterflies and moths; beetles, wetas and other insects; spiders, flies and geckoes, along with the herbs, reeds and grasses; fungi, lichens and mosses. We added all this to our extensive archive of marine life at the Poor Knights Islands and on the adjacent Tutukaka Coast garnered over five decades of diving. A compendium that, while not exhaustive, presents a pretty detailed and unique overview of the big picture on our coast, above and below water.

Looking back on it all now I recall that Jan and I got a great many pleasant shocks. So many new discoveries in an area we thought familiar to us. My second time to find treasure: the Tutukaka Coast.

# APPENDIX I

## EPILOGUE 10
## NON-WESTERN MIND: THE SHARK CALLERS OF LAULASI

### SHARK RATTLE EXPERIMENTS

A cassette tape from Honiara arrived in my letterbox at Matapouri and I learnt of Walt's adventures following my departure. When I left on the *Himalaya* he still had a few projects to complete.

The calling of sharks with a coconut rattle is a practice recorded from the Solomons by anthropologists, but unknown to the people of Laulasi, who would not kill a shark on any account. While there we had made up our own shark rattle, halves of coconut shell threaded on a cane hoop. We wanted to see if there was any truth in this "shark calling" business and whether the shark rattle worked. At 150 feet Walt had rattled his hoop in vain, a weird figure in his jailhouse suit, shrouded with a black cape. But he was determined to check it out with the Solomon's people to see if we were doing anything wrong. And we were!

At South Malaita Walt found a man named Toma at Tarapina village, who agreed to show how the shark calling was done.

"Toma turned out to be one helluva interesting guy," Walt said. "He's about forty-five years old, son of a famous warrior who, before his death, told his son: "When I die you must take the head from my body according to the custom. Otherwise I will cause you great trouble." Toma's village had been Christianised and the local missionary forbade Toma to remove the head from his father's corpse. Somehow Toma got hold of the body, stole it or whatever, and took the head. The missionary was outraged. He reported the 'crime' to the local constable and sent him to arrest Toma. The policeman went over, snatched up the skull and Toma and dragged him off to the jail. On arrival at the district centre, the seemingly healthy young constable dropped dead! The missionary was scared shitless, needless to say, and Toma got six months or so in jail.

"Toma said his village no longer had a large enough canoe for shark fishing so with the skiff we took him and several buddies about three miles out in the blue ocean. Before fishing began special prayers were chanted in their own language. They were calling to the spirit sharks, telling them to go to the bottom, so that any hooked would be wild sharks. If you catch an ancestor shark, you die.

"Then they stuck the rattles over the side and shook them vigorously at the surface with a lot of splashing, which is undoubtedly why our underwater experiments didn't work. The shark rattle mimics the sound of fish schooling on the surface. The sharks came in, very fast. I timed the interval until the first shark appeared. In two days of fishing at eight different locations, this time varied from one minute ten seconds to about eleven minutes, but in every instance sharks appeared. Usually several sharks at a time would come in. Six sharks were caught on baited hooks. The bait is tied on with a plant fibre believed to have a special power with regard to sharks. When a shark is boated its backbone is severed to immobilise it. This is customary since a thrashing shark can upset a canoe.

"After the first catch I decided to get in the water to film and see what I could of the response of the sharks to the rattle. The striped suit was a little of my own magic against the sharks. Its bold contrast it too much for the shark's eye. It probably sees only a series of black bars. They certainly are attracted to the rattles. Very aggressively they came charging in ready to grab anything.

"I was in the water in one of the early trials and a big, pale looking shark of some sort (I didn't recognise the species) about nine feet in length, streaked in, flat out. There I was beside the rattle and he hurtled directly at it. At the last second he apparently saw me. Braking with his pectoral fins, he suddenly turned and dived straight down. The striped suit again proved its value but I decided not to push my luck. I really thought he was going to nail me.

"Running back in the skiff, Toma explained that we had not been lucky. Normally the rattle brings about thirty sharks or more around the boat, and they can hook a great many in a day. But this time we had the *mary* with us, pidgin for woman, and he nodded at Janice. This was bad magic enough and only a few sharks came in. To make matters even worse, the *mary* had stepped across the fishing line, which is strictly taboo. That was why we only caught six sharks. Apparently not even a wild shark can stomach that. I told Janice that from henceforth she should keep her crotch away from our fishing gear. Even though she ruined things we got some great pictures and now understand how the Malaitans really do attract sharks by sound vibration."

# APPENDIX II

# LAULASI AND THE MODERN WORLD

From Wikipedia, 2011:

“Nowadays to look at Laulasi village, tourists come by war canoe down the Langalanga Lagoon from Auki — a twenty-minute trip, driven by outboard.

“On arrival a priest purges the visitors and they are challenged by warriors with bows and arrows, *kila kila*.

“This island is one of the few pagan, custom-observing communities left. Whereas the missionaries have involved the natives elsewhere in their own economic systems, these people have formed a company called ‘Laulasi Adventure Tours.’ The impetus came from a few Laulasi men who had been involved with churches at some stage, this being the main avenue towards Western education. They had dropped out, reverting to their custom religion, and decided to match the churches at their own game. The company has seven directors and fifty shareholders in the village. They charge tourists $19 to come down the lagoon and spend a day on the island watching them making shell money, carving, dancing and singing.

"While this commercialism undoubtedly influences their way of life, they could not possibly escape this anyway. Laulasi is not remote. This venture involves the whole village in activities, which place a high value on their traditions. In so doing the customary reverence for the old people and their knowledge is retained. All rituals, ceremonies and taboos are performed meaningfully. And in an increasingly Westernised world they have the wherewithal to maintain their stand off from the missionary influences.

"And so today most of these people live largely as they did a hundred years ago, rarely using European money, living off the sea, trading fish for vegetables with the bush people on the adjacent coast, and making shell money.

"Traditional authority in villages such as Laulasi has now been eroded. Exile once meant death at the hands of surrounding tribes. Now it is Honiara and the bright lights. Young men may shrug at taboos if they wish. The law will not enforce them and will step in if the elders get too tough. Only the regard for custom religion and its system of beliefs gives the elders any authority.

"Laulasi people have stood out against the churches and the aid they give in return for submission. Stepping naively into corporate business, they may be beyond their depth. The Solomon's Government will have its hands full to protect small community ventures such as theirs from being exploited by Westerners and Asiatics."

For photo disk essays to supplement text, please contact
Wade Doak Box 20 Whangarei NZ 0140

## WEBSITES

WEBSITE: www.wadedoak.com
BLOGSITE: http://wadedoak.blogspot.com
PUBLIC FIGURE FACEBOOK PAGE:
http://www.facebook.com/pages/WadeDoak/151318038214160?ref=ts&v=wall
PERSONAL FACEBOOK PAGE FACEBOOK (1) WADE DOAK:
http://www.facebook.com/profile.php?id=100001432936284
YouTube: http://www.youtube.com/user/wade47694
TWITTER: https://twitter.com/wadedoak
EMAIL: wade@igrin.co.nz

## WRITTEN WORKS
[Available in electronic form per website]

*The Elingamite and its Treasure* 1969
*Diving for Treasure* 1971
*Beneath New Zealand Seas* 1971
*The Cliff Dwellers — an Undersea Community* 1971
*Fishes of the New Zealand Region* 1972
*Sharks and Other Ancestors* 1975
*Islands of Survival* 1976
*Dolphin Dolphin* 1981
*The Burning of the Boyd* 1984
*Encounters with Whales & Dolphins* 1988
*Ocean Planet* 1989
*Wade Doak's World of New Zealand Fishes* 1991
*The New Zealand Diver's Guide* 1993
*Swimming With Dolphins in New Zealand* 1994
*Friends in the Sea — Solo Dolphins in New Zealand & Australia* 1995
*Deep Blue — A South Pacific Odyssey* 1997
*I Am a Fish* 1999
*New Zealand Sea Fishes* 2003

DIVINE ARTS sprang to life fully formed as an intention to bring spiritual practice into daily living. Human beings are far more than the one-dimensional creatures perceived by most of humanity and held static in consensus reality. There is a deep and vast body of knowledge – both ancient and emerging – that informs and gives us the understanding, through direct experience, that we are magnificent creatures occupying many dimensions with untold powers and connectedness to all that is. Divine Arts books and films explore these realms, powers and teachings through inspiring, informative and empowering works by pioneers, artists and great teachers from all the wisdom traditions.

We invite your participation and look forward to learning how we may better serve you.

Onward and upward,

Michael Wiese
Publisher/Filmmaker

DivineArtsMedia.com

DIVINE ARTS

# HERE ARE OTHER **DIVINE ARTS** BOOKS YOU MAY ENJOY

**THE SACRED SITES OF THE DALAI LAMAS**
by Glenn H. Mullin

"As this most beautiful book reveals, the Dalai Lamas continue to teach us that there are, indeed, other ways of thinking, other ways of being, other ways of orienting ourselves in social, spiritual, and ecological space."

— Wade Davis, Explorer-in-Residence, National Geographic Society

**YEAR ZERO:** Time of the Great Shift
by Kiara Windrider

"I can barely contain myself as I implode with gratitude for the gift of *Year Zero*! Every word resonates on a cellular level, awakening ancient memories and realigning my consciousness with an unshakable knowing that the best has yet to come. This is more than a book; it is a manual for building the new world!"

— Mikki Willis, founder, ELEVATE

**THE SHAMAN & AYAHUASCA:** Journeys to Sacred Realms
by Don José Campos

"This remarkable and beautiful book suggests a path back to understanding the profound healing and spiritual powers that are here for us in the plant world. This extraordinary book shows a way toward reawakening our respect for the natural world, and thus for ourselves."

— John Robbins, author, *The Food Revolution*, and *Diet For A New America*

**A HEART BLOWN OPEN:**
The Life & Practice of Zen Master Jun Po Denis Kelly Roshi
by Keith Martin-Smith

"This is the story of our time... an absolute must-read for anyone with even a passing interest in human evolution..."

— Ken Wilber, author, *Integral Spirituality*

"This is the legendary story of an inspiring teacher that mirrors the journey of many contemporary Western seekers."

— Alex Grey, artist and author of *Transfigurations*

**SOPHIA—THE FEMININE FACE OF GOD:**
Nine Heart Paths to Healing and Abundance
by Karen Speerstra

"Karen Speerstra takes us on a journey of the mind and heart through history, psychology, myth, archeology and architecture; through the width and breadth of time and culture. Hers is a tapestry of words that would have made weavers of the ages proud."

— Craig S. Barnes, author, *In Search of the Lost Feminine: Decoding the Myths That Radically Reshaped Civilization*

**1.800.833.5738 • 25% discount available online • www.divineartsmedia.com**